God and the Creative Ima

'Among contemporary theological voices, that of Paul Avis is always wide-ranging, constructive and sane, combining scholarship with a nuanced feel for tradition. This book covers the central questions in the philosophy of religious language in a way that is digestible and fresh.'

Rowan Williams, *Bishop of Monmouth*

'This is a book of scholarship and integrity. A unique combination of theology and literary methodology.'

R. William Franklin, *Berkeley Divinity School at Yale*

'*God and the Creative Imagination* is an extremely well written and carefully researched study of the place of metaphor, symbol and myth in religion and theology. I read this with considerable enjoyment.'

Robert Hannaford, *University College Chichester*

In *God and the Creative Imagination*, Paul Avis argues that metaphor, symbol and myth are the keys to a real knowledge of God and the sacred. Avis explores what he calls an 'alternative tradition', stemming from the Romantic poets Blake, Wordsworth and Keats, and drawing on the thought of Coleridge and Newman.

In his illuminating discussion, Avis shows us that Christianity lives from the imagination, that divine revelation is both given and received in imaginative modes, that theology requires imaginative insight, and that belief is a form of aesthetic perception.

Drawing on a range of non-theological disciplines, including literary theory, anthropology and philosophy of science, Avis clarifies the nature of metaphor, symbol and myth, and develops a critical, symbolic and mythic realism on the premise that God is appropriately likened to an artist or poet and that the greatest truths are expressed in imaginative form. This book challenges theological conservatives and liberals alike as it develops a realist, cognitive theology of the imagination.

Anyone wishing to further their understanding of God, belief and the imagination will find this an inspirational work.

Paul Avis is General Secretary of the Council for Christian Unity of the Church of England, Sub Dean of Exeter Cathedral and Director of the Centre for the Study of the Christian Church. He is also the author or editor of numerous books, including *Faith in the Fires of Criticism* and *Divine Revelation*.

God and the Creative Imagination

Metaphor, symbol and myth in religion and theology

Paul Avis

London and New York

First published 1999 by Routledge
11 New Fetter Lane, London EC4P 4EE

Simultaneously published in the USA and Canada
by Routledge
29 West 35th Street, New York, NY 10001

Routledge Ltd is a Taylor & Francis Group company

© 1999 Paul Avis

Typeset in Times by Routledge
Printed and bound in Great Britain by Clays Ltd, St. Ives PLC

British Library Cataloguing in Publication Data
A catalogue record for this book is available from the British Library

Library of Congress Cataloguing in Publication Data
Avis, Paul D. L.
God and the creative imagination: metaphor, symbol and myth in
religion and theology / Paul Avis.
p. cm.
Includes bibliographical references and index.
1. Imagination–Religious aspects–Christianity. 2. Metaphor–
Religious aspects–Christianity. 3. Christian art and symbolism.
4. Myth 5. Apologetics. I. Title.
BR115.I6A95 1999
230'.01'9–dc21   99–19282
CIP

ISBN 0–415–21502–1 (hbk)
ISBN 0–415–21503-X (pbk)

Contents

Preface   vii
List of abbreviations   x

PART I

1 Speaking of God in the language of the imagination   3
2 The fate of the imagination in modernity   14
3 The fate of the imagination in postmodernity   23
4 Affirming the truth of imagination: The alternative tradition 30

PART II

5 The world of biblical imagination   49
6 Creative theology and the making of doctrine   68
7 Imagination and the adventure of faith   78
8 Liturgy as literature   83

PART III

 9 Metaphor   93
10 Symbol   103
11 Myth   114

PART IV

12 Critical realism   137

13 Symbolic realism   152

14 Mythic realism   158

Bibliography   175
Name index   186
Subject index   190

Preface

How can we envisage God, who is beyond all human imagining? How can we speak of God, who transcends all human speech? These are ultimate theological questions for almost all religions. But theistic religions, particularly Judaism, Christianity and Islam, turn the question round, asking first not what we humans can do to express the truth of God, but what God does in divine revelation to make himself known to us. In what form and by what means does God reveal God's nature and purpose to us? Only when we have established the priority of divine revelation can we go on to ask how we receive, express and interpret that revelation.

Whichever way round we look at them, these divine–human encounters of revelation and response are invariably expressed in the highly figurative language of metaphor, symbol and myth. Is such figurative language capable of telling the truth about reality, or is it merely the expression of free-wheeling fantasy projected onto a void? Can metaphor, symbol and myth be vehicles of truth-giving insight into the sacred realm? Can they become paths to God?

My contention in this book is twofold: first, that it is primarily through the imagination and the genres typically generated by the imagination (metaphor, symbol and myth) that we are brought into living contact with our object (the sacred, the divine, revelation, God), both in living religion and in theological reflection; second, that these modes of discourse have a truth-bearing capacity and can support a critical-realist theology, one that does justice to both the subjective and the objective aspects of theology. The argument of this book develops in four stages:

- In Part I I set out my stall. I open up some of the key issues and explore the background in modernity and postmodernity, showing that both are inhospitable – for different reasons – to the symbolic and its truth-bearing capacity. I sketch an alternative tradition of epistemology that stems from the Romantic poets and thinkers and has been put to work in some modern philosophies of science.
- In Part II I explore the role of imaginative thinking and its expression in metaphor, symbol and myth in four key areas of the Christian religion: revelation through the Bible; theology and doctrine; faith and belief; worship and liturgy. I carry forward important questions for discussion later.
- In Part III I draw largely on non-theological disciplines, such as literary theory, anthropology, philosophy of language and philosophy of sci-

ence, to clarify the nature of metaphor, symbolism and myth, in prepa-
ration for deploying these concepts in the final part.

• Finally, in Part IV I tackle the fundamental questions of whether and
how figurative discourse – primarily metaphor, symbol and myth – can
bear truthful witness to the nature of reality and of God. I ask what
consequences this has for Christian beliefs and examine some thorny
doctrinal – mainly Christological – issues.

So the argument is cumulative and advances in a sort of spiral, coming back
to the central issues of the Bible, doctrine, faith and worship from several
different perspectives.

We can only adopt this critical, interpretative and evaluative approach to
the language of faith and theology when we recognise that religious imagery
is humanly and socially constructed. If the metaphors, symbols and myths
of Christianity were given, ready-made, whole and entire, and without
remainder in divine revelation, there would be little work that we could
appropriately do on them. It would be a question of receiving them in all
humility and merely presenting, arranging, elaborating and expounding
them. The critical, comparative and evaluative approach would be out of
place. It is, then, a presupposition of this study that religious imagery did
not fall ready-made from heaven, but emerges out of the human response to
the disclosing of divine presence in revelation. While revelation stands over
against all human subjectivity and social construction, it remains true that
(as Marx has taught us) man makes religion. The phenomena of religion –
beliefs, forms of worship, structures of organisation, moral codes – are
human artefacts derived from revelation but mediated through human
cultural perspectives. The response to revelation that is articulated in
religion is culturally and socially conditioned. Divine revelation and the
human response embodied in religion interact creatively and critically. This
realm of divine–human encounter and interaction may be called 'the sacred'.
In it the elements of givenness and of appropriation may be distinguished in
conceptual analysis but are difficult to separate out in lived experience. The
whole repertoire of religious imagery – primarily metaphor, symbol and
myth – forms the primary constituents of the sacred.

> The sacred is a set of related images that carry the sense of mystery. Sacred
> images are those that open a world to the transcendent. They mark the
> limits of the human world and the boundary points where men and
> women meet the unknown but felt reality that encompasses their world.
>
> (Davis, 1976, p.90)

My overall intention is to defend the rationality, coherence and credibility of the Christian faith. I do not make the assumption, however, that the
truth-claims of Christian theology can be established or defended merely by
analysing the figurative language in which they are expressed. What such an
analysis can and does show, however, I believe, is the unequivocal intention

of Christian discourse to speak of the nature of reality and of the true relation between God and humanity. The study of metaphor, symbol and myth can show us how such language works, as it serves as the vehicle for spiritual insight – evoked by the revelatory action and gracious presence of God – into ultimate mystery. I believe that such an analysis can demonstrate, as I have already suggested, that creative figurative language is significant, cognitive and unsubstitutable, though not veridical – that is to say, it is not a window into reality as it is, transparent and undistorted, but a reflection in human thought of the actual impact of objective reality, though refracted, dimmed and distorted by the psychological, sociological, political and cultural lenses through which we must inevitably look. 'For now we see through a glass, darkly' (1 Corinthians 13.12, AV).

Underlying my argument is the conviction that the creative human imagination is one of the closest analogies to the being of God. The mystery of imagination points to and reflects the mystery of God. As Coleridge (among others) suggested, human imaginative creativity is an echo, a spark, of the divine creativity that is poured out in the plenitude of creation. Religious thinkers as different as St Augustine and William Blake have (as we shall see) pictured God as a poet or artist who delights to reveal himself through the forms of the imagination: in the poetic and the symbolic. If not, why did Jesus choose to teach through parables?

To bring this discussion within reasonable bounds I have had to take out, in revision, much material that seemed interesting to me – particularly on the Enlightenment, modernity and postmodernity, and also on the construction of Christian identity and the role of symbols, ritual and narratives therein. This suggests the possibility of another project, on the construction of Christian identity in the postmodern age. I have made a start on this in my recently completed text on the pastoral mission of a national Church. I am sympathetic to those who will say – if I may attempt to anticipate a criticism or two – 'Why don't you clarify what you mean by postmodernity?' or 'How can you expound the nature of symbols without discussing identity-formation?' or 'How can you talk about myth without going into narrative theory and narrative theology?' In response, I would point out that I have gone as far into these matters as the argument seemed to require but no further. I merely ask any such critics to be patient.

Unfortunately, I did not see Keith Ward's helpful discussion of metaphor and analogy in *Religion and Creation* (OUP, 1996), Chapter 6, until this book was in press.

I am most grateful to Richard Bourne, my research assistant in the Centre for the Study of the Christian Church, for his work on the indexes.

As General Secretary of the Church of England's Council for Christian Unity I would like to make it clear that I am writing in a purely personal capacity.

Paul Avis

Abbreviations

AV	Authorised Version of the Bible (King James Bible), 1611
BCP	Book of Common Prayer (Anglican), 1662
LXX	The Septuagint (Greek) translation of the Old Testament (Hebrew Bible)
NEB	New English Bible
NRSV	New Revised Standard Version of the Bible
REB	Revised English Bible

Part I

1   Speaking of God in the language of the imagination

My thesis in this book is that Christianity lives supremely from the imagination. My central claim is that the role of the imagination is crucial to understanding the true nature of Christianity. Unless we attempt to do full justice to the part played by the imagination, we cannot understand the Christian faith and we cannot ourselves truly believe. My argument is perhaps parallel to H.U. Von Balthasar's massive, extended and sustained advocacy of the place of beauty in the theological realm. There is, he argues, a need for spiritual perception of the form of beauty that is perfectly expressed in Jesus Christ (Von Balthasar, 1982–9, vol.1). The present study is a sustained attempt to take the imagination or spiritual vision into account when considering Christianity, or (to put it another way) to evaluate Christianity – its scriptures, doctrines, faith and liturgy – in the light of imagination.

I set out to ask: given the imaginative provenance of the Christian faith, how can it also be true? I aim to show that Christianity is indeed true – that its revelation is real, that its central doctrines are informative, that belief in its object is well placed and that its worship is in touch with reality. So my thesis embraces four critical areas of concern: biblical revelation, Christian doctrine, religious belief and divine worship.

Biblical revelation

My starting point is the conviction that divine revelation is given above all (though certainly not exclusively) in modes that are addressed to the human imagination, rather than to any other faculty (such as the analytical reason or the moral conscience). But let no one accuse me of reducing divine revelation to mere human religious consciousness or projection. There is admirable precedent for my claim. As St Augustine saw, God is a poet and speaks to the world in metaphors, symbols and parables. The supreme revelation is the 'form' (as Von Balthasar would say) of Jesus Christ – the whole pattern of divine truth embodied in an historical person and shining out through him into human history. Blake said that 'the Whole Bible is fill'd with Imagination and Visions' (Ackroyd, 1995, p.27).

Austin Farrer, in his outstanding Bampton Lectures *The Glass of Vision* (1948), claimed that the revelatory character of the Bible resided in certain dominant images which lay at the centre of the teaching of Jesus: kingdom of God, Son of Man, restored Israel, suffering servant, sacrifice, covenant and so on. For Farrer, revelation was conveyed through the imagination of the Apostles and the Bible was the product of inspired imagining similar to poetic inspiration. 'Divine truth is supernaturally communicated to men in an act of inspired thinking which falls into the shape of certain images' (Farrer, 1948, p.57). It is the images that lend vitality and dynamism to the Bible, and determine its form and content. The inspired mind of the Apostles, Farrer claims, 'is a process of images which live as it were by their own life and impose themselves with authority' (ibid., p.113). Farrer's theory, in the form in which he states it at least, has not found acceptance, but it has the heart of the matter in it. If – as I hope to show – all insight is given through metaphorical perception, if the deepest truths are conveyed in symbols and if those symbols drive the narrative identity of the community when they are constellated in myth, it would be astounding if this were not true of biblical metaphors, symbols and myths, handed on by the biblical community – Israel and the Church.

That is not how the majority of Christians today – especially Bible-loving conservative evangelicals – see the scriptures: they tend to view them as a system of factual, descriptive propositions, bearing divine authority, to be taken at face value and as literally as possible. Conservative evangelicals remain uneasy about approaches to biblical interpretation that play down the imperative of factual accuracy and dwell on the import of such figurative genres as metaphor, symbol and myth. Like the true fundamentalist, the conservative evangelical believes that the Bible makes explicit claims for itself and sets forth divine revelation accordingly in factual statements or propositions. He is uncomfortable with the notion that scripture reveals the truth of God indirectly, obliquely, through images and similitudes, and in a manner constrained by its historical and cultural context. Augustine's hint that God communicates with us in a poetic mode and Blake's tenet that Jesus and the Apostles were artists would seem to conservative evangelicals to make divine revelation rest on the shifting sands of subjective, arrogant human subjectivity. A recent major study concludes that an obsession with factual accuracy, a penchant for literal interpretation and a predictable tendency to arrive at maximally conservative conclusions – whatever arguments are considered along the way – mark (and mar) the conservative evangelical approach to biblical interpretation and serve to stake out common ground with fundamentalism (Harris, 1998).

Literal interpretations of the most patently figurative parts of scripture are relinquished by conservative evangelicals long after they have ceased to be tenable and not without a violent struggle. For conservative evangelicals, Genesis 1 was first history, then a sequence of geological epochs, before being reluctantly accepted as myth. Mark Noll's *The Scandal of the*

Evangelical Mind (1994) traces the sorry tale of the corruption of sober, scholarly evangelical thinking in the nineteenth century by fundamentalism, resistance to evolution, distortions of geology and ultimately full-blown creationism. The virginal conception of Jesus in Matthew and Luke is interpreted as literal biology by some evangelical theologians, even when it is admitted that that stance creates insuperable problems from the point of view of genetics and is in any case not helpful in defending the doctrine of the incarnation, namely the assumption of complete humanity by the Logos. The conflicting presentation of the resurrection appearances in the Gospels (exacerbated by the lack of any resurrection appearances at all in the original ending of Mark) still gives scope for the ingenuity of the harmonisers.

This literalistic approach is defensive and impossible to sustain indefinitely. Perhaps that is why there are so many 'post-conservative evangelicals'; possibly it accounts for the fact that a number of prominent liberal theologians originally came from the conservative evangelical stable. The deeper study of biblical images, parables and symbolic narrative, at which the early Fathers excelled and which Barth and Von Balthasar have revived, is more commensurate with the character of divine revelation. Blake's dictum that the whole Bible is filled with imagination and visions needs only to be thought about in order to carry conviction. The question of the metaphorical, symbolic and mythic complexion of the biblical revelation will be taken up in Chapter 5.

Christian doctrine

My second claim is that Christian doctrines (though ultimately derived from divine revelation) are the high expression of human imaginative insight. Because God is a poet, as Augustine suggests, and communicates with us in the imaginative mode, our most appropriate response is also in that mode. Theology does its work in the realm of analogy. Doctrines as the authoritative ultimate outcome of theology – privileged theology, we might say – are equally stated by means of analogy. There is no escape from analogical theology. Our task, therefore, in this section will be to try to show that there is a connection, a continuity, between metaphor and analogy – so that analogy is seen as an unravelling of primal metaphors, a spelling out of the similes that are compressed in metaphors. As Farrer asserts, analogy 'is only another name for sober and appropriate images' and all our significant thinking about ultimate, unique meanings, whether in metaphysics or theology, is 'irreducible analogizing' (Farrer, 1948, pp.71, 74).

Doctrines are elicited from the Church as it comes under the sway of the pattern or form of revelation. The Church sees or perceives (or thinks it does) the import of revelation and articulates that perception in the most strenuous act of God-given reason. That act of reason is filled with ethical and aesthetic perception. The doctrines of the creed (to use Oliver Quick's phrase) are not divinely revealed in propositional form. As William Temple famously said, there are no revealed truths but there are truths of revelation. Divine revelation and human discovery are correlative terms not because revelation is not real or because the Bible is not full of it, but precisely because of the nature of revelation and its reception. It can only be given in the medium of the imagination and can only be appropriated in the same way.

That does not mean that doctrines are a matter of individual preference – every man his own magisterium – nor does it make them frivolous and ephemeral. Doctrines are weighty matters and carry the authority of the Church that teaches them. But, because the Church is not generally infallible, doctrines are not irreformable. In practice, the symbols are permanent but the way they are interpreted is constantly evolving. No one in their right mind wants to 'monkey with the creed' (in Hilaire Belloc's immortal phrase), but it is simply the case that the profoundly symbolic character of revelation constantly generates new insights in response to the contemplation of faith.

The contribution that metaphor, symbol and myth make to Christian doctrine – together with their refined, sophisticated and critical development into analogy – will be explored in Chapter 6.

Religious belief

My third contention is that the act and attitude of faith is born from the imagination. Faith sees the form or pattern of divine revelation as a whole. It sees it embedded in the literary genres of the Bible. It sees it radiating supremely from Jesus Christ as he lies in the manger of the scriptures (as Luther put it). It hears and heeds the witness of the Church in its teaching. It is seized by the truth of the central Christian doctrines of creation, the fallen human condition, atonement, salvation and sanctification in the Church, and the accomplishing of all this through the triune nature of God. The meaning of these doctrines is grasped by the believer through an act of imaginative assent. Faith is not only convinced that the gospel of Christ is worthy of credence and is no illusion, it is also drawn by the perfection of its form: it sees it as supremely beautiful, attractive and desirable. I wish to draw attention to the aesthetic dimension in faith. The imaginative–aesthetic dimension of faith and assent will be pursued in Chapter 7.

Divine worship

Finally, I want to argue that the answer that we make together to God-in-revelation – that is to say, in the Church's worship – is also enacted in the mode of imaginative expression. The touchstone of liturgy is its imaginative adequacy. In its heights and depths, its profundity and simplicity, liturgy must be commensurate with our most treasured moments of knowing that we are in touch with a reality that is unconditional, infinite and eternal – and, moreover, is the source of our deepest well-being. Human religious experience typically speaks of such moments in metaphor, symbol and myth. Liturgy needs to acknowledge this.

When we worship through the Church's liturgy we know whether or not we have a deep sense of satisfaction, contentment and fulfilment that the liturgy is doing its job – performing effectively. Not only should it be adequate to express our most significant intuitions – our deepest hopes, aspirations and longings – but it should transcend them, poor and unworthy as they are, and impart to us a sense of being gathered up into an action and an event that is infinitely greater than ourselves – in fact into the timeless prayer of the Church, with 'angels and archangels and all the company of heaven' surrounding us as we pray (BCP service of Holy Communion). When the liturgy fails to be such a vehicle we experience frustration and feel short-changed. The liturgy has failed the test of imaginative adequacy. The truth of the imagination in liturgy will concern us in Chapter 8.

So when I say that the Christian faith lives from the imagination, I mean that Christianity is a faith that subsists in the symbolic realm and is appropriated through imaginative indwelling. All the vital practical expressions of Christian existence bear witness to this fact. Prayer, liturgy and theology, as well as the Bible, speak the language of the imagination and articulate their truths in metaphor, symbol or myth. Whether we consider the nature of divine revelation found in scripture, the way that it is interpreted in doctrines and assented to in faith, or the response that it draws forth from the believer in worship – the centrality of imagination is clear. Now the characteristic expressions of imagination are comprised in the three figurative genres of metaphor, symbol and myth. But these are the very substance of religious discourse. Our enquiry is generated by the question of how these can be the vehicles of true utterances about the sacred.

To claim that the Christian religion is best understood as the truth of imagination is totally different from saying that Christianity is an *imaginary faith*. The great reductionist thinkers of modernity – Feuerbach, Marx, Nietzsche and Freud – claimed that Christianity was an imaginary faith, in the sense that its beliefs were merely projections of unconscious psychological tensions or of social and economic conflicts. For these makers of the modern worldview, Christian beliefs were a world of illusion, created by compensatory wish-fulfilment. The persons of the Holy Trinity were imaginary beings; experience of the grace and presence of God was an imaginary psychological state; heaven and hell were imaginary places, and so on. For example, Friedrich Nietzsche claimed in *The Anti-Christ* that neither Christian morality nor Christian piety made contact with reality at any point. Imaginary, occult causes (God, spirit, soul) were supposed to produce imaginary effects (sin, redemption, forgiveness) within the framework of an imaginary purpose or teleology (kingdom of God, last judgement, eternal life) (Nietzsche, 1968, p.125; for further discussion, see Avis, 1995).

However, when I make the claim that Christianity lives from the imagination, that Christian beliefs are to be found embodied in metaphor, symbol and myth, and that the Christian faith can only be appropriated by a corresponding act of imaginative insight, I am asserting the opposite of the reductionist theses of Feuerbach, Marx and so on. I am defending the truth and reality of what the Christian faith postulates. The truth of Christian belief is not something that is purely immanent in and reducible to mundane, human and social factors, as the reductionists claimed; it infinitely transcends them – it remains ineffable. And because it transcends this-worldly factors, this truth and reality can only be grasped meaningfully in the realm of imagination which takes images of earth and uses them to evoke a realm beyond. The greatest truths can only be expressed in imaginative form – through images (metaphor, symbol, myth). We know the truth only through the imagination. Creative imagination, rather than some supposedly objective, rationally specifiable procedure that lies outside the domain of personal knowledge, is the key to knowing reality. The truth is contained in symbols and the symbols are materially embodied. That is, it seems to me, a corollary of the incarnational and sacramental character of Christianity.

John Keats wrote in 1817 at the age of twenty-two: 'I am certain of nothing but of the holiness of the Heart's affections and the truth of Imagination – What the imagination seizes as Beauty must be truth' (Keats, 1954, p.48). We know the truth through the whole person. As Newman wrote autobiographically, 'it is the concrete being that reasons ... the whole man moves' (Newman, 1959, p.225). In his sustained reflections on how we know the truth in the *Grammar of Assent* (Newman, 1903), with its concept of the illative (truth-seeking, truth-sensing, truth-seizing) sense, Newman gave a central place to the imaginative grasp of the truth. Unlike Keats, Newman – an ascetic – could not fully trust himself to beauty. As Vargish has pointed out, there is a dichotomy in Newman's thought between truth as beauty to be enjoyed and truth as power to be obeyed. 'In Newman's epistemology the perception of beauty and the realization of religious truth are disparate intellectual actions' (Vargish, 1970, p.156). But imagination is for Newman, just as for Keats, the power that kindles insight into reality. 'Real assent' (or, as Newman had called it in an early draft, 'imaginative assent') is 'more vivid and forcible' than notional assent. 'Real apprehension ... excites and stimulates the affections and passions, by bringing facts home to them as motive causes' (Newman, 1903, pp.9f., 12). Whether as beauty (for Keats) or as moral claim (for Newman), the truth is embodied immanently in material symbols, including words which are linguistic material symbols.

Christian truth is both immanent in the world and transcendent of the world. Once we have dealt with the destructive distortion that restricts the truth of faith to a function of immanental processes, we must make the vital corrective claim that these processes, that are so firmly of this world, can become the sacramental channels of the truth of God. They may be persons (prophets, Apostles, saints, the incarnate Jesus Christ) or liturgical actions (poured water, broken bread, lighted candles, icons) or special words and propositions (metaphors, linguistic symbols, narratives, parables, myths). Newman believed that Christ lives to our imaginations by his visible symbols (Prickett, 1986, p.217). The ultimate logic of this is found in the Christian doctrines of creation, revelation, incarnation, sanctification and consummation. These doctrines are all of a piece. They presuppose that mundane, worldly, created realities can become the vehicles and means of divine presence and purpose. They affirm that the material, the human and the historical can reflect the glory of God. The world is bound to God in ontological dependence, yet preserved at an epistemic distance that gives scope for human freedom, created contingency and divine involvement in revelation and redemption.

These pivotal Christian doctrines, from creation to consummation, also confront the sort of high-sounding deistic dualism that denies that the ultimate reality can be encountered through contingent, historical and human forms. Such extreme transcendentalism cannot make sense of the idea of God being involved in the mess and muddle, the tragedy and futility of the human condition. It cannot cope with the notion of a God who is 'the fellow sufferer who understands' (in A.N. Whitehead's unforgettable phrase; Whitehead, 1929, p.497). It cannot see the point of the Church as a divine–human society with God-given ministries and sacraments to bring us through earth to heaven. It cannot make philosophical sense of the Creator indwelling the creation, the absolute implicated in the relative, the necessary involved in the contingent. Its misplaced motivation is to preserve God's dignity. It assumes that it is appropriate for us to decide what is suitable to God. It forgets Luther's great war cry: 'Let God be God!' This damaging dualism has lost its grip on the paradigm doctrine of Christianity – the incarnation.

The incarnation may be variously understood, but essentially it speaks of a unique, unsurpassable involvement of God in an individual human life. It designates a single contingent fact as God. But that unique involvement is offset against the background of God's action and presence in the whole created process: the shaping of creation, the providential ordering of history to bring good out of evil and manifest the salvific purpose of God, the calling and teaching of Israel which provides the essential *locus* within which Jesus could be (and could be known to be) the Christ, and the sending of the Holy Spirit to the Church in order to constitute it as a general participation (*koinonia*) in the relationship between God and humanity that is seen definitively in Jesus Christ. The pattern of God's universal redemptive purpose provides the backcloth, the matrix for that definitive and unique act in Jesus Christ. The scandal of particularity is not a function of the perversity of some Protestant theologians, nor does it derive from a desire to shock our inherited Platonic susceptibilities. It does not stand alone, but forms a polarity with the *general* involvement and self-giving of God in God's world. One lights up the other and sets it in relief. But Christianity is a creational, incarnational and sacramental faith or it is nothing.

The same transcendental, Platonic dualism underlies the suspicion of the symbolic realm in post-Enlightenment culture. The Enlightenment could not see how particular facts could be the key to universal truths. Lessing's dictum, 'Accidental truths of history can never be the proof of necessary truths of reason' (Lessing, 1956, p.53), sums up modernity's scepticism about the truth-carrying capacity of the particular. Fichte reinforced this dualism when he said that 'only the metaphysical can save, never the historical.' Kant, similarly, laid it down that the historical could serve only for illustration, not for demonstration. In modernity, symbols (which belong to the particular and historical) are regarded merely as rhetorical gestures created by human subjectivity. They cannot point beyond themselves to an ultimate reality. They can only point reflexively back to their subjective, socially conditioned source.

But Christianity, we have been compelled to acknowledge, is creational, incarnational and sacramental in its very essence. It therefore pins its truth to the particular. If we think about it, what is the alternative? What else is there that provides a sure foundation? Blake, of all people, said that 'Strictly Speaking All Knowledge is Particular' (Wilson, 1978, p.246). Historical events, given the interpretation, can become windows into eternity. Symbols, as Coleridge so often insisted, unite the particular and the universal. A symbol, he wrote, 'is characterized by a translucence of the Special in the Individual or of the General in the Especial or of the Universal in the General. Above all by the translucence of the Eternal through and in the Temporal' (Coleridge, 1972, p.30). It is no accident that the Coleridge who affirmed the truth-bearing capacity of symbols was the Coleridge who had moved from Unitarianism to Trinitarian orthodoxy, who believed that the Holy Trinity was the ultimate Idea (eternal truth, seminal symbol) and who at one point wondered whether it was right to say that the sacraments of baptism and the eucharist were an important part of Christianity when truly they were Christianity itself (Coleridge, 1884, pp.249f.).

Kierkegaard celebrated the paradox intolerable to human reason that eternal truth is located, through that Pauline foolishness of God which is wiser than the wisdom of men, in a particular moment – 'the fullness of time'. Through passionate ethical intensity we may perceive that a moment is pregnant with eternal significance (Kierkegaard, 1946, p.13; 1945, pp.505, 88, 138). David Jenkins, with his characteristic reiteration of the theme of 'transcendence in the midst', has well said that 'there is no contradiction between the universality, infinitude and absoluteness of God and his giving himself in, through and to historical particularities. Jesus Christ ... confirms to us ... that particular moments, historical processes and embodied persons are the places where God is met, known, received and responded to' (Jenkins, 1976, p.21).

The fundamental challenge is that the 'truth of imagination' (to use John Keats' famous phrase), expressed in metaphor, symbol and myth, is cheapened and devalued in our postmodern culture just as it was in the modernity of the Enlightenment. For both ideologies, the symbolic belongs to the category of empty rhetoric. The challenge to a view of imaginative, figurative discourse as cognitive and capable of being the vehicle of true insight – to a notion of 'symbolic realism' – emerges from both quarters. In this book, I will contest the assumption made by both the Enlightenment and postmodernism that metaphors, symbols and myths belong to the realm of the trivial, the arbitrary and the false. I will show that symbols are not arbitrary or at our disposal, but powerful, cognitive and to be handled with care. I will claim that metaphors are the vehicles of fresh insight and thus constitutive of our apprehension of truth; that symbols mediate the transcendent because they participate in what they symbolise, and that myths, which are archetypal stories studded with numinous symbols, embody a sacral narrative of human identity in the face of the divine reality.

In the first instance, I will be arguing for 'metaphoric realism', then I will be moving on to 'symbolic realism' and from there progressing to 'mythic realism'. I will be arguing that the images that belong to these various kinds or genres, such as metaphor, symbol and myth, are *first* significant and to be taken seriously, though critically and with discrimination; *second* informative or cognitive, as embodying genuine insight into reality, albeit an insight that is shaped and conditioned by the psychological, social and cultural context, and *finally* unsubstitutable or irreducible, that is to say, incapable of being translated into some supposedly 'straight' or literal and non-figurative language.

What I will certainly not be claiming, needless to say, is that images are veridical – a perfect fit with reality. Figurative realism does not claim that images are descriptive of the world: there are incompatible symbol systems, for one thing. Linguistic symbols give insight into reality in the sense that they are the vehicle of our human imaginative apprehension of truth. But they do not guarantee the truth of that apprehension. That judgement, as to the truth of an insight, can only be made on other grounds, by applying criteria that bring our fresh insights into contact with our overall worldview and assess them by reference to science, history, experience, ideological criticism and so on. To put the point in Kantian terms, the truth of imagination is phenomenal, not noumenal. Linguistic images enrich our experience of the world. They are incremental in that they add to our understanding. We see more profoundly into reality through the truth of imagination than we do when we pursue the illusion of precise, specifiable, purely objective, literal description. So an analysis of metaphor, symbol and myth is not merely telling us about our mental processes – though it is at least telling us that – but it is showing how we attain reliable knowledge of the world. That penetration of reality is heuristic, not definitive; it is fragmentary, not total; it leaves the ocean of being largely unexplored. The knowledge it gives is not like the noonday sun, but (as Locke used to say) like the light of a candle in a dark room, sufficient to see our way – to make the moral commitment of faith that we are called to exercise as persons in a moral universe.

I attempt, then, to take the vital steps *from metaphoric realism to symbolic realism and from there to mythic realism.* Unlike some modern theologians in the Barthian tradition, I do not shy away from acknowledging substantial mythic elements both in the Bible (including the New Testament) and in Christian beliefs (including the Creed). In fact I hold that *all the really important affirmations of the Christian faith are expressed in mythic form.* Now this is a purely formal point, based on the premises that the central affirmations of the Christian faith tend to take a narrative form, that this narrative is not primarily historical in its intention and that it is studded with numinous symbols. It is simply a recognition of the conceptual, linguistic and literary modes concerned, though it has implications for how we interpret the narratives and it affects the sense in which we are able to claim that they are 'true'.

When we have accounts in narrative form, embodying potent symbols, concerning the encounter of humanity and God, describing realities that transcend our normal categories of space and time – to do with *origins* (the creation of the world and humanity), *divine interventions* (incarnation, atonement, resurrection, ascension) and *destiny* or *consummation* (eschatology) – we are compelled, I believe, to recognise the presence of myth. But we should not jump too hastily from epistemological premises to ontological conclusions. My claim that the really important affirmations of the Christian faith are expressed in metaphor, symbol and myth does not imply any pre-judgement on the truth-value or credibility of the message that those sacred and normative myths convey to us – though it does enable us to discern that the mythological stage scenery often belongs to a worldview that in any other context we would judge to be obsolete.

The mention of the notion of obsolete worldviews raises the spectre (as some would certainly see it) of Rudolf Bultmann and the concept of 'demythologisation'. I do not completely subscribe to Bultmann's demyth–ologising programme and I will be arguing that the question of myth in Christianity is a separate issue from many of the presuppositions that Bultmann brought to it and that it should be detached from them. I also recognise the need for remythologising, for I do not believe that any culture or faith can hope to supersede myth entirely – nor, on my premises, is this either possible or desirable – nor do I believe that there is a higher mode of articulating the truths of faith than the mythopoeic. By exploring the examples of the incarnation, the resurrection and eschatology (among others), I hope to indicate what I am striving for here. So in my conclusion I will be focussing on the crucial question of how we are to understand the truth of Christian beliefs when those beliefs clearly have mythic elements. What sort of realism can we claim for Christian doctrines?

2   The fate of the imagination in modernity

'A mere metaphor', 'an empty symbol', 'just a myth' are phrases that we often hear in conversation, journalism or political rhetoric. They signal the hostility of public discourse in our culture to imaginative truth. These tell-tale phrases disparage the figurative aspects of language and suggest that they are furthest removed from its truth-bearing aspects. They seem to imply that there is an alternative linguistic repertoire available to us – a more correct, more precise and somehow 'straight' kind of language. This supposed alternative is sometimes called 'the literal truth', 'the honest truth', 'plain prose' or 'factual language'. With wearisome monotony politicians insist that their policies are 'perfectly clear' – and we know that the more politicians protest that they have made it perfectly clear, are making it perfectly clear and will continue to make it perfectly clear, the more completely opaque and indeed dubiously murky 'it' really is.

The prejudice against the figurative is by no means confined to colloquial or popular culture. That merely takes its cue, long in arrears, from the discourse of academic disciplines such as philosophy and the natural and social sciences. In this approach the supposed literal use of language is taken as the norm from which figurative use is a deviation. 'Literal' language carries greater moral prestige; figurative language is regarded as somehow lightweight, frivolous and lacking in moral *gravitas*. If, without resorting to figurative language – to metaphor, symbol and myth, and in the process becoming hazy, imprecise and unclear – we cannot address the 'higher' realm, of which theology, metaphysics, ethics and aesthetics aspire to speak, so much the worse for these disciplines.

Modern philosophy in the analytical tradition was obsessed with the search for a precise, disciplined, stripped-down language, purged of ambiguity and without fuzzy edges, that would correspond as directly as possible to what is actually the case in the real world. Wittgenstein memorably began his *Tractatus Logico-Philosophicus* of 1922 with the definition: 'The world is all that is the case.' His early logical atomism represents, perhaps, the ultimate quest for a pure relation between words and things. Wittgenstein is exploring the conditions for a logically perfect language. The first requirement of such a language is that there should be strict correlation between word and thing – one name for every irreducible piece of information, so that to each fact is allocated one name and to each name only one fact corresponds. Because it is concerned with this relation between words and things, names and facts, logical atomism does not stand alone but corresponds to and in a sense depends on ontological atomism. Wittgenstein postulated irreducible, 'simple' (i.e. not complex) objects which could be named, which form the constituents of complex atomic facts or 'states of affairs'. Together all the atomic facts or states of affairs comprise all that is the case – the world. Objects in states of affairs are the way in which we represent logically the reality of things in situations. When we attempt to describe these basic units of reality as accurately as possible (i.e. scientifically), we need a correspondingly basic language. 'Atomic facts' are articulated in 'elementary propositions'. 'To states of affairs which are concatenations of simple objects there correspond elementary propositions which assert the existence of states of affairs; elementary propositions are concatenations of names for simple objects' (Kenny, 1975, p.85). The totality of true propositions is by definition identical with the whole body of knowledge of the natural sciences.

The relationship between a proposition and the reality it expresses cannot be expressed in propositions. To put it another way, alluding to Wittgenstein's 'picture theory of language', a picture cannot depict its pictorial form but can only display it. The common structure that must pertain between thought and fact, language and reality, the logical and the ontological, Wittgenstein calls 'the mystical'. He excluded the 'mystical' from the realm of philosophically correct discourse: the 'mystical' was 'inexpressible' and could only 'show' itself. The precise language of science was incapable of expressing the mystical. 'There are, indeed, things [*sic*] that cannot be put into words. They make themselves manifest. They are what is mystical' (Wittgenstein, 1961, p.73: 6.522). As Wittgenstein famously concluded: 'What we cannot speak about we must pass over in silence' (ibid., p.74: 7). For Wittgenstein there can be no genuine propositions of a metaphysical nature – to do with ultimate values and religious truth. No proposition can express the meaning of life or the point of the world, for all propositions are contingent since they refer to contingent states of affairs. 'How things are in the world is a matter of complete indifference for what is higher. God does not reveal himself in the world. The [contingent] facts all contribute only to setting the problem, not to its solution' (ibid., p.73: 6.432, 6.4321).

If philosophy cannot state the mystical and science cannot describe it, that shows the limitations of philosophy and science. There are undoubtedly experiences, thoughts, hopes, aspirations, longings and insights that are not exhausted by philosophical analysis or capable of being scientifically verified. Wittgenstein suggests that we can climb beyond him, throwing away the ladder after us: the reader who understands 'must transcend these propositions, and then he will see the world aright' (Wittgenstein, 1961, p.74: 6.54). Is it a permissible extrapolation from Wittgenstein to suggest

that once we have left behind the ladder of logical analysis, we can be helped
to mount further by means of the ladder of metaphorical insight? Wittgenstein is not himself shy of figurative language. The *Tractatus* and other
writings are full of it and it flashes illumination on the argument as it is
meant to do: 'logical space', 'substance of the world', 'objects are colourless'
and (from *Philosophical Investigations*, 1968) 'language games'. We wonder
whether, for Wittgenstein, metaphor can transcend the contingent and
trigger insight into 'the mystical'. His own metaphor of the ladder suggests
that it can and that while the mystical cannot be stated logically, it can be
signalled metaphorically.

> To view the world sub specie aeterni is to view it as a whole – a limited
> whole.
> Feeling the world as a limited whole – it is this that is mystical.
> (Wittgenstein, 1961, p.73: 6.45)

Wittgenstein's early views reflected, amongst other influences, the empiricist tradition of Bacon, Hobbes and Locke. His immediate predecessor on
the Continent was Rudolf Carnap, the author of the notorious 'verification
principle' which tests the propositions of physical science against immediate
sense experience and simple relationships, expressed in 'protocol sentences'.
Wittgenstein's legatee in English philosophy, A.J. Ayer, took the argument a
crucial step further. By applying the 'verification principle' to all kinds of
statements, he was able to claim that propositions which were neither
analytic and tautologous (such as the symbols of logic and mathematics),
nor synthetic and descriptive of the world (and therefore derived from sense
experience), were strictly meaningless – sense-less.

Clearly the logical empiricist approach, of which Carnap, the early
Wittgenstein and Ayer are representatives, takes its cue from certain
presuppositions about the methods of the physical sciences. It is widely
assumed within this tradition that the proper language of science is one that
is literal, factual and precise. Science, it is claimed, presents facts rather than
interpretations, realities rather than illusions, objectivity rather than
subjectivity, precision rather than broad generalisations, descriptions rather
than suggestive models.

Pierre Duhem (1861–1916) was a noted proponent of this view. For
Duhem, scientific descriptions should shun images in favour of abstract
formulae. Louis de Broglie wrote of Duhem:

> Essentially a systematic mind, he was attracted by axiomatic methods
> which lay down exact postulates in order to derive by rigorous reason-
> ing unassailable conclusions; he prized their solidity and rigour, and was
> far from repulsed by their dryness and exactness.
> (Duhem, 1954, p.vi)

All theories based on images were vague and unstable; only hypotheses that could be expressed algebraically were pure and reliable (ibid., p.vii). Duhem was able to adopt this scornful attitude to symbolic descriptions in science because he held that it was not the business of science to venture beyond phenomena and to attempt to provide ultimate explanations – where, it seems, symbolic statements are the best that we can hope for.

The literary critic D.J. James, though presumably an amateur in this field, contends that all scientific language must 'abhor metaphor'. Scientific language is literal; poetic language is metaphorical. His view rests on the assumption that the task of science is to provide information, that of poetry to express states of mind. So James asserts:

> Poetry in its pure secular nature ... advances no statements and pro-
> pounds no doctrine ... Poetry ... affirms nothing in its great play of
> symbolism; it stakes, or utters, no claim – it does not put itself out for
> knowledge; it only shows how it imagines things.
>
> (James, 1949, p.99)

James is driven to make the implausible assertion that 'philosophical poems', such as Lucretius' *De Rerum Naturae*, Wordsworth's *The Prelude* and Tennyson's *In Memoriam* (and what about Dante's *La Divina Commedia*?), are less poetical than purely lyrical poems and fall short of the poetic ideal (James, 1949, p.102).

The foundations of the social sciences are infected with the same preju-dice. In his classic work in the sociology of religion, *The Elementary Forms of the Religious Life*, Durkheim argued that religious language needed to be translated into the rigorous conceptualities of science: 'Logical thinking is always impersonal thinking, and is also thought *sub specie aeternitatis* – as though for all time. Impersonality and stability are the two characteristics of truth' (Durkheim, 1915, p.436). Disciplines such as theology, philosophy, ethics and metaphysics that are inimical to such disciplined speech are looked upon as belonging to a lower order of discourse – as dealing in opinion rather than knowledge, values rather than facts, subjective preference rather than objective entities.

As our argument develops, we will challenge this interpretation of sci-ence. We shall see that thinking in images is essential to scientific explora-tion and that broad, illuminating symbols are needed to interpret data. We shall also question the assumption that poetry makes no statement about the nature of reality and is purely non-cognitive. This will enable us to see an affinity between the perceptions expressed in poetry and the language of religious belief. Science, poetry and religion are all energised by the imagination and all tell us something about reality, appropriate to their various methods.

Metaphor, symbol and myth are the main constituents of figurative language and are therefore regarded by those influenced by this caricature of science as the prime culprits in the debasement of language. The terms metaphor, symbol and myth are commonly used in a pejorative and reductionist sense. The implication is that when we want to say something important, true and real we naturally shun metaphor, symbol or myth and speak plainly. They are deemed to carry a 'logical taint', to borrow Middleton Murray's phrase (Murray, 1937, 2nd series, pp.1ff.).

Some theologians, captivated by the prestige of the physical sciences, are suspicious of figurative language. T.F. Torrance, for example, has argued consistently for the primacy of aural over visual models of revelation and its reception. Torrance has claimed that thinking in images should be regarded as strictly subordinate to thinking in concepts, the word (*logos*), rational discourse, to guard against as a prophylactic for idolatry (Torrance, 1965, pp.20f., 50f., 87f.; 1969, pp.17ff.).

At the other extreme there are theologians who exploit the figurative forms of metaphor, symbol and myth, but take them in a non-cognitive or non-realist sense. For example, it is not clear to me that Sallie McFague in *Metaphorical Theology* believes that the metaphors or images that she advocates so persuasively do actually refer in the real world to a transcendent 'object' or whether she is 'bracketing out' the question of realism and working purely immanently with expressions of human subjectivity. On the one hand she speaks acceptably of 'dominant, founding metaphors as true but not literal', while on the other hand she insists that in theological language we are not dealing with 'reality as it is' but solely with perspectives on reality (McFague, 1982, pp.28, 134). The 'heavily projectionist' tenor of McFague's view of theological metaphors has been usefully exposed by Colin Gunton (in Kimel, ed., 1992).

The legacy of the Enlightenment

Suspicion of metaphor and the figurative generally belongs to the mentality of the Enlightenment. As we shall see when we discuss metaphor specifically, this suspicion can be traced back to Aristotle. But its author in modern thought is the founder of empirical science, Francis Bacon (1561–1626). Bacon is the originator of the analytical view of language, a tradition that runs through Descartes, Hobbes, Locke and Bentham to the linguistic analysis of the twentieth century. Bacon advocated a literary style to match the rigour and self-discipline of his empirical method. It was to be a style marked by 'chastity'. This austere ideal of expression was premised on the view that words were 'counters' or 'signs' and had an exactly quantifiable value. Metaphor and other figures of speech were an encumbrance to the truth. 'And for all that concerns ornaments of speech, similitudes, treasury of eloquence, and such like emptinesses, let it be utterly dismissed' (Bacon, 1905, p.403). Though Bacon spends considerable time elucidating the wisdom concealed in myths, he regards the figurative generally as primitive: 'As hieroglyphics came before letters, so parables came before arguments' (ibid., p.822; cf. Rossi, 1968, ch.3). Vico adopted the chronology but made the opposite valuation: 'The first nations,' he asserted in his *New Science*, 'thought in poetic characters, spoke in fables and wrote in hieroglyphs' (Vico, 1961, p.139, para.429). These were the wellsprings of insight.

Fundamental to the analytical view of language are the two criteria of clarity and distinctness. When Descartes (1596–1650) set out to eliminate all that he could not be certain of and to build his knowledge from scratch by indubitable stages, his first rule was 'never to accept anything as true that I did not know to be evidently so: that is to say ... to include in my judgements nothing more than what presented itself so clearly and so distinctly to my mind that I might have no occasion to place it in doubt' (Descartes, 1968, p.41). His momentous conclusion, *Cogito ergo sum*, was the paradigm of a clear and distinct idea. Descartes inferred from this that 'I could take it to be a general rule that the things we conceive very clearly and very distinctly are all true' – though there remained the problem that it is difficult to recognise for certain which things we do see distinctly (ibid., p.54). Elsewhere Descartes elaborated his germinal insight. An idea is clear when it is 'present and apparent to an attentive mind' and distinct when it is 'so precise and different from all other objects that it contains within itself nothing but what is clear' (Schouls, 1989, p.21, citing *Principles of Philosophy*). Though Descartes' criteria have been judged, ironically, to be far from clear and distinct themselves (see Ashworth, 1972), they were destined to have a long and interesting history right up until they were explicitly challenged by the later Wittgenstein.

Thomas Hobbes (1588–1679) was Bacon's secretary and colleague. Though he developed a conception of science that diverged radically from Bacon's, being determined by the deductive rather than the inductive method, he shared Bacon's atomistic view of language as made up of counters or signs with a designated meaning. Hobbes asserts in *Leviathan*: 'Words are wise men's counters, they do but reckon by them; but they are the money of fools' (Hobbes, 1962, p.78). Metaphor, for Hobbes, is at best an aberration, at worst pathological. A metaphor is a word used in a sense other than the intended or ordained one and is therefore deceptive (ibid., p.75). Rhetorical figures such as metaphors usurp the function of 'words proper' and lead us astray (ibid., p.85). They are a will-o'-the-wisp and 'reasoning upon them is wandering amongst innumerable absurdities' (ibid., p.86). For Hobbes language is a matter of naming, as Adam named the creatures. It is a product of the will and is therefore arbitrary. Names are mechanical devices for tagging and recalling thoughts. From names we construct definitions and by computing definitions we pursue rational thought. Hobbes' method consists in reasoning from definitions by what he calls adding and subtracting.

John Locke (1632–1704) combines Bacon's empirical method, Descartes' critical principle of clear and distinct ideas, and Hobbes' passion for precision and suspicion of metaphor. For Locke thinking is conscious, explicit cogitation – there are no subliminal creative depths – in which the units of thought are the familiar Cartesian and Hobbesian clear and distinct ideas. Locke, however, takes this approach a step further when he puts forward the notion of 'determinate' or 'determined' ideas, meaning that we have an idea and we know exactly what we mean by it (Locke, 1961, vol.1, pp.xxxviii, 306ff.). The 'articulate sounds' that we call words have 'no natural connection with our ideas, but have all their signification from the arbitrary imposition of men' (ibid., vol.2, p.77). Locke finds the imperfection of words in their incorrigible vagueness and advocates the counsel of perfection that 'men should use their words constantly in the same sense and for none but determined and uniform ideas' (ibid., vol.2, p.106). The aim is the conjunction of clear and distinct ideas with precise and unambiguous terms: let us, he urges, 'fix in our minds clear, distinct, and complete ideas, as far as they are to be had, and annex to them proper and constant names' (ibid., vol.2, p.239). Figurative language is mere adornment and poetry a waste of time (cf. James, 1949, Part II; for further discussion on Bacon, Descartes, Hobbes and Locke, see Avis, 1986b).

All these thinkers were harbingers of the Enlightenment: they shaped the philosophical assumptions of the *philosophes* of the eighteenth century. Lacking an integrated psychological model in which reason and imagination could be seen as two interrelated aspects of the mind working as a whole, analytically and synthetically, the *philosophes* privileged reason at the expense of imagination. For them the notion of imaginative truth was a contradiction in terms. As Voltaire (1694–1778) wrote in the *Philosophical Dictionary*: 'Ardent imagination, passion, desire – frequently deceived – produce the figurative style ... too many metaphors are hurtful, not only to clarity but also to truth, by saying more or less than the thing itself' (White, 1973, p.53). This self-denying ordinance excluded myth, legend and fable from the category of evidence that should be taken seriously. Manuel tells us that Turgot 'was ultimately led by his worship of reason to prefer the purest mathematical abstraction over all other forms of knowledge and to look upon metaphors and images ... as a sort of baby-talk' (Manuel, 1962, p.32).

The Utilitarians Jeremy Bentham (1748–1832) and James Mill (1773–1836) perpetuated the Enlightenment's rationalistic view of language and its hostility towards imaginative truth into the nineteenth century. Bentham believed that metaphors, such as 'body politic', applied to society had led to numerous 'false and extravagant ideas' as 'poetry had invaded the domain of reason'. Metaphors of the health, vigour, corruption, dissolution, death and resurrection of a society are sheer mystification. 'Simple language' is best fitted to convey the truth (Preyer, 1958, pp.52f.). Bentham's scorn for 'vague generalities' was discussed by John Stuart Mill, son of James Mill. 'He did not heed,' observes the younger Mill, ' ... that these generalities contained the whole unanalysed experience of the human race.' While the assertion of a generality does not constitute an argument, adds Mill, 'a man of clear ideas errs grievously if he imagines that whatever is seen confusedly does not exist: it belongs to him, when he meets with such a thing, to dispel the mist, and fix the outlines of the vague form which is looming through it.' The proper use of words, for Bentham, was to articulate precise logical truth and anything less than this, say in poetry, was a perversion of their purpose. The dictum 'All poetry is misrepresentation' is attributed to Bentham. The obsessive striving for logical precision and clarity rendered Bentham's later works obscure and unintelligible according to Mill, who regarded this as the nemesis of Bentham's hostility to figurative language. In striving to avoid anything that savoured of a poetic turn of phrase 'he could stop nowhere short of utter unreadableness and after all attained no more accuracy than is compatible with opinions as imperfect and one-sided as those of any poet or sentimentalist breathing' (Mill, 1950, pp.59, 61, 95, 97).

Thomas Babington Macaulay (1800–59), in his critique of James Mill, commented on the illusions entailed in the striving for clarity and distinctness:

It is one of the principal tenets of the Utilitarians, that sentiment and eloquence serve only to impede the pursuit of truth. They therefore affect a quakerly plainness, or rather a cynical negligence and impurity of style ... They do not seem to know that logic has its illusions as well as rhetoric – that a fallacy may lurk in a syllogism as well as in a metaphore [*sic*].

(Macaulay, 1978, p.100)

When the mathematico-deductive method is applied to the great moral themes of human experience, claims Macaulay, the results are ludicrous: 'When men begin to talk of power, happiness, misery, pain, pleasure, motives, objects of desire, as they talk of lines and numbers there is no end to the contradictions and absurdities into which they fall' (ibid., p.107).

However, Macaulay (who has a foot in both the Enlightenment and Romanticist camps) is not entirely consistent in his view of imaginative truth. In his essay on Milton he suggests that as civilisation advances, poetry almost inevitably declines. To write poetry in these enlightened times requires 'a certain unsoundness of mind'. The truth of poetry is 'the truth of madness'. Shakespeare's *Hamlet* and *King Lear* represent 'the despotism of the imagination over uncultivated minds'. Macaulay capitulates to Bentham and James Mill when he claims: 'We cannot unite the incompatible advantages of reality and deception, the clear discernment of truth and the exquisite enjoyment of fiction' (Macaulay, 1905, pp.3f.). The rationalist assumption that metaphor, symbol and myth – which are the constituents of poetry – are the antithesis of truth and reality could hardly be more clear.

The cul-de-sac into which the Enlightenment's suspicion of imagistic thinking led, has been well summarised by Gouwens:

Neither continental rationalism, with its emphasis on clear and distinct ideas, nor British empiricism, with its stress on the concreteness and vividness of sense-impressions, could adequately account for the faculty of imagination or for aesthetics as a realm of activity. For rationalism, the imagination did not possess the clarity of rational ideas; for empiricism, the imagination seemed to lack the concreteness and vividness of sense-impressions.

(Gouwens, 1989, p.17)

The modernity that stems from the Enlightenment assumes a dichotomy between rational discourse, on the one hand, and imagistic thinking, on the other. It privileges *logos* over against *eidos*. The former is hailed as the vehicle of knowledge, mastery and progress; the latter dismissed as the source of ignorance, superstition and illusion. The first is the path to truth; the second to falsity. The burden of my argument in this book is not to reverse that (as postmodernism does) and to set image over logic, but to challenge the dichotomy – to argue that rational discourse and imagistic thinking are not mutually exclusive but actually entail each other, because discourse is composed of images and metaphors are the stuff of thought.

3   The fate of the imagination in postmodernity

Transition to postmodernity

We might be forgiven for assuming that in some respects the Enlightenment's hostility to the figurative representation of truth is no longer our problem. The pendulum has swung: the Enlightenment is suspect along with its own suspicion of the figurative, the imprecise, the mystical and the mysterious. In our postmodern age there is plenty of scope for mystery in the form of the occult and the New Age openness to the non-rational. Along with this goes a new receptivity to images, symbols and myths. Combined with consumer-led capitalism, this generates a market-place of images where metaphors, symbols and myths are freely and arbitrarily created, traded, syncretised and dissolved – especially in the mass media, advertising and information technology. As Richard Kearney has commented in his history of the imagination, 'one of the greatest paradoxes of contemporary culture is that at a time when the image reigns supreme the very notion of a creative human imagination seems under mounting threat' (Kearney, 1988, p.3).

This is not the place to discuss the general nature of postmodernity and its relation to modernity – the vexed question of whether it represents a reaction against or an intensification of modernity (for this see Avis, *Mission After Modernity*, forthcoming). What concerns us here is to note that postmodernity adopts the same dichotomy between rational discourse and imagistic thinking as the modernity that stems from the Enlightenment, but it reverses modernity's valuation. Postmodernity privileges image over discourse, *eidos* over *logos*. It has lost faith in any order inherent in things and is suspicious of all attempts to impose it. The image – or rather the plurality of images – is all. Experience is a passing show of discrete, disconnected images, lacking in coherence, depth and substance. Culture reflects and intensifies experience: it is inchoate, fragmentary and ephemeral. We have the power to produce such a succession of images, but not to elicit them from a real world that is intrinsically ordered, by the operation of a mind that reflects that order. Kearney (1988) distinguishes between the 'mimetic' imagination which belongs to the biblical and classical worlds, the 'productive' imagination which is characteristic of humanist, Romanticist and capitalist culture, and the 'parodic' imagination which is typical of postmodernity or late capitalism. While the imagination which we see at work in Homer or the Old Testament achieves an imitation or copy of the truth of existence, and the imagination of the Romantic poets and artists rises above this to enhance and intensify the truth of existence, the best that the postmodern imagination can do is merely to parody, to play games with, to subvert the truth of existence – because at heart it does not believe that there is such a truth.

Deconstruction

The extreme version of postmodernity that goes by the name of deconstruction is a metaphysical reflection on this state of affairs – a metaphysic to end all metaphysics. (For Derrida generally and what follows immediately here, see Hart, 1989, esp. pp.1–15, 24–33.) Metaphysics is defined by Derrida as any science of presence – the study of the signs that are claimed to represent the wholeness and integrity of reality. For Derrida any discourse is metaphysical to the extent to which it claims that presence absolutely precedes representation. Derrida's *différance* means that absence is prior to presence, fragmentation prior to wholeness, disintegration prior to integration. The weight that metaphysics, including theology, places on the sign is misplaced, for the sign cannot deliver; presence cannot fulfil its promise to provide a ground for ontological security. The notion of full presence – prelapsarian (before the Fall) or eschatological (in the fulfilment of God's purposes in the End Time) – is an illusion, for it assumes that there is something outside the sign system that can escape its determination, it forgets that the ground of the sign is interpretation, the mutual mediation of the totality of signs. There is no knowledge – no revelation, we might say – that is thus unmediated.

Deconstruction challenges the theological claim that the ultimate ground of all meaning is God. Theology cannot escape the gravitational pull, as it were, of the sign system; it is trapped within it. There is no isomorphism between word and reality. An endless accumulation of words will never attain to the Word. No plethora of images, however rich and diverse, can ever reflect the Image of God. Like postmodernism generally, deconstruction's bitterest argument is with the aspiration to totality. For Derrida, any claim that a particular text can be totalised, so as to be of universal and absolute import, is theological. He regards 'God' as an instrument of totalisation. The terms 'metaphysical' and 'theological' identify a lust for totality. What then does it mean to practice deconstruction? To deconstruct a given discourse is to show, by reference to the assumptions that it makes, that it depends on prior differences that prevent it becoming a candidate for totalisation (Hart, 1989, p.67).

In her formidable *After Writing: On the Liturgical Consummation of Philosophy* (1998), Catherine Pickstock accepts the challenge of Derrida and deconstruction, seeing it as the outcome (not the antithesis) of premodern and modern culture. She exposes its roots in the complex of broadly rationalist and secularist ideas and practices that began to emerge in the late medieval period, were reinforced in the Reformation, acquired momentum in seventeenth-century empiricism and received ideological form in the instrumentalism of aspects of the Enlightenment. She shows how these tendencies achieved dominance in technological modernity and finally ran into the sand in the fragmentation and nihilism of postmodernism. For Pickstock, our increasingly information-based culture represents the nemesis of the domination of the world by the alienated analytical intellect, in which an original whole and integrated vision of the world is chopped up into discrete data, spread out and moved around, commodified, packaged and manipulated (for which Pickstock employs the terms 'spatialisation' and 'pure immanence'). The tyranny of the media-induced sound bite (she claims) mirrors the totalitarian pretensions of state-owned political power which began to absorb all areas of life within its control in the early modern period, and so parodied the medieval wholeness of communal life that was permeated by the sacramental structure – thus forcing religion into the private sphere of interior subjectivity.

Pickstock highlights the destructive dualisms of late modernity: the dominance of writing over conversation, of space over time and of subjectivity over objectivity. Where Derrida believes that it is writing that reveals the nature of language (and therefore of what is real), she appeals to the example of Socrates and Jesus to argue that speech is closer to reality because it is expended in passing time, invites an immediate response and is rooted in physical embodiment and the particularity of circumstance (however, this seems to overlook the crucial place of Plato's Socratic dialogues and the Gospels). The supreme instance of speech rising into transcendence and therefore putting all that is importantly immanent in its rightful place, she asserts, is liturgy. Doxology receives reality as a gift, sanctifies it through prayer and offers it back as a sacrifice. Only in total oblation to God as a living sacrifice does the worshipper unwittingly receive back self, life and the world. Liturgical action bestows meaning on the world and only in liturgy does language ultimately make sense. In other words, she accepts and glories in Derrida's accusation that talk of totality is irreducibly theological. She wants to recover a non-dualist theological paradigm in which the whole of creation and of human life is sanctified by worship.

Pickstock identifies her salutary paradigm historically in the early Middle Ages, when liturgical action was embedded in a sacramental world and ritualised culture, and paradigmatically in the Roman Rite of the Mass, which ensured an appropriate spiritual discipline by allowing for the reality of the physical and contingent, and for the hesitancy and inarticulateness of the worshippers, but at the same time leading them to the point at which they could receive a true, integrated, yet fragile identity as a gift of grace.

After Writing advocates (as does the present work) a symbolic realism in which equal weight is placed upon both halves of that term. Symbolism is crucial to its epistemology. It takes the realm of sign and figure as constitutive. 'The liturgical city ... is *avowedly* semiotic. Its lineaments, temporal duration, and spatial extension are entirely and constitutively articulated through the signs of speech, gesture, art, music, figures, vestment, colour, fire, water, smoke, bread, wine, and relationality' (Pickstock, 1998, p.169). But Pickstock is not advocating retreat into an intranarratival enclave, a sort of fideism where the semiotic code is merely posited. Hers is a symbolic *realism* – linguistic, sacramental and ecclesial. 'These signs are both things (*res*) and figures or signs – of one another and of that which exceeds appearance' (ibid., p.170). The symbolic and the realist pivot (for her as for me) on the Christological. Reality comes closest to us in Christ-centred worship, for here language fulfils its intended purpose and makes its best sense. But liturgy is an 'impossible possibility' for fallen creatures and becomes possible only through Christ – his incarnation, sacrifice, exaltation and inspiration of the Church through the Holy Spirit. The Christological realist symbol – both immanent and transcendent, truly human and fully divine – saves us from the postmodernist trap where symbolism is all pervasive but meaningless.

In postmodernity everything has the potential to become a symbol, but nothing is a symbol of the transcendent. This pan-symbolism is purely immanent. Symbols, images and myths interpret one another, interacting immanently, but none of them points beyond the symbolic realm. They do not symbolise a reality in which they participate. Roland Barthes can include soap-powders, steak and chips, striptease, Einstein's brain and the new Citroën (the DS) in his *Mythologies*. Anything can become a myth. Myth, for Barthes, simply refers to a type of speech in which the mode, not the message, is dominant. Myth means the elevation of petit-bourgeois culture to the level of universal nature, depoliticising icons of capitalist society so as to distort the true representation of society (Barthes, 1972, pp.9, 109, 121f., 142f.).

George Steiner has encapsulated modern deconstructive linguistics:

> There is in words and sentences no pre-established affinity with objects, no mystery of consonance with the world. No figura of things, perceived or yet to be revealed, inheres in the (purely arbitrary) articulations of syntax. No phonetic sign, except at a rudimentary level ... has any substantive relation or contiguity to that which it is conventionally and temporarily held to designate. The linguistic marker is as 'coded' as the algebraic symbol.
>
> (Steiner, 1989, p.105)

We have become the victims of our jargon: the 'mere metaphor', the 'empty symbol' and the 'exploded myth' now comprise the postmodern linguistic universe.

Nietzsche

The prophet of postmodernity is Friedrich Nietzsche (1844–1900), with his deeply cynical, mordantly suspicious view of language. Language and especially the figurative is a veil concealing the true nature of the universe as hostile to humanity. As far as Nietzsche is concerned, language is one big lie. In his early work 'On Truth and Falsity in their Ultramoral Sense', Nietzsche asks: 'What is a word? The expression of a nerve-stimulus in sounds' (Nietzsche, 1873, p.177). The nearest we come to things themselves is through metaphor, but metaphors do not at all correspond to the reality. We forget that our metaphors of perception are metaphors and take them for the things themselves. The generation of metaphors is intrinsic to humanity and an aspect of our inveterate projection of inner needs, desires and fears onto the 'external' world. Myth and art are both the products of metaphoric projection. We do not possess truth, only illusion. The boundary between dreaming and waking is blurred (ibid., p.188). 'What, therefore, is truth?' Nietzsche asks. He replies:

> A mobile army of metaphors, metonymies, anthropomorphisms: in short a sum of the human relations which become poetically and rhetorically intensified, metamorphosed, adorned ... truths are illusions of which one has forgotten that they are illusions; worn out metaphors which have become powerless to affect the senses; coins which have their obverse effaced and have lost their currency, becoming again mere bits of metal.
>
> (ibid., p.180)

Elsewhere Nietzsche asserts: 'Every word has become a prejudice' (Nietzsche, 1986, p.323).

However, in his first book, *The Birth of Tragedy*, Nietzsche has a positive view of the symbolic in the sense of myth. Myth is 'the concentrated image of the world'; without myth, culture loses its vitality and creative power; 'only a horizon surrounded by myths can unify an entire cultural movement.' Nietzsche mourns the passing of the unified mythic world and with it the notion of tragedy as perfected by the Greek dramatists. He sees the analytical spirit of the Enlightenment (personified by Socrates) as the solvent of all myths and the modern world as one marked by 'the loss of myth, the loss of the mythical home, the mythical womb'. Demythologisation, says Nietzsche in effect, leads to secularisation. But we cannot live without myths and, just as the Greeks descended into superstition, the Enlightenment degenerates into the bazaar of mythologies that (we would say) is typical of postmodernism: 'a pandemonium of myths and superstitions piled up and accumulated from all over the place' (Nietzsche, 1993, pp.109–12).

Postmodernist hostility to narrative

Lyotard has identified antipathy to grand narratives as the dominant characteristic of postmodernity. Modernity was structured by such grand narratives. Its intellectual disciplines or sciences legitimated themselves by reference to some normative 'metadiscourse' – 'making an explicit appeal to some grand narrative', such as Hegelian dialectics of the Spirit, Marxist emancipation of the proletariat, capitalist creation of wealth, rationalist positivism and so on. The most impressive of all was the grand narrative or metadiscourse of the Enlightenment, with its faith in reason and its hope in progress. But that is absent from postmodernity. 'Simplifying to the extreme,' writes Lyotard, 'I define postmodern as incredulity toward metanarratives.' Metanarratives, which give overarching meaning to a society, a science or a cause, are the victims of the undermining of all narratives – of the narrative structure of identity and human life. In traditional societies, the social bond is transmitted through the pragmatic rules embedded in narrative. But in postmodernity, knowledge exists no longer in narrative form but in the form of information technology, bringing a 'loss of meaning'. Narrative knowledge is self-authenticating in a way that is foreign to postmodernity: 'it certifies itself in the pragmatics of its own transmission without having recourse to argument and proof.' Narrative statements seem then – to those schooled in the culture of information technology – to belong 'to a different mentality: savage, primitive, underdeveloped, backward, alienated, composed of opinions, customs, authority, prejudice, ignorance, ideology. Narratives are fables, myths, legends, fit only for women and children' (Lyotard, 1984, pp.xxiii–xxiv, 21–7).

But this line of argument is, we must say, merely a republication – with a vengeance – of the Enlightenment's arrogant misconception of myth, which reached its culmination (as we shall see) in the work of Sir James Fraser in the late nineteenth and early twentieth century. An attack on narrative is an attack on metaphor, symbol and myth. As we shall see as we go on, metaphor is elaborated into symbol and symbols are constellated in narrative form to create myth. Postmodernity is as hostile to the values of realist symbolism, as is the modernity stemming from the Enlightenment. Postmodernity is clearly as inhospitable to a realist (reality-referring, truth-bearing) concept of imaginative truth as is the modernity deriving from the Enlightenment. In this book we are addressing the question: how does the relegation of metaphor, symbol and myth to the realm of the trivial and the unreal in both modernity and postmodernity affect the way we evaluate the truth-claims of the Christian faith?

Francis Fukuyama famously prophesied 'the end of history' – the cessation of the historical process of development on account of the final triumph of liberal democracy and of capitalist free-market economics, where the freedom to seek one's own advantage is mysteriously subsumed by the common good. Fukuyama foresaw the triumph of modernity, the high noon of Enlightenment (Fukuyama, 1992). When Communism was crumbling it was not difficult to prophesy what was already being fulfilled. When it became apparent what was immediately taking its place in former Marxist regimes – industrial paralysis and social disintegration – Fukuyama began to have second thoughts. Only thus belatedly did he discern the acids of postmodernity that are the decadent waste-product of modernity's undermining of the end of history – alienating, fragmenting, sapping the common purpose and preventing benevolent capitalism from generating its blessings of work, free exchange and prosperity! This led Fukuyama to publish a sequel to *The End of History and the Last Man* and he called it *Trust: The Social Virtues and the Creation of Prosperity* (Fukuyama, 1995). Only those societies that foster an attitude of trust and build fruitful relationships outside their own kinship systems can flourish economically, he argued. Thus Fukuyama has proposed a fiduciary basis for economics.

All this is a parable. In place of modernity's disparagement of the figurative in language – its contempt for metaphor as mere adornment, its suspicion of symbol as superstition and its patronising of myth as primitive history – and in place of postmodernity's devaluation of the figurative by divorcing it from rational discourse and making it a frivolous end in itself, I want to argue for an alternative tradition that invites us to trust ourselves in the first instance to a language that is greater than ourselves, and in particular to trust ourselves to metaphor, symbol and myth. Trust, openness and receptivity are the first steps in discernment of the truth. They do not, of course, remove the need for suspicion, interrogation and criticism as we pursue our enquiry to its conclusion. The aesthetic does not supplant the ethical, nor does imagination do away with reason. Kierkegaard's critical appropriation of the legacy of the Romantic imagination is a case in point. To a reappropriation of an alternative tradition we now turn.

4 Affirming the truth of imagination
The alternative tradition

It is of course to the Romantic movement that we owe the recovery – even the discovery – of the imagination in its modern sense. But Romantic imagination swung to excess and Kierkegaard was among those who was wary of its more extravagant claims, while ultimately vindicating its vital role. Gouwens sums up the 'apotheosis' of imagination in Romanticism:

> 'Imagination' in Romantic thought had become a central category, complex and subtle in its permutations. It was not only the heart of poetic creativity, but also the central human faculty and the locus of the Romantic quest for wholeness, a wholeness in which the world is poeticized and redeemed, and in which the individual is even able to find union with the infinite.
>
> (Gouwens, 1989, p.16)

Kierkegaard mounted an attack on the absolutising of the imagination and the aesthetic by the Romantics to the detriment of the ethical, but he combined this with a refutation of idealist (Hegelian) disparagement of images or mere representation as inferior to pure conceptual truth. Kierkegaard ultimately vindicated the imagination as necessary to the ethical disposition which was superior to the aesthetic and a stage on the way to true religion. Kierkegaard calls imagination 'the capacity *instar omnium*' – the capacity of all capacities (op. cit.). To speak of the truth of the imagination is not to fall for the excesses of Romanticism, but to make a critical and discriminating appropriation of that tradition. Let us now begin to try to do this.

Trusting and testing

The fiduciary tradition in epistemology insists that we have to trust in order to test. We cannot make a judgement, on proposals that are offered for our assent, from outside – from the detached position of an observer. As Isaiah says: 'Unless you believe you will not understand' (Isaiah 7.9 LXX). Faith, insists Augustine in his sermons *De verbis Domini*, ought to precede understanding, so that understanding may be the reward of faith. And Anselm speaks in the same tradition when he confesses: 'I believe in order to understand' (*Credo ut intelligam*). This insight of Anselm catalysed Karl Barth into a creative interpretation of Anselm, published in 1931 as *Fides Quaerens Intellectum* – faith seeking understanding (Barth, 1960).

Isaiah's oracle and Augustine's dictum were among Coleridge's mottoes. In the appositely titled *Aids to Reflection*, Coleridge considers that: 'To believe and to understand are not diverse things, but the same thing in different periods of growth' (Coleridge, 1993, p.194). That is why Coleridge could claim that we may be said to comprehend what we cannot properly be said to understand. In the *Notebooks*, Coleridge interprets the Gospels' use of 'faith' as 'a moral act or habit', adding: 'Believe, says St Augustine, and most profoundly too – and thou wilt receive an intellectual conviction (perception of its rationality) as the reward of thy faith' (Coleridge, 1990, vol.3, p.3,888). Again Coleridge comments on the same theme: 'Try it … travel along it, trust in it and … obey in all respects the various guideposts both at its entrance and those which you will find along it – and this is the method, nay, this is from the nature of the thing the only possible method of converting your negative knowledge into direct and positive Insight … In all things worth knowing our knowledge is in exact proportion to our faith: and all faith begins in a predisposition, analogous to instinct' (Coleridge, 1990, vol.4, p.4,611).

Michael Polanyi's account of 'personal knowledge' may be considered as a sustained exposition of the rule that one must trust in order to test. Polanyi insists that 'we know more than we can tell'. This tacit knowledge that cannot be fully specified or articulated is absorbed from the environment that we test for its truth and adequacy by trusting ourselves to it. This environment is constituted by the symbolic. As Coulson says: 'The Christian is one who places himself within an order of signs' (Coulson, 1981, p.162). Polanyi calls this the 'fiduciary' approach to truth. He insists that 'truth is something that can be thought only by believing it' (Polanyi, 1958, p.305). Polanyi's personalist philosophy affirms that all truth is held in a framework of trust. Truth is not an external, objective entity that we can analyse, discuss and decide to accept if we will. It is not at our beck and call. We are responsible for our beliefs and cannot be relieved of that responsibility by appealing to a supposed set of objective criteria that will do the work of making up our minds for us. We grasp the truth only through the disciplined pursuit of a moral quest.

> On a huge hill,
> Cragged and steep, Truth stands, and hee that will
> Reach her, about must, and about must goe;
> And what the hill's suddenness resists, win soe.
>   ('Third Satyre'; Donne, 1950, p.107)

Personal knowledge is heuristic and reaches out to the truth, indwelling it by anticipation, led on by intimations and clues that are picked up by our tacit awareness searching within the gravitational field (so to speak) of the object. For Polanyi, the interpretation of phenomena, whether in basic perception or in scientific research, is effected by acts of personal judgement that cannot be replaced by specified acts of explicit reasoning according to a formula. All our experience is of unities, rather than of atomistic facts in isolation. We have tacit knowledge of particulars through apprehending the whole structures within which they subsist. 'The efforts of perception are evoked by the scattered features of raw experience suggesting the presence of a hidden pattern which will make sense of the experience.' Thus 'knowing is always a tension alerted by largely unspecified clues and directed by them towards a focus at which we sense the presence of a thing' (Polanyi, 1962, p.11). Polanyi emphasises the need to recover the ability to deliberately hold unproven beliefs for heuristic purposes (Polanyi, 1958, p.268).

Seeing and shaping

The analytical tradition in epistemology that emerged in the pre- and early Enlightenment period was mesmerised by the ideal of a completely dispassionate, totally objective, perfectly clear and absolutely certain act of knowing. Bacon believed that an unmitigated realism was possible for science. Descartes' method confined itself to 'what we can clearly and perspicuously behold and with certainty deduce'. It was an ideal of knowledge without the knower, objectivity alienated from subjectivity, a god-like knowledge. In reaction the 'turn to the subject' in modern philosophy has produced an alternative conception, that of 'personal knowledge' (identified particularly with Michael Polanyi) which takes as its watchword 'no knowledge without a knower'. In *The Knower and the Known*, Marjorie Grene (developing Polanyian insights) has systematically challenged the Cartesian position, opposing to it a basically Kantian position. All knowledge is 'the achievement of the whole, inalienable psycho-physical person ... not the work of a disembodied intellect' (Grene, 1966, pp.81f.; see also Crewdson, 1994, pp.28ff.).

Polanyi argued that 'the structure of scientific intuition is the same as that of perception' (Polanyi, 1962, p.12). Perception is paradoxical: in our knowledge of the physical world we are receptive but not passive, constructive but not inventive. We work hard – in the realm of the imagination – to arrive at reliable knowledge of the world. It was a core tenet of Romanticism that perception is creative, that the mind has the making of reality. So Blake pronounced: 'As a man is so will he see.' And in *The Everlasting Gospel* he wrote:

This Lifes dim Windows of the Soul
Distorts the Heavens from Pole to Pole

And leads you to Believe a Lie
When you see with not thro the Eye.
>   (Blake, 1977, p.860)

In *The Prelude*, Wordsworth gave poetic elaboration to this fundamental insight of the Romantics (Wordsworth, 1971). The poetic faculty enhances what is objectively out there:

An auxiliar light
Came from my mind, which on the setting sun
Bestowed new splendour ...
>   (Part II [1805], ll. 87ff.)

... and the midnight storm
Grew darker in the presence of my eye.
>   (ibid., ll. 392f.)

The creative power of nature inhabits the poetic imagination and its expression in words:

... the great Nature that exists in works
Of mighty Poets. Visionary power
Attends the motions of the viewless winds
Embodied in the mystery of words.
>   (Part V [1850], ll. 594ff.)

With the image of the 'viewless winds' Wordsworth is not only borrowing a phrase from *Measure for Measure* (III.i.122) but, more importantly, is echoing John 3.8: 'The wind bloweth where it listeth, and thou hearest the sound thereof, but canst not tell whence it cometh, and whither it goeth.' He is hinting at the divine source of poetic inspiration. This is of course a classical as well as a biblical metaphor and it is as the former that it is employed by Shelley: 'The mind in creation is as a fading coal, which some invisible influence, like an inconstant wind, awakens to transitory brightness' (Shelley, 1888, vol.2, p.32).

The pre-established harmony between the mind and nature was to have been the theme of Wordsworth's projected philosophical poem 'The Recluse' and he announced his subject in a 'Prospectus':

How exquisitely the individual Mind
   ... to the external World
Is fitted:– and how exquisitely, too –
Theme this but little heard of among men –
The external World is fitted to the Mind;
And the creation (by no lower name

Can it be called) which they with blended might
Accomplish:– this is our high argument.
(Wordsworth, 1920, p.755)

While Wordsworth was writing *The Prelude* (1799–1805), Coleridge was already expressing similar ideas in 'Dejection: An Ode' (1802; Coleridge, 1969, pp.362ff.). Coleridge laments the fading of poetic inspiration which had lit up the natural world. Though he knows that the world is still beautiful, it has lost that transcendent aura that resonated with the poetic gift. 'I see, not feel, how beautiful they are!' (ibid., l. 38). The direction is not from outer reality to inner experience, but vice versa. The poet does not imitate nature but transforms it through creativity:

I may not hope from outward forms to win
The passion and the life, whose fountains are within.
(ibid., ll. 45f.)

In a classical statement of the Romantic creed that imagination can transfigure the impersonal Newtonian universe, Coleridge continues:

O Lady! we receive but what we give,
And in our life alone does nature live:
Ours is her wedding garment, ours her shroud!
And would we ought behold of higher worth,
Than that inanimate cold world allowed
To the poor loveless ever-anxious crowd,
Ah! from the soul itself must issue forth
A light, a glory, a fair luminous cloud
Enveloping the Earth –
And from the soul itself there must be sent
A sweet and potent voice, of its own birth,
Of all sweet sounds the life and element!
(ibid., ll. 47–58)

Coleridge goes on to ask 'what this strong music in the soul may be',

This light, this glory, this fair luminous mist,
This beautiful, and beauty-making power.
(ibid., ll. 62f.)

'Joy' is 'the spirit and the power' that reveals a new heaven and a new earth, the luminous cloud that envelops the earth, and from it flows all beauty of sight and sound:

All melodies the echoes of that voice,
All colours a suffusion from that light.

(ibid., ll. 74f.)

'Joy' is another name for the 'shaping spirit of Imagination' (ibid., l. 86).
Coleridge's final benediction to his beloved reiterates the Romantic
philosophy of creative perception:

To her may all things live, from pole to pole,
Their life the eddying of her living soul!

(ibid., ll. 135f.)

The insights of the Romantics are corroborated by modern psychology.
Anthony Storr has explored the connection between the inward quest for
harmony and wholeness in the psyche, and the outward quest for order and
structure in the world. He points out that 'the human mind seems so
constructed that a new balance or restoration within the subjective,
imaginative world is felt as if it were a change for the better in the external
world, and vice versa'. Storr adds: 'The hunger of imagination which drives
men to seek new understanding and new connections in the external world
is, at the same time, a hunger for integration and unity within.' Artistic
creation and aesthetic appreciation depend on this correlation of subject and
object, this 'creative apperception' that colours the world around us with the
hues of our own imagination. Storr quotes Winnicott's remark that: 'It is
creative apperception more than anything else that makes us feel that life is
worth living' (Storr, 1989, pp.124, 71). It seems that, provided our basic
human needs are already met, nothing is more likely to induce a sense of
spiritual well-being and wholeness than seeing the form of beauty that is not
ourselves and knowing that we have a part in it.

Thinking and speaking

We need now to take a firm grasp of a connection that has been hovering on
the edges of the argument throughout – the connection between imaginative
insight and its articulation in words. The effect is actually reciprocal. Insight
needs verbal expression both to reflect it back to the subject, so clarifying
the experience, as well as to communicate it to others in order that they may
share in it and verify it for themselves (or not, as the case may be). But the
words that are available to us (together with their logical combination in
concepts) actually condition how we interpret reality. They enlarge or
restrict the scope of experience that is possible for us. There is no insight or
imaginative experience that can be had in the absence of words, for the
words we inherit inform all our experiences. Profound words and luminous
conceptualities facilitate imagination. There is a genuine hermeneutical circle
here. The words of poets (or prophets) open a window on reality – as

Shelley says: 'Poetry lifts the veil from the hidden beauty of the world' (Shelley, 1888, vol.2, p.11). But what is revealed there will change the meaning of the words from within.

Our environment of meanings is our symbolic world and it is primarily constituted by language. Heidegger called language 'the House of Being'. Karl Kraus said that language was 'the mother, not the handmaiden of thought' (quoted in Gombrich, 1972, p.130). The 'order of signs', that is the *milieu* within which we position ourselves in order to try to test its adequacy as a faith to live by, is larger than the linguistic – it includes tangible symbols such as sacraments – but its prime constituent is language. Words are the go-betweens that make connections and mediate meaning from one unique and unrepeatable situation to another. Through the medium of words we are enabled to share the same 'personal space' as other persons. Communication creates community.

Shelley wrote in *Prometheus Unbound*:

He gave man speech, and speech created thought,
Which is the measure of the universe.

(Shelley, n.d., p.260)

For Wordsworth, poetic vision was 'embodied in the mystery of words'. Coleridge claimed that 'things take the signature of thought' (Coleridge, 1993, p.36). Words, for Coleridge, have constitutive force: 'For if words are not THINGS, they are LIVING POWERS, by which the things of most importance to mankind are actuated, combined, and humanized' (ibid., p.10). The 'shaping spirit of imagination' works through words and gives them their creative power.

In Blake's writings, whether poetry or prose, his words have the power, authority and inevitability of the Bible in the Authorised Version. This is not unconnected with the fact that Blake earned his living for forty years – and expressed his extraordinary vision – by engraving on copper. As Ackroyd says: 'Words were for him objects carved out of metal'; they had a material, tangible reality (Ackroyd, 1995, p.44; cf. p.142). So strong was his sense of the objectivity of those words and that they were not under his control that he testified to Henry Crabb Robinson that he only wrote when commanded to do so by his angels and that, the moment he had written them, he saw 'the words fly about the room in all directions' (ibid., p.342).

When the Romantics claim, as Coleridge does, that words are 'living powers', they are asserting the objectivity of the meaning of words – that they are already given, that they are not arbitrarily manufactured, that they have authority and vitality. They are not falling into the crass error of postulating an exact correspondence between words and what they signify. As Urban has observed: 'For any but the most primitive and naive views of language, the word is never identical with the thing, and the relation is, therefore, in some sense and to some degree, symbolic' (Urban, 1939, p.37).

As proponents of symbolism themselves, such thinkers as Coleridge knew this better than most. When Coleridge affirms that truth and being are correlative (Coleridge, 1965, pp.80, 144f., 149ff.), he is continuing his protest against purely analytical notions of truth that would confine truth to propositions. He is explicitly reiterating the medieval scholastic principle that truth is the conformity of the mind to reality ('the truth is universally placed in the coincidence of the thought with the thing'; ibid., p.144). He is not saying that language and reality, word and thing are exactly correlative. Similarly Newman consistently affirmed against all forms of propositional fundamentalism that 'revelation is not of words', ultimate truth is 'beyond words' and the saints know the truth 'without words'.

Language expresses our *experience* of reality rather than reality itself. Max Black writes:

> the concept of language as a mirror of reality is radically mistaken ... Language must conform to the discovered regularities and irregularities of experience. But in order to do so, it is enough that it should be apt for the expression of everything that is the case. To be content with less would be to be satisfied to be inarticulate; to ask for more is to desire the impossible. No words lead from grammar to metaphysics.
>
> (Black, 1962, p.16)

Of course the medium of language refracts as well as reveals reality

> like the pearl-diver's hand trembling under water
> Towards his store of food and beauty ...
> (Conquest, 1988, p.32)

Understanding and indwelling

If words are not counters but living powers, we now need to ask what it is about the nature of language that endows it with this potency. Words spoken or written with full intent, that have survived the vicissitudes of the centuries and have been handed down from generation to generation, are an extension of being in the personal mode. They embody the perceptions of gifted individuals who have given those words to their community through its tradition. We are enabled to indwell the meaning of those words by participating – through myth and ritual, as we shall see – in the life of the community that owns them and so become initiated into the truths and realities to which they point. Philosophers of language refer to 'speech communities' and insist that meaning exists only in communication: 'intuition and expression are one' (Urban, 1939, p.67). Polanyi suggests that words have this seminal power because they are over-determined, being made up of countless layers of meaning derived from innumerable human experiences. Therefore they transcend any single use to which they might be put. Words can transmit meanings from a deep social source. Robert Conquest has spoken of

> The inexact impressions of a phrase
> That draws strength only from the hard-won stock
> Of image flowering from
> Our speech's core.
>
> (Conquest, 1988, p.10)

Augustine reflected on the relation between teacher and disciples: 'So powerful is the feeling of a mind which sympathises that, whilst they are moved as we speak, and we as they learn, we have our dwelling in one another, so both they, as it were, in us speak what they hear and we in a certain way learn in them what we teach' (Augustine, *De Catechizandis Rudibus* 17; cited in Harrison, 1992, p.55).

Vico's insight into the philosophy of history was essentially that we are enabled to understand historically remote societies because they still indwell, as it were, their language and culture, and we who share a common human nature with them are able to indwell them too, through strenuous historical research combined with profound imaginative insight (Vico, 1961, p.67, para.161). Vico elaborates his basic axiom of *verum factum* – humans have made culture/reality, therefore humans can understand it:

> In the night of thick darkness enveloping the earliest antiquity, so remote from ourselves, there shines the eternal and never failing light of a truth beyond all question: that the world of civil society has certainly been made by men and that its principles are therefore to be found within the modifications of our own human mind.
>
> (Vico, 1961, p.96, para.331)

Herder claimed that to think and speak is to 'swim in an inherited stream of images and words; we must accept these media on trust; we cannot create them' (Berlin, 1976, p.168).

F.D. Maurice well understood the notion of indwelling words in order to indwell a community when he wrote that when we use words with care and respect, we are enabled to enter into sympathy and fellowship with those who have used them before us. We begin to sense that words have stored within them wisdom that can lead us to a better understanding of the world and God. Taken on trust, they put forth their 'living, germinating power' (Maurice, 1904, p.35). (George Steiner has said something very similar in connection with the art of the translator: 'When using a word we wake into resonance, as it were, its entire previous history ... To read fully is to restore all that one can of the immediacies of value and intent in which speech actually occurs' (Steiner, 1975, p.24).) Maurice confessed that he had learned from Coleridge, by example, 'how one may enter into the spirit of a living or a departed author, without assuming to be his judge; how one may come to know what he means, without imputing to him our meanings' (Maurice, 1958, vol.2, p.354). Within this 'common tradition' of fiduciary hermeneutics, to which John Coulson has so salutarily recalled us, Maurice believed that the Oxford Movement (of which he was in some other respects fiercely critical) had played its part in restoring the 'great principle of a social faith', namely that 'we exist in a permanent communion which was not created by human hands, and cannot be destroyed by them' (Maurice, 1843, p.10).

We are inevitably reminded here of Burke's attack on the theory of the contractual basis of society and his affirmation of a partnership between the generations that alone produces the highest good of human community:

> It is not a partnership in things subservient only to the gross animal exis-
> tence of a temporary and perishable nature. It is a partnership in all sci-
> ence; a partnership in all art; a partnership in every virtue, and in all
> perfection. As the ends of such a partnership cannot be obtained in many
> generations, it becomes a partnership not only between those who are
> living, but between those who are living, those who are dead, and those
> who are to be born.
>
> (Burke, 1910, p.93)

In *Real Presences*, George Steiner has defended a fiduciary hermeneutic: an act of trust, he insists, underlies our universe of discourse (Steiner, 1989, pp.89f.). Expounding the dictum 'a sentence always means more', Steiner suggests that meaning spreads outwards like the ripples on a pond:

> These comprise the individual, subconsciously-quickened language
> habits and associative field-mappings of the particular speaker or writer.
> They incorporate, in densities inaccessible to systematic inventory, the
> history of the given and neighbouring tongues ... As the ripples or shot-
> silk interference effects expand outward, they become of incommensu-
> rable inclusiveness and complexity. No formalization is of an order
> adequate to the semantic mass and motion of a culture.
>
> (Steiner, 1989, p.82)

As a parting shot Steiner adds that the equation Wittgenstein made in the *Tractatus* between the limits of our language and the limits of our world 'is almost a banality' (ibid., p.83). Our language, rightly understood, is actually unlimited in its suggestiveness, if only we trust ourselves to it and indwell it, allowing it to lead us further. Edwin Muir spoke of the utterance of divine creation and of human creativity as 'spontaneous syllables, bodying forth a world' (Muir, 1984, p.165). We have to recover the dying art of appropriat-ing in order to read and to hear the language of poetry, liturgy and scripture that can open up new worlds.

The power of language to move our emotions, to open up new experiences, to act as midwife at the birth of religious belief lies in its deep social source. Because it is chronically over-determined, its range of possible meanings is inexhaustible. As John Coulson has put it:

> The inherited language of faith, to which we make an imaginative assent ... is of an uncompromisingly symbolic character: it is a many-faced challenge which never yields a final paraphrase: in fact its linguistic mode seems deliberately chosen thus to preserve it for infinite use for all generations.
>
> (Coulson, 1981, p.78)

Analysing and integrating

We prosecute our grasp of reality by a combination of analysis and synthesis, of discrimination and integration. We discern ever finer differences and we apprehend ever wider similarities. We are enabled to isolate discrete features of experience but also to create more ambitious combinations of them. We switch our attention from the part to the whole and from the whole to the part. In this dialectic of analysing and integrating, of attention to the part and to the whole, the analytic and fiduciary traditions place their emphases differently. Rationalistic modernity gives priority to the first part of the equation, concentrating its attention on the analysis and interaction of the parts, especially their mechanical interaction in the manner of Bacon, Hobbes and Locke. The alternative tradition privileges the second: we only know particulars because we apprehend the wholes in which they subsist; we can engage in analysis because we already hold the complete picture in a tacit synthesis. Gestalt theory, holistic philosophies and systems theory contribute to a consensus that pertains here. In a system the parts are arranged within the whole and subsist in mutual connection rather than as an aggregate of discrete components. We do not know the components without the connections or the contents apart from the framework. We respond to the symmetry within the whole pattern and we respond as whole persons.

Burke suggested in his essay *On the Sublime and the Beautiful* that 'the mind of man has naturally a far greater alacrity and satisfaction in tracing resemblances than in searching for differences' and the reason for this is 'because by making resemblances we produce new images; we unite, we create, we enlarge our stock; but in making distinctions we offer no food at all to the imagination' (Burke, 1834, p.26). Shelley states in *A Defence of Poetry* that 'reason respects the differences, and imagination the similitudes of things' (Shelley, 1888, vol.2, p.1). Wordsworth, similarly, awards to imagination the

... observation of affinities
In objects where no brotherhood exists
To passive minds.
(*The Prelude* [1850], Part II, ll. 384–6, in Wordsworth, 1971)

For Coleridge – the supreme theorist of the imagination among the Romantics – imagination is the faculty that perceives connections, creates combinations and extrapolates from these to new insights. He calls it variously 'the coadunating power', 'the shaping spirit', 'the esemplastic gift', 'the reconciling and mediatory power', 'the completing power'. In *Biographia Literaria* Coleridge gives his most powerful account of imagination, distinguishing it from mere fancy, just as reason soars above understanding:

> the imagination, or shaping or modifying power: the fancy, or the aggregative and associative power: the understanding, or the regulative, substantiating and realizing power; the speculative reason – vis theoretica et scientifica, or the power by which we produce, or aim to produce, unity, necessity and universality in all our knowledge by means of principles a priori.
>
> (Coleridge, 1965, p.160)

Coleridge distinguishes – but, as he would be the first to insist, distinguishes without dividing – the primary from the secondary imagination. The first is our complicity with God: 'the living power and primary agent of all human perception' and 'a repetition in the finite mind of the eternal act of creation in the infinite I AM'. The second is the source of human creativity: 'an echo of the former', differing only in degree and mode of operation, it 'dissolves, diffuses, dissipates, in order to re-create' (ibid., p.167).

Coleridge operates with the old distinction, which he drew from Hooker and Milton (among others), between intuitive and discursive rationality, the former being vastly superior to the latter – just as the intellect of angels excels that of humans (*Paradise Lost*, Book V, ll. 485–90, in Milton, 1913; Coleridge, 1965, p.93). Reason, Coleridge writes in *Aids to Reflection*, 'is the Power of universal and necessary Convictions, the Source and Substance of Truths above Sense, and having their evidence in themselves'. It is the faculty of 'Contemplation': in words that Coleridge quotes from Hooker, reason is 'a direct Aspect of Truth, an inward Beholding'. Understanding, on the other hand, is discursive, lacks authority in itself and is dependent on a higher judgement; it is the 'Faculty of Reflection' rather than 'Contemplation'. Understanding is 'the Faculty judging according to Sense'. Reason is spiritual, understanding material (Coleridge, 1993, p.216ff., 223).

J.S. Mill, in a celebrated essay, took Bentham as representative of the Enlightenment and the power of reason, on the one hand, and Coleridge as representative of Romanticism and the power of imagination, on the other.

The strength of the first was in analysis; of the second in synthesis. Mill justly pointed out that no one's synthesis could be more complete than his analysis (Mill, 1950, p.58). Coleridge had some observations on analysis and synthesis. In effect, he is countering Mill and asking what is the use of analysing without then integrating? 'It is a dull and obtuse mind, that must divide in order to distinguish; but it is a still worse that distinguishes in order to divide' (Coleridge, 1993, p.33: Introductory Aphorism XXVI).

In his *Essay in Aid of a Grammar of Assent*, Newman argued that 'our most natural mode of reasoning is not from propositions to propositions, but from things to things, from concrete to concrete, from wholes to wholes' (Newman, 1903, p.330). To explain the phenomenon that it is the whole mind – indeed the whole person – that reasons, Newman postulated the 'illative sense'. This is 'the living mind' on the track of truth. We grasp innumerable particulars – whether in empirical science, historical research, or theological interpretation – and arrive at a judgement without being able to specify how we have reached it. The mind itself, asserts Newman, is 'more versatile and vigorous than any of its works [i.e. functions].' It contemplates the ingredients of its own thought 'without the use of words, by a process that cannot be analyzed' (ibid., pp.353, 359, 360f.). Newman's holistic epistemology takes its place in that 'common tradition' discerned by John Coulson (Coulson, 1970), a tradition that runs from Coleridge through Maurice and Newman in the nineteenth century, and was renewed by Polanyi and his followers in the twentieth (cf. Grene, 1966; Crewdson, 1994).

Clarifying and enlarging

An abiding suspicion of spurious clarity is a key feature of the alternative tradition. If we have cited the Wittgenstein of the *Tractatus* on behalf of the analytical tradition and its obsession with clarity, we can now invoke the later Wittgenstein of the *Philosophical Investigations* against it. He brings out the heuristic value of concepts that are admittedly vague, defends inexactness as more helpful than great exactitude for some tasks and challenges the common assumption that ' "inexact" is really a reproach, and "exact" is praise' (Wittgenstein, 1968, pp.41f.).

Polanyi also has attacked the Cartesian legacy of obsession with precision. In the social and human sciences, where interpretation is the dominant method, the personal factor is crucial. For all the objective disciplines that we may employ, our conclusions are ultimately grounded in personal insight into the actions and motivations of persons. At the same time, these disciplines are rich in factual content. When we move along the scale of increased formalism, however, from the exact to the deductive sciences, the personal factor diminishes steadily and so too does the informativeness of scientific statements until we reach the level of broad abstractions or laws. From (say) history at one end of the spectrum to (say) pure mathematics at the other, it is a sequence of increasing formalisation and symbolic manipulation, combined with decreasing contact with experience. Higher degrees of formalisation make the statements of science more precise, its inferences more impersonal and correspondingly more 'reversible'; but every step towards this ideal is achieved by a progressive sacrifice of content.

(Polanyi, 1958, p.86)

Whitehead argued that in our exploration of reality we should resist the temptation to seek for smaller and smaller units of meaning, and for ideas which are ever more clear and distinct. Instead we should look outwards, exploring the further reaches of connection, reference and context. Whitehead insists that for every statement we make 'there is always a background of presupposition which defies analysis by reason of its infinitude' (Whitehead, 1941, p.699). Our ideas are therefore 'ignorantly entertained' since we are oblivious to the 'infinitude of circumstances' to which they are relevant. Philosophical method is then, according to Whitehead, 'a resolute attempt to enlarge the understanding of the scope of application of every notion which enters into our current thought' (Whitehead, 1938a, pp.233f.). Whitehead points out that we do our thinking 'under the guise of doctrines which are incompletely harmonised. We cannot think in terms of an infinite multiplicity of detail', so we marshal particulars under general ideas with all their haziness and crudity. Except for the simpler notions of arithmetic, even our familiar ideas, which we accept at face value, are infected with an incurable vagueness. These ideas subsist in symbolic form, 'metaphors mutely appealing for an imaginative leap' (Whitehead, 1938b, p.217).

Baron Von Hügel, giving principles of theological discipline to a correspondent, writes: 'Pray get this point quite definite and firm,- that to require clearness in proportion to the concreteness, to the depth of reality, of the subject-matter is an impossible position,- I mean a thoroughly unreasonable, a self-contradictory habit of mind.' This is necessarily so, Von Hügel goes on, because only abstract ideas and numerical and spatial relations are perfectly clear, undeniable and readily communicable. And they are thus because they do not directly involve any assertion of real particular existences. As soon as we assert specific facts, Von Hügel seems to be saying, everything becomes contestable (Von Hügel, 1921, p.100).

Turning from these modern allies to historical figures: Vico knew that, in the realm of historical research and reconstruction, Descartes' criteria of clarity and distinctness were counterproductive. We are enabled to grasp the nature of primitive societies, not because we see their elements laid out clearly and distinctly, but only by a strenuous effort of empathy and imagination, by which through the mists of time we intuit obscurely what their life was like. But this insight is only just possible for it is 'beyond our power to enter into the vast imagination of those first men whose minds were not in the least abstract, refined or spiritualized, because they were entirely immersed in the senses, buffeted by the passions, buried in the body' (Vico, 1961, p.118, para.378).

Burke pointed out the limitations of clarity in his treatise on *The Sublime and the Beautiful*, observing: 'It is one thing to make an idea clear, and another to make it affecting ... In reality, a great clearness helps but little towards affecting the passions' (Burke, 1834, p.39). In other words, clarity is irrelevant to experiencing the sublime – above all in the hearing of scripture. Obscurity mixed with terror are the elements of the sublime. Besides biblical examples, Burke points to Milton's description of Death in *Paradise Lost*, Book II: 'In this description all is dark, uncertain, confused, terrible, and sublime in the last degree' (ibid., p.38). He did not have available to him then Blake's 'The Tyger' – an extraordinary evocation of sublimity.

Burke claims that poetic images are inherently obscure and where they invoke boundlessness extremely obscure: 'The ideas of eternity and infinity, are among the most affecting we have: and yet perhaps there is nothing of which we really understand so little, as of infinity and eternity' (ibid., p.39). Burke suggests that infinity fills us with 'that sort of delightful horrour [*sic*], which is the most genuine effect and truest test of the sublime' (Burke, 1834, p.43). He could have instanced Pascal's 'the eternal silence of these infinite spaces fills me with dread' (Pascal, 1966, p.95).

Blake evokes infinity and eternity with wonder rather than with fear (perhaps because he finds them in the microcosm rather than the macro-cosm) in the opening lines of 'Auguries of Innocence', which have the structure of biblical parallelism:

> To see a World in a Grain of Sand
> And a Heaven in a Wild Flower
> Hold Infinity in the palm of your hand
> And Eternity in an hour.
>
> (Blake, 1977, p.506)

A theology that set its sights on clarity and distinctness would be hard pressed to make sense of infinity and eternity as attributes of God! Burke administers the *coup de grâce* to misplaced clarity and distinctness with the comment:

> Hardly anything can strike the mind with its greatness, which does not make some sort of approach towards infinity; which nothing can do while we are able to perceive its bounds; but to see an object distinctly, and to perceive its bounds, is one and the same thing. A clear idea is therefore another name for a little idea.
>
> (Burke, 1834, p.40)

Newman warns against the deceptions of clarity when he remarks that the vividness of an image is no indication of truth: 'The fact of the distinctiveness of the images, which is required for real [as opposed to notional] assent, is no warrant for the existence of the objects which those images represent.' Newman explicitly takes issue with Descartes' method when he insists that strength of mental impression is no guide to reality (Newman, 1903, p.80).

Coleridge mused 'whether too great definiteness of terms in any language may not consume too much of the vital and idea-creating force in distinct, clear, full-made images, and so prevent originality' (Coleridge, 1895, p.19). He opposed to the method of ever-smaller refinements of definition, the method of exploring grand, pregnant, luminous generalities – 'Ideas'. In *The Statesman's Manual* (1816), Coleridge proclaimed: 'Every idea is living, productive, partaketh of infinity and (as Bacon has sublimely observed) containeth an endless power of semination.' Ideas galvanise the mind into activity:

> At the enunciation of principles, of ideas, the soul of man awakes, and starts up, as an exile in a far distant land at the unexpected sounds of his native language, when after long years of absence, and almost of oblivion, he is suddenly addressed in his mother tongue. He weeps for joy and embraces the speaker as his brother.
>
> (Coleridge, 1972, p.24)

'An IDEA, that most glorious birth of the God-like within us,' he enthuses (ibid., p.50).

In his work on Church and state, Coleridge defines an idea teleologically, by reference to its 'ultimate aim' (Coleridge, 1976, p.12). Ideas are the prerogative of the Reason for their attribute is universality, while the Understanding deals in mere 'conceptions' which are simply categories of particulars (ibid., pp.13, 58). Ideas emerge in the form of symbols, which contain contraries and these can only be reconciled at the level of the Reason; for the Understanding they are sheer contradictions. In *Aids to Reflection*, Coleridge cryptically remarks: 'A symbol is a sign included in the Idea, which it represents' (Coleridge, 1993, p.263 n.).

A substantial notebook entry expands on what Coleridge meant by Idea. Ideas mediate between finite and infinite, particular and universal, the absolute and the qualified. Ideas have not only a metaphysical but a theological basis: 'The Trinity is indeed the primary Idea, out of which all other ideas are evolved – or as the Apostle says, it is the Mystery (which is but another word for Idea) in which are hid all the Treasures of Knowledge.' An Idea is inherently inconceivable. The Understanding 'reflects and refracts' the Ideas of the Reason in two contradictory positions (Coleridge, 1990, vol.4, no.5,294).

Coleridge leaves open, at least in his earlier work, the question whether Ideas are the true representation of reality or simply a helpful clue. 'Whether Ideas are regulative only, according to Aristotle and Kant; or likewise

CONSTITUTIVE, and one with the power and Life of Nature, according to Plato and Plotinus ... is the highest problem of Philosophy' (Coleridge, 1972, p.114).

George Tyrrell brought out the continuity in the 'common tradition' between Coleridge and Newman in their use of 'Idea'. Recalling that in his *Essay on the Development of Christian Doctrine* (Newman, 1974), Newman had spoken about the development of the 'idea' of Christianity, Tyrrell observed that this had misled those for whom 'ideas' in theology mean 'intellectual concepts, universals, definitions, from which a doctrinal system could be deduced syllogistically'. Tyrrell pointed out that Newman had meant 'a spiritual force or impetus' – which was, of course, how Tyrrell himself, the so-called 'modernist', understood Christianity (Tyrrell, 1910, pp.29–33).

There is no need for us to try to swallow Coleridge neat. I am not going to attempt to defend Coleridge's Ideas as tantamount to Platonic Forms. But there is no denying that such luminous general ideas as Unity, Freedom, Immortality, Transcendence, Grace, Truth, Goodness, Beauty, Justice, Providence, Love and Creativity have the power to arouse the human spirit both to intellectual achievement and to outstanding actions. We do not need to deny that they have their ultimate source in the mind and being of God – indeed it is vital to theism to affirm that – but it is sufficient to say that they acquire their aura of transcendence and their power of motivation from the fact that they have been invoked in the aspirations of generation after generation. They lend themselves to our indwelling because they have been preached, prayed, intoned, sung, debated, written and read, lived for and died for by an innumerable company of our brothers and sisters who have walked the earth before us. The power, though not the reality and validity (we are talking about the *ordo cognoscendi* rather than the *ordo essendi*), of these ideas can be accounted for sociologically, as Wittgensteinian 'forms of life', rather than theologically, as Platonic Forms. The common tradition is a convivial tradition!

Men created the logos-concept, but it was pre-ex, in the 'mind' of god, who created the men who created it.

Part II

5 The world of biblical imagination

Karl Barth memorably spoke of 'The Strange New World within the Bible'. The phrase is the title of a sermon in *The Word of God and the Word of Man* (Barth, 1928, p.28–50). Barth's early writings unlocked this strange new world. More than anyone else, he helped modern theology to rediscover the otherness, the difference of the Bible. He evoked its numinous power and reminded us that to enter the Scriptures is to tread on holy ground.

> It is not the right human thoughts about God which form the content of the Bible, but the right divine thoughts about men. The Bible tells us not how we should talk with God but what he says to us; not how we find the way to him, but how he has sought and found the way to us; not the right relation in which we must place ourselves to him, but the covenant which he has made with all who are Abraham's spiritual children and which he has sealed once and for all in Jesus Christ. It is this which is within the Bible. The Word of God is within the Bible.
>
> (ibid., p.43)

Barth recovered those awesome sayings that liberal theology did not know what to do with: 'Our God is a consuming fire'; 'It is a terrible thing to fall into the hands of the living God'; 'No man can see God and live'; 'Who is sufficient for these things?'; 'Woe is unto me if I preach not the gospel'; 'The foolishness of God is wiser than the wisdom of men'. Barth was right to suggest that the words of men (the sexist substantive seems right for the biblical writings which were not only written but read, interpreted and enforced by men) can never be identified with the Word of God. But he went too far, in this early stage of his development, in placing them in opposition. The perfect, paramount speech of God is contrasted with the blind and corrupt utterances of men. This is to simplify the unique phenomenon of divine revelation and to do less than justice to the humanity of God (to invoke Barth's own suggestive phrase).

Barth here eclipsed a fundamental fact about the Bible: that in it God speaks by the mouths of men and accommodates the divine speech to what human minds can grasp and human lips can utter. The Word of God is not so much in opposition to the word of man as in critical tension with it. Scripture is not so much a dialogue between God and humanity – still less merely a polite conversation – as a summons, a search, a calling by name, on the one hand, and a relentless quest, an on-going argument, on the other: 'the LORD hath a controversy with the nations' (Jeremiah 25.31 AV). This character of Holy Scripture as a divine–human encounter is brought home to us not only in the fact, so often reflected on by divines, exegetes and commentators in the past, that God deigns to communicate through ancient Hebrew and *koinē* Greek, and subjects his majestic discourse to the constraints of grammar, but equally by the fact that God's revelation is conveyed or articulated not with clarity, precision and literalness, but in the obscure and opaque figures of metaphor, symbol and myth. Nowhere do we see more clearly the truth of Barth's great dictum that 'revelation comes to us clothed in the garments of creaturely reality' than in the fact that the Word of the Lord which is mightier than the sound of many waters obeys the universal genres of figurative discourse.

Edwyn Hoskyns was influenced by Barth and translated his commentary on Romans into English. In one of his Cambridge sermons Hoskyns seems to echo Barth's phrase about the strange new world of the Bible: 'Can we rescue a word and discover a universe? Can we study a language and awake to the Truth? Can we bury ourselves in a lexicon, and arise in the presence of God?' (Hoskyns, 1970, p.70). Clearly we can. In this chapter we shall attempt to evoke something of the vast biblical world of the imagination and draw out its texture as metaphor, symbol and myth.

Metaphors of revelation

'Ah Lord GOD,' Ezekiel cried, 'they are always saying of me, "He deals only in figures of speech" ' (Ezekiel 20.49 REB). The language of the Bible is the language of the sanctified imagination. Blake claimed that the Bible was addressed to the imagination and declared that 'the Whole Bible is fill'd with Imagination and Visions'. Spinoza, one of the founders of modern biblical criticism, stated:

> Scripture does not explain things by their secondary causes, but only narrates them in the order and the style which has most power to move men, and especially uneducated men, to devotion; and therefore it speaks inaccurately of God and of events, seeing that its object is not to convince the reason, but to attract and lay hold of the imagination.
>
> (Watson, 1994, p.297, n.2)

A useful guide to the figurative character of scripture is G.B. Caird's *The Language and Imagery of the Bible* (Caird, 1980). There is now J.C.L. Gibson's *Language and Imagery in the Old Testament* (Gibson, 1998). Sue

Gillingham has surveyed the poetry of the Hebrew Bible, including the Psalms, analysing its form and structure in a way that the Hebrews themselves never of course attempted. They did not draw our basic distinctions, such as that between poetry and prose: the two flow into each other so that we find poetic elements within prose and prosaic tendencies within poetry in the Old Testament (Gillingham, 1994, p.43).

John Keble, a child of Romanticism, believed that the biblical revelation was intrinsically poetic, in the sense of being both the product of the imagination and addressed to the imagination. The art of poetry is to conceal at the same time as it reveals and so to point to the beyond, the unknown, the infinite. Keble prefaced his rendering of the Psalter into English verse with the observation that in revelation God intends 'to disclose, rather than to exhibit, his dealings and his will; to keep himself, to the generality [of people], under a veil of reserve ... a certain combination of reserve with openness being of the very essence of poetry' (Gillingham, 1994, pp.15f.). Keble may help us to see that figurative, imaginative language is the appropriate vehicle of divine revelation, preserving as it does, through its combination of disclosure and concealment, the transcendence and mystery of God.

Psalms, hymns and prayers speak of God in the metaphors of king, rock, shepherd, husband, brother, friend and even mother. One Psalmist runs through much of the repertoire: 'I will love thee, O Lord my strength,' he cries. 'The Lord is my stony rock, and my defence: my Saviour, my God, and my might, in whom I will trust, my buckler, the horn also of my salvation, and my refuge' (Psalms 18.1 BCP). These images are edifying, comforting and moving, as the case may be, but laying them end to end for cumulative effect is somehow self-defeating. The shock waves seem to diminish; they certainly do not generate a theological earthquake. So let us go, without more ado, straight to the heart of this matter. It is not the saying of metaphors, but the being a metaphor that is so explosive in biblical revelation. Let me explain that cryptic statement.

In the New Testament Jesus Christ is said to be both the image of God (Colossians 1.15) and the Word of God (John 1.1ff.). Here metaphors of expression – 'image' and 'word' – are employed to express a relationship that is beyond human expression, the identity-in-distinction between the Godhead and the human being Jesus of Nazareth. An individual existence not only is a metaphor (as we shall see later), but is described by a metaphor. A person not only becomes a statement, but is stated by an image. A life not only serves as a symbol, but its significance is expressed by a symbol.

Jesus' distinctive teaching is given in the form of parables which are symbolic narratives, sometimes simply conveying one central message or meaning, but certainly demanding an act of imaginative insight on the part of the hearer to understand their meaning. 'Those who have ears to hear, let them hear.' Ricoeur says that a parable is a metaphorical process in narrative form (Ricoeur, 1980, p.26). But there is, once again, a further significant step: the Jesus who speaks in parables is himself a parable, a narrated life imaging the divine. 'Jesus proclaimed God in parables, but the primitive Church proclaimed Jesus as the parable of God' (J.D. Crossan, cited in McFague, 1982, p.48).

The words spoken by the Word and the images poured forth by the Image become vehicles of the same one truth. The Johannine Christ announces: 'The words that I have spoken to you are spirit and life' (John 6.63). But those words in the discourse following the feeding of the multitude (as elsewhere) are full of cryptic metaphors and oracular symbols in which Jesus warns that only those who eat his flesh and drink his blood will attain eternal life. In these Johannine texts we see clearly that Christian faith depends on the truth-bearing capacity of metaphor, symbol and myth – indeed is hostage to it, so to speak. The coming together in scripture of being and meaning through the mediation of language undergirds the validity, dignity and authority of the image and the word. They are elevated to become the bearers of transcendent meaning. Our task, therefore, must be to demonstrate that truth-bearing capacity.

Biblical symbols: spirit, light, love

Already in the Bible, the spontaneous metaphors generated by engagement with God in religious experience are reflectively refined into conceptual symbols. Abstracted from their original context in the address to God of prayer and praise, sacred symbols stand in their own integrity as windows on the transcendent. But they continue to have a living connection with liturgy (though this becomes even more pronounced in the case of myth – reference the long debate on the priority of myth or cult). The Johannine symbols of spirit, light and love stand out here. In the Johannine literature – the Fourth Gospel and the three Epistles of John – God is described in the symbols of spirit, light and love. Three great primary affirmations are made in the symbolic mode: 'God is spirit' (John 4.24), 'God is light' (1 John 1.5), 'God is love' (1 John 4.8, 16). Though these statements seem to have an almost metaphysical status, as apparently abstract and ethereal assertions about the nature of ultimate reality, in their biblical context they are fundamentally practical, down-to-earth symbols, inextricably connected with right Christian worship and ethical behaviour.

1 *Spirit* 'God is spirit' is found embedded in a doubly polemical setting reflecting the rivalry between the Jews and the Samaritans as to where Yahweh was rightly to be worshipped, and between Jews and Christians about the location of worship now that the Temple had been destroyed and the Christians driven out of the synagogues. God requires a new worship of the heart rather than the outward forms – 'in spiritual reality'. Location is irrelevant, for Jesus has already spoken of the new spiritual temple of his

crucified and risen body (John 2.19–22). The Church will offer worship to
God through Jesus Christ 'at all times and in all places', as the liturgy puts
it. 'The hour is coming, and is now here, when the true worshippers will
worship the Father in spirit and truth, for the Father seeks such as these to
worship him. God is spirit, and those who worship him must worship in
spirit and truth' (John 4.23f.).

John defines God as *pneuma*. The Logos, being one with God ('the Word
was with God and the Word was God'; John 1.1), also has the nature of
pneuma. The Johannine symbols of God – spirit, light, love – are also
Christological symbols. What is said of God is also said, directly or by
implication, of Jesus Christ. 'What God was, the Word was' (John 1.1
NEB). Unless this is allowed to have its full force, the shock, scandal and
miracle of the Incarnation is lost: 'And the Word became *sarx* (flesh)' (John
1.14). We have just been told that believers have been born 'not of the will
of the flesh' (John 1.13) and shortly we shall hear that they are born of
water (baptism) and the Spirit, 'for what is born of the flesh is flesh and
what is born of the Spirit is spirit' (John 3.5–6). 'Being the vehicle of life,
pneuma is the medium of rebirth' (Dodd, 1953, p.224). In John, flesh and
spirit are opposed. They are set over against each other, in an antithesis
which comes to focus and tension in Jesus Christ, the Word made flesh.

There is no implication in John 4 that spiritual worship can dispense with
the symbolic and the sacramental, or that it can be so ethereal as to rise
above the embodied nature of our humanity, like some 'out of the body'
experience. In John the symbols, expressed as physical forms (flesh, blood,
word, vine), enable the mutual indwelling of Christ and the believer (John
6.56; 8.31; 15.4). As Hoskyns wrote in his great commentary on *The Fourth
Gospel*:

> The contrast between false and true worship does not, therefore, lie in a
> distinction between that worship which is directed towards some visible
> and material object and that which is abstracted from all contact with
> the visible world; nor does it lie in a distinction between sacrificial or
> outward and non-sacrificial or inward worship. False worship is wor-
> ship directed towards a visible object regarded as in itself complete and
> final [i.e. idolatry] ... True worship is directed towards the flesh and
> blood of Jesus ...
>
> (Hoskyns, 1947, p.245)

Hoskyns' emphasis resonates with our reiterated insistence throughout
this book on the bodily location of the truth of God. Images derive from the
senses. Metaphor is the brain function of superimposing two images whose
meanings have a hidden connection. Symbols elaborate images to become
sacramental of what they symbolise. Narrative is a creative, idealised and
stereotyped relation of the paths and journeys on which individuals and
communities find themselves. Myth is the numinous symbolic narrative of

spatio-temporal happenings and the realities that permanently ground them. This embodied identity of the figurative modes of discourse coheres well with a religion that was provocatively described by William Temple as the most materialistic of all religions. Temple may well have been reading Chesterton's Father Brown stories, for in one of the earliest (published in 1911) the unprepossessing priest lays it down in a typically outrageous Chestertonian paradox that 'there is one mark of all genuine religions: materialism' (Chesterton, 1950, p.121). Christianity is a religion that begins by rehearsing the reality and goodness of physical creation and goes on to recount God's salvific revelation in history, before telling of an incarnation of God's Word in a specific human life and the community that arose from this which is held in existence through sacraments that employ water, bread and wine.

As well as the continuum that Hoskyns postulated in his Cambridge sermons and elaborated in his posthumous work with Noel Davey – *Crucifixion-Resurrection* – there is also the continuum that we might associate with William Temple, which forms the biblical presupposition of the former: creation-incarnation is the basis for crucifixion-resurrection (see Hoskyns and Davey, 1981).

George Pattison gives a salutary reminder of the irreducibly material and 'carnal' basis of art – even, or should I say especially, sacred art: 'God, to put it at its boldest, is not revealed otherwise than in the modes of bodily vision, colour, space, light ... The Christian God is the God whose self-expression is altogether and utterly compatible with the flesh' (Pattison, 1991, pp.146f.). This is merely a deduction from the incarnational, sacramental character of the Christian faith which brings us, as Hilary of Poitiers insisted, 'into fellowship with Christ's flesh' (Kelly, 1965, p.409). The 'Prayer of Humble Access' from the 1662 *Book of Common Prayer* puts the communicant's participation in Christ in powerfully physical language: 'so to eat the Flesh of thy dear Son Jesus Christ, and to drink his Blood, that our sinful bodies may be made clean by his Body and our souls washed through his most precious Blood.' Teilhard de Chardin said, 'I worship a God who can be touched' (Habgood, in Brown and Loades, 1995, p.20).

2   *Light*   'God is light and in him is no darkness at all' in 1 John 1.5 complements the prologue of John's Gospel where the Word who was with God and was God is the source of the (eternal) divine life that, permeating all creation, is experienced as light. In the Gospel light belongs not in the sphere of pure contemplation (*theoria*) but of *praxis*. It has ethical import. God, life and knowledge of the truth are symbolised by light, and their opposites – evil, death and ignorance – by darkness. In the epistle the symbol of God as light 'in whom is no darkness at all' is the presupposition of an exhortation to 'walk in the light', renouncing one's sins, and so enjoy fellowship with the Father and the Son and with one another (1 John 1.5–10;

on the symbolism of light in John and 1 John, see Koester, 1995, pp.123–54; Dodd, 1953, pp.201ff.).

As we have seen in connection with the symbol of Spirit, symbols of God in the Johannine literature are also symbols of Jesus Christ. 1 John defines God as light. In the Gospel the Logos is described as the creative source of life which became 'the light of all people' and as 'the true light, which enlightens everyone' (John 1.4, 9). The great dominical utterance 'I am the light of the world. Whoever follows me will never walk in darkness but will have the light of life' (John 8.12) echoes the prologue and leads into the story of the healing of the man born blind. God is light; Christ is light – this is the implicit deity of Jesus Christ as conveyed by the Johannine books.

3 *Love*   The twice stated 'God is love' of 1 John (4.8, 16) may not look like a symbol. Love has no essential visible form, unlike light. But here a word normally used to designate an action or an attitude is used as a definition, to sum up the very being and nature of God. Those who dwell in the symbol (love), dwell in what is symbolised (God). As throughout Johannine symbolism, 'the symbol is absorbed into the reality it signifies' bringing about an 'intrinsic unity of symbol and thing signified' (Dodd, 1953, p.140). But the symbol of God as love is introduced almost incidentally to reinforce an exhortation to love one another. One of the most stupendous utterances of all scripture is mentioned in passing. Once again the ethical import is primary: there is no fellowship or communion with God apart from loving fellowship with one's fellow Christians. 'God is love and those who abide in love abide in God, and God abides in them' (1 John 4.7–21).

In the Johannine writings the central symbols of God are also symbols of Jesus Christ. There is no explicit designation in either Gospel or Epistles of Jesus Christ as love. But there is ample implicit identification of Christ and love. The last verse of the prologue echoes the frequent Old Testament warning that no man can see God and live, when it says: 'No one has ever seen God.' But it brings out the new situation or dispensation created by the Incarnation in what follows: 'It is God the only Son, who is close to the Father's heart, who has made him known' (John 1.18 NRSV). The loving fellowship between Father and Son is more than hinted at here. The first Epistle consciously echoes this and draws out the Christological significance when it says: 'No one has ever seen God; if we love one another, God lives in us, and his love is perfected in us' (1 John 4.16). That is to say that God becomes visible in Jesus Christ, beloved Son of the Father, and God becomes visible too in the love that Christians show for each other. This points to the mutual indwelling, the coinherence of Father, Son and children of God: 'As the Father has loved me, so I have loved you; abide in my love' (John 15.9); 'so that the love with which you have loved me may be in them, and I in them' (John 17.26).

At the core of biblical faith there are profound and powerful symbols that focus the essence of Christian belief and life. They gather up into a concentrated intensity the theological import of the revelation of Jesus Christ. 'Spirit', 'light' and 'love' can be predicated of God in the light of Jesus Christ and can be predicated of Jesus Christ as the Incarnation of God. 'Spirit' is the metaphysical nature of God. 'Light' is the moral nature of God. 'Love' is the personal nature of God. These must be at the heart of what Christianity affirms about God – its Theo-logy – and about Jesus Christ – its Christology. The Christian faith has a vested interest in the proper understanding of symbols. It could never tolerate the phrase 'an empty symbol' being applied to its dearest imagery.

The profundity, purity and power of these Johannine symbols, which permeate Christian spirituality, worship and theology, have a normative influence on the Christian understanding of imaginative truth. They inform the critical perception that Christians have of the symbolic world of the culture in which they live. They are a standing reminder of the true nature of symbolism and expose as superficial, fraudulent or obscene the manufactured symbols of commercialism which exploit particularly the humanity of women and the dignity of creation. It might seem that these do deserve the expression 'empty symbols': they are indeed hollow and unwholesome. But it would be a mistake to underestimate their power to shape our thinking, our worldview. There are evil symbols that bring moral decay and spiritual death. They must be combated on the symbolic plane – by the promotion of Christian symbols properly understood and critically expounded.

> Lift high the cross, the love of Christ proclaim
> Till all the world adores his sacred name.

Biblical myth?

Is there myth in the Bible? While that might strike some as a rhetorical – and indeed superfluous – question, there have been biblical scholars who have answered it, in effect, in the negative. Such scholars collude with popular misunderstandings of myth and the strong aversion to recognising myth in the sacred scriptures among Christian believers. Frei denies that the Bible contains substantial mythic elements. He argues that the concept of 'narrative meaning' avoids the dilemma of choosing between the literal meaning and a mythic meaning (Frei, 1974, pp.270, 280). He claims that to acknowledge biblical myth would be to locate the meaning of the Bible beyond the text in universal timeless truths. Thus he asserts in *The Identity of Jesus Christ* that 'the Gospel story's indissoluble connection with an unsubstitutable identity in effect divests the saviour story of its mythical quality' (Frei, 1975, p.59; cf. Watson, 1994, p.23). So Frei recognises that there is a certain truth of myth, but it is not one that is appropriate to the Gospels. He does not believe in the possibility of mythic realism, that myth can convey the universal significance of particular historical events and persons through symbolic narrative. Frei does not raise similar questions about narrative, which he seems to regard as unproblematic. As Francis Watson points out, Frei does not attempt to establish the truth of narrative but treats it as an irreducible datum (ibid., p.25).

I find Frei's position peculiarly elusive: it is difficult to see what could be entailed in a narrative meaning that related neither to history or to myth, but only to the positive world of the text itself. Frei states: 'The direction in the flow of intratextual interpretation is that of absorbing the extratextual universe into the text, rather than the reverse (extratextual) direction' (Frei, in McConnell, ed., 1986, p.72). For Frei, the text is self-referring and self-sufficient. There is nothing to be explored beyond the text. Sense and reference are one. Meaning and subject-matter coincide (for exposition and critique of Frei, see Fodor, 1995, pp.258–330).

Frei's hermeneutic appears to be an attempt to insulate the meaning of scripture from public canons of truthfulness. No wonder his narrative approach is so appealing to conservatives: they can take refuge in the notion of 'realistic narrative' and bracket out the intractable problems of myth, history and truth. Appealing to narrative brings no escape from the hard questions raised by the presence of myth in the Bible. Narrative and myth are actually correlative concepts. When archetypal, numinous symbols, with a cosmic, universal reference, are incorporated in narrative, we have myth. To take flight from myth into narrative is illusory.

A more apposite question than whether there *is* myth in the Bible, would be whether there is anything *but* myth in the Bible. As J.C.L. Gibson insists, the people of the Old Testament not only breathed the general mythological atmosphere of their time, 'they themselves also became mythmakers' (Gibson, 1998, p.91). Edmund Leach has written in the essay 'Genesis as Myth': 'All stories which occur in the Bible are myths for the devout Christian, whether they correspond to historical fact or not' (Leach, 1969, p.7). Elsewhere, Leach amplifies this provocative assertion.

> In saying that the Bible is not a history book but a mythology, I am not arguing that the events it records could not possibly have happened in real time. It is simply that spatial and chronological relations within biblical texts always have symbolic significance whether or not they happened to correspond to reality as ordinarily understood. The patterning is determined by literary-aesthetic considerations rather than by historical or geographical facts.
>
> (Leach, 1989, p.581)

In the Old Testament, Leach continues, at every stage events are presented as the fulfilment of what has come before and as the foreshadowing of what will follow. The symbolic unity of the Bible is like that of a Shakespearean tragedy or a novel by Tolstoy. Leach, a Fellow of King's College,

Cambridge, with its magnificent choral tradition and breathtaking chapel, concluded that the Bible should be read 'as a total work of art, much as one listens to choral singing, echoing from the vaulted roof of a gothic cathedral' (ibid., p.597). Thus it was the unity, symmetry, harmony and teleology of the Bible, expressed through the medium of its governing symbols, that led Leach to call the Bible a mythology.

Now the same unity, symmetry, harmony and teleology that impressed the social anthropologist are also brought out by Von Balthasar and by Karl Barth. To immerse oneself in their work, especially to the extent that it is conducted by means of an ongoing exposition of vast areas of biblical typology and symbolism, is to be made aware of the symbolic character of scripture. But it requires a further step to designate this as myth. Barth is notoriously cavalier about questions of genre and related problems of historicity. For him, the Bible is a given narrative world, the only sphere of revelation. Von Balthasar acknowledges the similarities between the myths of pagan antiquity and the symbolic narratives of the Bible: they both give shape to the divine in response to revelation. The Bible is both the definitive revelation and the fulfilment of non-biblical aspirations.

> Christian revelation will, it is true, empty the myths of the 'world's archons' of all power, replacing them with the glory of God's true epiphany, just as the distance between myth and biblical revelation can be so emphasised that its original meaning and content is reversed. But this does not alter the fact that biblical revelation occurs in the same formal anthropological locus where the mythopoeic imagination designed its images of the eternal.
>
> (Von Balthasar, 1982–9, vol.1, p.145)

If Barth could be blithely neglectful of questions of myth because of his complete absorption in the hermeneutical circle (reinforced by his naive realism in biblical epistemology), Von Balthasar could be equally relaxed owing to his Platonic assumption of the unity of *mythos* and *logos* (reinforced by his Catholic doctrine of the mutual directedness of nature and grace). Von Balthasar recognises that the language of myth is 'nothing other than the common fund of images understood by every human being'. While he acknowledges that classical myths have 'no vision for the sin of the world and for the humiliation of divine love even unto death', he insists that, in seeing the world as a sacred theophany, the mythological understanding of the world has an intimation of the eschatological vision of the Christian faith – of the world as the 'body' of God (ibid., vol.1, pp.144, 608, 677, 679).

A great deal depends, of course, on one's definition of myth and one's evaluation of myth. These issues will have to await further clarification in Part III of this book. But there is a prima facie case for allowing that the Bible contains at least reconstructed or transfigured myth. Gibson describes the first creation account, that of the six days and the Sabbath (from the priestly tradition) as 'a particularly cool example of myth' in that 'it avoids the wilder mythology of the creation references in Israel's poetic literature' (Gibson, 1998, pp.91f.). Gibson elaborates:

> The priestly authors of Genesis did not like the more lurid furniture of myth in composing their careful account of how the world began, though they still spoke mythologically in what they considered a more fitting way. But in their almost modern delicacy of taste they stand nearly alone in the Old Testament.
>
> (ibid., p.92)

This qualified acceptance of myth in the Bible is as far as some scholars are prepared to go. Brevard Childs argued in *Myth and Reality in the Old Testament* (1960; second edition, 1962) that the biblical understanding of reality, grounded on the redemptive activity of God in history, came into conflict with the inherited mythic conception of reality where Nature was regarded as active, living and powerful, communicating her vitality through dreams, visions and apparitions. It seems that Childs is operating with a distinction between an immanent profane and a transcendent sacred, but that antithesis will not do to demarcate natural religion from biblical revelation. Nevertheless, Childs is right to advocate that the Old Testament reflects the presence of myth, though of 'broken myth', and to insist that the Old Testament worldview is not constituted by the mythic – that is to say, pagan, naturalistic, immanental – understanding of reality but by divine revelation. But he is wrong to call a halt to the presence of myth in the Old Testament at that point. His 'broken myth' is actually a Trojan horse.

Pannenberg offers an important discussion in 'Myth in Biblical and Christian Tradition' (Pannenberg, 1973, vol.3). Like Leach, he accepts that time and space in the Old Testament are significantly mythical, as are the cultus and monarchy, but he asserts that the demonology of the New Testament and its cosmology (the 'three-decker universe') are not inherently mythical, though they do represent an obsolete worldview. Furthermore, according to Pannenberg, the apocalyptic account of eschatology in the New Testament 'cannot be understood as mythical without qualification' (ibid., p.67). On the other hand, Pannenberg affirms that the creation of myth by the early Church cannot be ruled out and he suggests that 'the function which the figure of Jesus came to have for the Christian Church is reminiscent of the archetypal elements of myth' (ibid., p.68). The crucial problem is created by the way the originally non-mythical story of the man Jesus of Nazareth could have turned into the characteristic mythologisation of his person which is found as early as Paul. The Church generated a 'new myth', that of the Redeemer coming down from heaven, which has parallels with the mythic world of antiquity (ibid., p.69). The identity that early Christian theology postulated between this mythical figure descending from heaven and the unique historical event of Jesus of Nazareth strained the limits of myth and Pannenberg concludes that 'the function of the mythical language remains only that of an interpretative vehicle for the significance of a historical event' (ibid., pp.70–4).

I must confess that I find these attempts to apologise for the presence of myth in the Old and New Testaments unpersuasive. Myth is reluctantly admitted on the condition that it is entirely subservient to something other than myth. I do not believe that there is something other which can be postulated in abstraction from myth, or at least from the symbolic in its broad sense. Let us take Childs first: how is the understanding of reality that is grounded in divine revelation expressed, if not in myth? How are the redemptive acts of God in history recounted, if not in myth? Where is the biblical worldview located, if not in myth? It must subsist in the mythic realm because only this has the capacity to articulate symbolic narrative with sacred meanings. As often as not these myths of the redemptive acts of God in history, etc., are reconstructed and transfigured versions of earlier, less appropriate, less theologically profound myths.

Now let us turn to Pannenberg: he seems to assume that the mythical was the contingent or accidental form which the significance of Jesus assumed – as though his unique status as the embodiment of God's revelatory and redemptive act could be articulated and elaborated, theoretically, in some other way. The formula 'Jesus Christ' contains a fact and an interpretation – but they are inseparable, inextricable and indissoluble. There never was an historical Jesus of Nazareth who did not already have interpreted significance (just as there is no bare sense-datum that is not already in some sense an interpreted perception); there is no interpreted significance that is not already part of a symbolic narrative, and there is no symbolic narrative that does not have mythic features which it shares with its mythic milieu.

As Fawcett has argued, it is a fallacy to set myth and history in sharp antithesis. The Old Testament and the New offer ample evidence of both the historicisation of myth, as mythic elements are assimilated to a more sophisticated understanding of salvation in history (e.g. the Exodus theme), and also of the mythicisation of history, as actual events are assimilated to archetypal symbols (e.g. New Testament Christology). Thus 'historicization made myth relevant while mythicization made history meaningful' (Fawcett, 1973, p.30).

My approach, in contrast to the reluctant mythographers, is to accept that the Bible contains substantial mythic components (as do Christian beliefs, for that matter). But I go further and claim that all stories about the interaction of God and the world – stories that transcend the diurnal framework of space and time by speaking of the remote past (origins) or the remote future (destiny) or historical purpose (teleology) – have the status of myth as a narrative genre. But of course Barth and Von Balthasar, Childs and Pannenberg have the heart of the matter in them: their priority is to let divine revelation stand forth in its integrity. It is an aspiration that I share.

But I believe that they are misguided in thinking that the integrity of revelation is compromised by its mythic form. However, I can only substantiate that claim by developing a 'mythic realism' before I finish.

The poetical character of revelation

Let us take six examples of writers who have brought out the poetical, figurative and symbolic character of the Bible: Augustine, Aquinas, Burke, Coleridge, Newman and Blake.

1   Few theologians have reflected more deeply than St Augustine on the imaginative complexion of Holy Scripture. For him, as Carol Harrison has shown, scripture is one of the primary ways in which God addresses humanity in concrete form – others being creation, incarnation and the Church – through the tangible signs of images, parables, allegory, poetry and ascending levels of meaning. The nature of the Bible demands and suggests an approach that is more characteristic of the artist than of the philosopher. The embodied forms of divine revelation, Harrison suggests, become sacramental and require of us 'an intuitive, imaginative, symbolic, image-making apprehension of God's Word, expressed in a manner which is more characteristic of a poet than of a philosopher' (Harrison, 1992, pp.82, 95). She quotes Marrou's summary of Augustine's thought on this aspect:

> If Holy Scripture is not just the history of sinful humanity and the economy of salvation ... if it is also this forest of symbols that through the appearances of figures suggests to us these same truths of the faith, one must have the courage to conclude that God is also a poet himself. To manifest himself to us he chose a means of expression which is also poetic ...
>
> (ibid., p.80)

2   St Thomas Aquinas asks near the beginning of the *Summa Theologiae* whether it is appropriate for Holy Scripture to employ metaphorical or symbolic language. His reply is:

> Holy Scripture fittingly delivers divine and spiritual realities under bodily guises. For God provides for all things according to the kind of things they are. Now we are of the kind to reach the world of intelligence through the world of sense, since all our knowledge takes its rise from sensation. Congenially, then, holy Scripture delivers spiritual things to us beneath metaphors taken from bodily things.
>
> (Aquinas, 1964–81, Ia.1.9, *Responsio*)

But it is not only human nature that invites revelation to employ figurative language: it is also the nature of God. Aquinas sounds rather like his supposed antithesis Karl Barth when he suggests in *Quaestiones quod-libetales* that God can make words mean whatever he chooses:

> Any truth can be manifested in two ways: by things or by words. Words signify things and one thing can signify another. The Creator of things, however, can not only signify anything by words but can also make one thing signify another.
>
> Therefore, as well as the plain or 'literal' sense of scripture, there are spiritual truths that can be derived by allegorical or figurative interpretation. But owing to the ambiguities of symbolism (for example, the lion in the Bible can stand for God or the devil), 'no compelling argument can be derived from the spiritual sense'.
>
> (Gombrich, 1972, pp.13f.)

3   The first major work of the young Edmund Burke was *A Philosophical Enquiry into the Origin of our Ideas of the Sublime and the Beautiful* in 1756. His discussion of the nature of the sublime touches on the figurative character of biblical language. Burke's approach had already been anticipated by Robert Lowth's *Lectures on the Sacred Poetry of the Hebrews* (1787). The imagination, argues Burke, detects resemblances between disparate things and generates fresh images. In so doing, 'we unite, we create, we enlarge our stock' and this gives peculiar pleasure to the mind (Burke, 1834, p.26). Images that evoke the sense of the sublime are of a particular kind:

> Whatever is fitted in any sort to excite the ideas of pain and danger, that is to say, whatever is in any sort terrible, or is conversant about terrible objects, or operates in a manner analogous to terrour [*sic*], is a source of the sublime; that is, it is productive of the strongest emotion which the mind is capable of feeling.
>
> (ibid., p.32)

Burke acknowledges that 'the Scripture alone can supply ideas answerable to the majesty of this subject. In the Scripture, wherever God is represented as appearing or speaking, everything terrible in nature is called up to heighten the awe and solemnity of the divine presence' (ibid., p.42; see also Prickett, 1986, pp.105ff.).

4   Coleridge knew this passage in Burke – though he did not have a very high opinion of Burke's essay on the *Sublime and the Beautiful* (Coleridge, 1884, p.63). For the Romantics, as Abrams (1971) has pointed out, biblical imagery and natural phenomena were eclipsed on the scale of the sublime by the wonders of the human psyche; they could not compete with

such fear and awe
As fall upon us often when we look
Into our Minds, into the Mind of Man.
('Prospectus' to 'The Excursion'; Wordsworth, 1920, p.755)

Nevertheless, in his lectures on Shakespeare, Coleridge remarked that he was impressed by the fact that the language of the Bible was universally regarded as being of 'a high poetic character', particularly from 'the stately march of the words'. In setting out to discover the cause of this general experience, he found that in the passages (presumably in the English translation, the Authorised Version – though that is celebrated for retaining the rhythms of the original Hebrew and the idioms of the Greek) that were particularly affecting, there was metre and often poetry. The language of the Bible was the product of strong emotion held in check by metrical form (Coleridge, 1960, vol.2, pp.52f.; cf. Coleridge, 1965, p.173).

5 Newman echoes Burke and Coleridge (for, as John Coulson has reminded us, there was a 'common tradition' here; see Coulson, 1970) when he argues (in 1829, before the launch of the Tractarian Movement) that the Christian revelation is 'poetical' in nature:

While its disclosures have an originality in them to engage the intellect, they have a beauty to satisfy the moral nature. It [revelation] presents us with those forms of excellence in which a poetical mind delights, and with which all grace and harmony are associated. It brings us into a new world – a world of overpowering interest, of the sublimest views, and of the tenderest and purest feelings ... With Christians, a poetical view of things is a duty.

(Newman, 1895, vol.1, p.23)

Newman reflected later that one of the essential notes of the poetical was its ability to move the affections through the imagination. For Newman – raised on the Romantic poets, devourer of the novels of Sir Walter Scott, Platonist in his ontology, imaginative indweller of the early Church – the Christian revelation, in scripture and the teaching of the Church, appeals primarily to the imagination and its language is the language of poetry.

6 William Blake belongs, chronologically, before Coleridge and Newman. Blake derives from an earlier age (he was born in 1757, Coleridge in 1772, Newman in 1801), that of the late eighteenth century and the violent, instinctive reaction against the clinical rationalism of the early Enlightenment – a reaction that took the form of a fascination with the occult and esoteric and bizarre experiments with mesmerism, electricity and phrenology. But I place him last in our list of witnesses to the imaginative nature of divine revelation, partly because he is not an orthodox Christian theologian and partly because his is the most powerful and extreme voice of them all.

Influenced by Swedenborg and other spiritualistic visionaries, Blake held communion with the spiritual world. Imagination was the strongest clue to the nature of the divine, the great primal Imagination that lay behind, not unformed, unshaped nature, but works of artistic genius and the world of spirits and visions that came to the assistance of artists and poets. In his antipathy to nature in the raw, Blake reveals himself as of a different spirit to the true Romantics like Wordsworth, Shelley, Keats and Coleridge. It seems that, unlike Wordsworth, say, Blake did not enter imaginatively into nature, indwelling it and sensing the diffused presence of the divine, but absorbed it into the intensity of his artistic vision. Blake's utterances are exceptionally oracular and cannot be interpreted more than tentatively, but that is what he seems to mean. 'Nature & Fancy [imagination] are Two Things & can Never be joined; neither ought anyone to attempt it, for it is Idolatry & destroys the Soul' (Ackroyd, 1995, p.226).

> Every body does not see alike. The tree which moves some to tears of joy is in the Eyes of others only a Green thing that stands in the way ... But to the Eyes of the Man of Imagination, Nature is Imagination itself ... To Me This World is all One continued Vision of Fancy or Imagination.
>
> (Ackroyd, 1995, p.209)

Imaginative vision was the criterion of truth for Blake, not only in art but in theology. Imagination is our complicity with God and the company of heaven. Through imagination God communicates with humanity – primarily in the Bible which was Blake's single most fruitful source of inspiration. When as a boy he 'wander[ed] thro each charter'd street/Near where the charter'd Thames does flow' of eighteenth-century London, Blake actually saw a city filled with spangled angels and bearded Old Testament prophets: he saw, as Ackroyd says, a biblical city (Ackroyd, 1995, p.34). Blake was deeply imbued with the images and cadences of the Bible, even from his mother's knee, and testified to the sort of book it is. 'The Whole Bible is fill'd with Imagination and Visions' (ibid., p.27). Since the Christological divine humanity – 'The Eternal Body of Man' – is 'The IMAGINATION [*sic*]', and Christ is 'the True Vine of Eternity The Human Imagination' (ibid., p.297), it follows that 'Jesus & his Apostles and Disciples were all Artists' (ibid., p.351) who had visionary perception of divine truth and communicated it in imaginative modes: prophecy, parable, cryptic utterance and similitudes of various kinds. 'I know of no other Christianity and of no other Gospel', Blake wrote, 'than the liberty both of body & mind to exercise the Divine Arts of the Imagination' (ibid., p.148).

Indwelling revelation

I am engaged in arguing that the Christian faith – in all its departments: revelation through the Bible, theology and doctrine, faith and belief, worship and liturgy – is inextricably wedded to figurative language and cannot be abstracted from it. Christianity's understanding of the nature of truth is that of Keats – 'the truth of imagination'. A moment's reflection will show, I believe, that this is inevitable. It follows from the nature of Christian revelation (for resources for the study of divine revelation, see Avis, (ed.), 1997).

In scripture, divine revelation is mediated through the vicissitudes experienced by a people, a nation. It is through imaginative empathy and the discernment that comes from indwelling that the revelation is mediated at several removes to us. The Incarnation is the central paradigm of the biblical revelation: it represents the presence of God uniquely indwelling a human person who was in himself totally transparent to the divine truth and love. Jesus Christ is a symbolic Person. He has been called the metaphor of God. We respond to him in the same way that we respond to the truth of imagination in poetry, drama, novel, pictorial art or music – by a moral, spiritual and aesthetic indwelling and commitment – though in his case infinitely heightened as his claim over us is the claim of God to whom we owe everything, even our very being. Our indwelling of the Person Jesus Christ is unlimited in its possibilities and our commitment is in principle absolute. And the way that this indwelling is enhanced and this commitment is expressed and strengthened is sacramental. It is precisely through the living and effectual metaphors and symbols of the water of baptism and the bread and wine of the eucharist that we are caught up into the revelation and salvation of God that is incarnated in our mortal flesh. These sacramental actions are accompanied and interpreted by a symbolic narrative or myth – such as the prayer of thanksgiving at the eucharist that rehearses the wonderful works of God in salvation history from creation to the consummation of all things and culminates in the words of institution.

Conclusion

As J.C.L. Gibson has well said, in his recent survey of the Old Testament's language and imagery, what the Bible gives us is not doctrinal propositions, but 'an imaginative vision of God' and God's dealings with human beings. He adds: 'It is the stories and poetry of Scripture and especially perhaps its figurative language which create that vision' (Gibson, 1998, p.13). Gibson's point was already understood, as we have seen, by Augustine and Newman, Blake and Coleridge. Augustine's and Blake's insights, that God is a 'poet' and that Jesus and the Apostles were essentially 'artists', are profoundly suggestive. It means that the Bible is full of figurative discourse – of metaphor, symbol and myth – not merely because early cultures would naturally have expressed themselves in that way, as Vico, followed by Herder and Rousseau, realised in the eighteenth century when they discovered with the force of revelation that the first philosophers were poets (Vico, 1961, pp.21, 71, paras 34, 86), but primarily because that is how the profoundest living truths are best communicated. Thus Jesus did not teach in parables simply because he was a first-century rabbi preaching to first-century peasants and fishermen, but because his gospel was addressed to the whole person in its depth and integrity – to the heart as well as to the head, to children to whom the kingdom of heaven belonged as well as to the intelligentsia of scribes and Pharisees, to the alienated and outcast as well as to the aristocracy of the Sadducees. It was meant to evoke a response from the whole person as it was quickened by the Holy Spirit into repentance and faith and awoke to a new world of grace. The one request that Jesus could not accede to was: 'If you are the Messiah, tell us plainly' (John 10.24).

Revelation is not the downloading of information or the elaboration of a metaphysic: it is the disclosure from person to person of existential insight. In it the heart of God speaks to the human heart: *Cor ad cor loquitur* (Newman's motto). Such wisdom is most effectively imparted in forms that are vivid, concrete, narrative, oblique, intriguing and personal. The parables and pithy sayings of Jesus were not meant to be understood at a glance, so to speak; indeed we may say that they were intended not to be understood at first glance at all. Their first purpose was to announce eschatological judgement and to summon to repentance, their second was to convey an offer of unconditional salvation.

> To you has been given the secret [or mystery, for the disciples did not understand even so] of the kingdom of God, but for those outside, everything comes in parables; in order that [Greek: *hina*, introducing a final (or purposive) clause: 'in order that'] 'they may look and look and not perceive, and may listen and listen and not understand; so that they may not turn again and be forgiven'.
>
> (Mark 4.11–2)

Probably some of his hearers only understood the parables and sayings ten, twenty, thirty years later, when experience and circumstances had prepared them for the moment that Ian Ramsey so well evoked in his writings on religious language: light dawned, the penny dropped, the scales fell from their eyes, things fell into place – and the truth that Jesus had spoken, like a delayed-action depth-charge, was detonated. In Iris Murdoch's novel *Bruno's Dream*, the dying Bruno is troubled by his persistent unfaithfulness to his wife and a particular memory that he refused to go to her when she called to him from her deathbed. He was afraid that she was going to reproach him once again. Only at the end of his life, many years later, does it dawn on him that she had summoned him in order to forgive him. Whole stretches of years have to be reinterpreted retrospectively – just as when a word-processor progressively reformats a large tract of text (see Murdoch, 1970).

If these reflections faithfully bring out the character of divine revelation, it appears to follow that we have to respond to it not primarily cognitively, by intellectual analysis, but aesthetically, by indwelling its beauty – just as we would respond to a work of art or beauty: reading poetry aloud, listening to music, enjoying a painting, relaxing in a garden, relishing a good meal, taking delight in the face of a beloved. The aesthetic response is not our whole response, but it is an important – and neglected – part of it. We have always known that Jesus was a poet as well as a prophet, but we have tended to overlook the profound *theological* significance of the Johannine saying, 'He who has seen me has seen the Father.'

who is 'me'?

6   Creative theology and the making of doctrine

It is not only the primary speech of religion – in revelation mediated through the Bible – that is ineradicably figurative, but also the language of theology and the doctrine that it articulates. Theology, as a second order critical reflection on the first order utterances of faith, finds it neither desirable nor possible to escape from the all-embracing realm of figurative language which is generated by the primary encounter of individuals and communities with the reality of the sacred. Sallie McFague, who favours the notion of 'model' rather than our preferred term 'symbol', points out that 'there is an intrinsic relationship between religious language and theological language suggested in the notion of model, since models have characteristics of both imagistic and conceptual language' (McFague, 1982, p.193). The metaphors of religious language and the models of theological discourse have a common semantic structure in their dependence on analogy (cf. Leatherdale, 1974, p.1; on models in theology and science, see Barbour, 1990, pp.41ff.). Though its language is shaped by reflection rather than spontaneity and by criticism rather than ecstasy, theology has no other tools with which to operate than those of metaphor, analogy, symbol and myth, for (as we shall see later in the argument) no significant, meaningful statement can be made without them.

Religion evokes reality

In two major works – *Language and Reality* (1939) and *Humanity and Deity* (1951) – W.M. Urban has explored the language of religion and theology. In the first of these, Urban insisted that the language of religion was not only 'evocative' but also 'invocative': 'It evokes feelings, but it also invokes objects' (Urban, 1939, p.573). This dictum is suggestive. Poetry also, of course, evokes feelings, but it does not invoke objects. That is not to claim (with D.G. James) that pure poetry is simply lyrical. Poetry evokes not only emotions but also perceptions. Furthermore, it may even elaborate the interpretation of those perceptions into the broad framework of a metaphysic: it may articulate a worldview. Wordsworth evokes the poet's emotions ('recollected in tranquillity'), but he also interprets the object of those emotions and articulates a metaphysical vision that celebrates divine immanence:

And I have felt
A presence that disturbs me with the joy
Of elevated thoughts; a sense sublime
Of something far more deeply interfused,
Whose dwelling is the light of setting suns,
And the round ocean and the living air,
And the blue sky, and in the mind of man:
A motion and a spirit, that impels
All thinking things, all objects of all thought,
And rolls through all things.

('Lines Composed a Few Miles Above Tintern Abbey';
Wordsworth, 1920, p.207)

So poetry may describe objects and the poet's emotional response to them. It may also apostrophise them rhetorically, as Wordsworth did the skylark, Shelley the west wind and Keats the nightingale. Here the poet addresses the object of his muse as though it were a person. And sometimes poems are addressed to persons, as are love poems. But to invoke an invisible and transcendent reality as personal belongs peculiarly to religion. Poems that invoke God and call for an answer, such as Donne's 'Batter my heart, three-person'd God ... ' and Gerard Manley Hopkins' 'Terrible Sonnets', bridge the distinction between poetry and religion. They speak the language of religion – of address to God or contemplation of God – in the form of poetry. Hymns do the same (and of course many hymns are originally religious poems that have been set to music); the music intensifies both their poetic and their religious character, creating the *milieu* of oblique, aesthetic assent to the realities presupposed or celebrated in the hymn. The distinction between poetry and religion is not clear-cut: they feed from each other; they illuminate each other. But Urban's assertion that it is invocation that distinguishes religion from poetry seems broadly valid. Urban suggests in this pre-war work that religious language is lyrical because it expresses emotion, dramatic because it rehearses narrative or myth, and theological because it contains propositions that are metaphysical and make assertions about the nature of the world. That is not to deny that the language of religion is fundamentally poetic: Urban suggests that religious expressions may be described as numinous poetry (Urban, 1939, pp.571–6). The invocative character of religious language points to the issue of realism.

In his post-war work *Humanity and Deity*, Urban continues to insist that the language of religion is poetic (even when it is expressed in prose) because it is emotional, intuitive and figurative. The lyrical and the dramatic are the primary forms of religious language, but instead of subsuming theological propositions under religion generally, Urban distinguishes the language of theology from the language of religion. While religious language is evocative and invocative, theological language is reflective and deals at second-hand with the feelings and objects that are the subjects of primary religious experience, mediated to us through language. But theology cannot avoid mythic and symbolic speech. It retains the dramatic character of the language of religion because it must discourse in the narrative mode. Even when formulating statements of a more metaphysical nature, theology is compelled to use symbolism and to reflect on the consequences of so doing. This raises the question of analogy which Urban regards as both more fundamental than symbol and its presupposition (Urban, 1951, pp.55–8, 225, 229, 246). This is our cue to discuss Aquinas, Barth and Pannenberg.

Analogy and metaphor

Thomas Aquinas believed that the metaphorical and symbolic language of scripture is perpetuated in the study of theology, the ministry of holy teaching (see Ernst, 1979, ch.6: 'Metaphor and Ontology in *Sacra Doctrina*'). I want to argue that the doctrine of analogy – according to which attributes drawn from the realm of human experience are predicated of God neither univocally nor equivocally (that is neither in the same sense nor in a completely different sense) but analogically, incorporating both identity and difference – is a refinement of the more spontaneous metaphorical and symbolic language of the Bible and of Christian worship, and functions on a continuum with it.

In the cold light of logic nothing could be more inappropriate than to take qualities like love, justice, peace, mercy, kindness, faithfulness, compassion, purity, etc., drawn from mundane human experience, and to apply them without more ado to the ineffable God. There is an 'infinite qualitative distinction' that it seems analogy cannot bridge. The doctrine of analogy is peculiarly vulnerable to knock-down refutations (for an attack on the classical theological concept of analogy, from a linguistic analysis point of view, see Palmer, 1973), but it also needs to be protected from some of its would-be supporters.

The recent claim by W.P. Alston that there is not a problem here is absurd. Alston asks what all the fuss is about. By relabelling traditional attributes of God, such as knowledge, will and love, as psychological functions, Alston believes that he has overcome the great theological dilemma addressed by Aquinas: how can we speak truly of God if all we say is meant neither univocally nor equivocally? Alston believes that there is 'a significant commonality of meaning between psychological terms applicable to God and to man'. 'Even though there is no carry-over of the complete package from one side of the divide to the other,' he says, 'there is a core of meaning in common. And the distinctive features on the divine side simply consist in the dropping out of creaturely limitations.' This is surely no more than Aquinas' *via negativa* which discounts inappropriate creatureliness in analogical language: it does not itself remove all the problems of analogy. Thus, Alston triumphantly concludes, it is possible to 'create psychological concepts that literally [*sic*] apply to God, thus generating theological statements that unproblematically [*sic*] possess truth values' (Alston, in Morris, 1987, p.39).

The expressions 'literally' and 'unproblematically' cause loud alarm bells to ring immediately. The truth-claims of theology are actually intrinsically and incurably 'problematical'. It is thanks to the ambiguities inherent in analogy that all doctrinal statements about the divine nature, purpose and action (there are three analogies straight away!) remain tantalisingly elusive. That does not mean that we cannot attempt them: we are bound to do so in our faltering efforts to discern and interpret divine revelation. It does not mean that analogy is worthless: it is all we have and, sensitively handled, it is a useful tool. But we deceive ourselves if we believe that we can speak of God either literally or unproblematically.

We must reaffirm the insuperable principle of the ineffability of God who 'dwells in light unapproachable'. God is the all-transcending reality. Among other things this must mean that God infinitely transcends all human designations and descriptions. The First Vatican Council (1869–70) insisted that 'divine mysteries by their very nature so excel the created intellect that, even when they have been communicated in faith, they remain covered by the veil of faith itself and shrouded as it were in darkness' (Neusner and Dupuis, 1983, pp.45f.). As Karl Rahner has emphasised, in revealing himself the hidden God becomes present 'as the abiding mystery', and that mystery – that hiddenness – will remain even in heaven (Rahner, 1965–92, vol.16, p.238). Theology, with its inveterate tendency to domesticate God and to be comfortable with burning truths, needs reminding continually of the great dictum of the mystic Tersteegen: 'A God comprehended is no God.'

Pannenberg does well to preface his treatise on the Godhead in the first volume of his *Systematic Theology* with an acknowledgement of the surpassing majesty and mystery of God: 'Any intelligent attempt to talk about God – talk that is critically aware of its conditions and limitations – must begin and end with confession of the inconceivable majesty of God which transcends all our concepts.' Pannenberg concludes: 'Between this beginning and this end comes the attempt to give a rational account of our talk about God' (Pannenberg, 1991, p.337).

Because God is the all-transcending reality, there has always stood, alongside affirmative theology (*via affirmativa*), negative or apophatic theology. Whatever we want to say about God stands in its literal sense only to be negated and cancelled out. Analogy works dialectically, taking away with one hand what it first proffers with the other. God is love, says the New Testament, but we are immediately conscious that our most consuming experiences of love are shot through with ambiguity: the Freudian 'hidden agenda' in the love of a child for its parent or of a parent for its child, the mixed motives of mutual friendship, the tempestuous episodes of some erotic love. Human love at its noblest remains an unworthy and hopelessly inadequate analogy of the great 'fire of love' that is the 'heart' of God.

Again, God's wisdom is perfect and unerring – not as we humans become wise: learning from painful experience, piecemeal, by trial and error, by arduous study; 'older and wiser', 'a sadder and a wiser man' (Coleridge, 1969, p.209). And after all those qualifications, we are completely trumped by the biblical insight that 'the foolishness of God is wiser than [the wisdom of] men' (1 Corinthians 1.25).

From the fourteenth century, *The Cloud of Unknowing* insists: 'Of God himself can no man think.' 'Therefore,' the anonymous English mystic continues, 'I will leave on one side everything I can think and chose for my love that thing which I cannot think. Why? Because he may well be loved but not thought. By love he can be caught but by thinking never.' Then *The Cloud* instructs us: 'Strike that thick cloud of unknowing with the sharp dart of longing love' (Wolters, 1961, pp.59f.). But even this strategy – forceful as it is in bringing home once again the ineffability of God – cannot escape the ambiguities of analogy: what can it mean to 'love' or even 'think' God?

But, one might reply, God can be thought and loved in Jesus Christ. 'The light of the knowledge of the glory of God' shines out from the 'face of Christ' (2 Corinthians 4.6). However, this unveiling is at the same time a veiling, for God transcends even God's self-revelation. It is precisely the 'glory', that is to say the ineffable nature of God, that is revealed. As Von Balthasar puts it:

> It is true that in Jesus Christ the mystery of the ground of the world burns out more brightly than anywhere else. But on the other hand, it is precisely in this light that for the first time and definitively we grasp the true incomprehensibility of God.
>
> (Von Balthasar, 1975, p.22)

or, quoting Markus Barth, in *The Glory of the Lord*:

> The full import of God's transcendence comes to light only on the basis of and in connection with his condescension.
>
> (Von Balthasar, 1982–9, vol.1, p.311)

The more we ponder on the holy child of Bethlehem and the stricken man of Calvary, the more we realise how little we know of God and God's counsels: 'O the depth of the riches and wisdom and knowledge of God! How unsearchable are his judgements and how inscrutable his ways!' (Romans 11.33). The Christian tradition has long known that theology is not an accumulation of positive knowledge, but a form of learned ignorance (*docta ignorantia*). Herbert McCabe, the translator of Aquinas' treatise on analogy in the Blackfriars edition of the *Summa Theologiae*, draws the sting of some tiresomely familiar criticisms of analogy when he remarks: 'Analogy is not a way of getting to know about God, nor is it a theory of the structure of the universe; it is a comment on our use of certain words' (Aquinas, 1964–81, vol.3, p.106).

This consideration alone justifies Barth's protest against any complacent or arrogant appeal to analogy. His great theological principle, that God can only be known through God, is well taken. It was this that led Barth to suggest that the direction of analogy was not from below to above but precisely from above to below. Analogies were selected in the sovereignty of God and graciously bestowed to enable us to speak of God at all meaningfully. Here, as so often, Barth had a point but overstated it. In spite of Barth's intentions as a dialectical theologian, his 'analogy of faith' (*analogia fidei*) is not dialectical enough: it lacks reciprocity. It actually distorts and misrepresents Aquinas and the 'analogy of being' (*analogia entis*). In Aquinas there is a satisfying symmetry and reciprocity in analogy. It is not at all an arrogant, idolatrous human attempt to scale the heights of infinite mystery, a theological Tower of Babel, a negation of God's ineffability or an attempt to bypass revelation. Analogy rests on the self-communication of God to the creation, God's impartation to it of being. 'Although philosophy ascends to the knowledge of God through creatures while sacred doctrine grounded in faith descends from God to man by the divine revelation, the way up and the way down are the same' (Gilson, 1964, p.39). Analogy is viable because it operates in a divinely ordained context of meanings bounded by the divine actions in creation and redemption. Aquinas brought out the ontological framework of analogy.

But there is an epistemological framework too. There is a context in human knowing that brings out the nature of analogy in theology, not as a logic-defying piece of metaphysical speculation but as a serviceable tool of unpretentious theological work – in preaching, catechising and biblical interpretation, for example. Of course Barth was not unaware of the epistemological aspects of analogy and its problems, but he did not achieve a satisfying resolution of them. Barth worked with an epistemological dualism. In the sphere of revelation he postulated an extreme realism. The import of revelation can be 'read off' and the role of human construction and interpretation is minimal. There is a strong isomorphism between word and thing in this 'passive-copy' theory of language. But Barth, deeply versed in European culture as he was, understandably did not apply such a crude theory to the language of poets, visionaries and prophets outside of revelation. He could not allow divine revelation to be subjected to such open-ended mediation – to be at the mercy of human interpretation. Barth's dualism entails that the mind, through language, has the making of worldly reality but not of divine revelation.

Barth is content that the givenness and otherness of revelation rules out the possibility that there could be a humanly correct theory of how language works in such a context. As Graham Ward puts it:

There is no coherent account of the Word in words ... It is Barth's Christology that bears the weight of any possible explanation or synthesis ... A keystone analogy holds up the edifice of Barth's theology, the *analogia Christi*: the Word is to Jesus of Nazareth as the Word is to the words of human beings. 'The Word was made flesh: this is the first, original and controlling sign of all signs' ...

(Ward, 1995, p.31)

Ward argues that Barth's gambit of bringing in Jesus Christ – a *deus ex machina* with a vengeance! – to solve his epistemological incoherence is deliberate: 'Theology for Barth takes place as a continual negotiation and renegotiation of a problematic that cannot be, cannot be allowed to be, resolved. The fact that it remains unsolved, unanswered and illogical is the very point' (ibid., p.239). Ward presents it as 'a rhetorical strategy presenting both the need to do and the impossibility of doing theology' (ibid., p.247). This dialectical deadlock or *aporia* will only be resolved eschatologically when God will vindicate the truth of his revelation.

Graham Ward seems to take that as a merit in Barth and believes that his equivocation about the language of revelation can be clarified by bringing in Derrida's concept of *différance*. But, as Ward himself admits, Barth does not distinguish metaphorical from other forms of language in theology. And Barth is not interested in distinguishing genres in biblical revelation. I see Barth as actually a virtuoso who makes free with the material of scripture and tradition (Avis, 1986c, pp.35ff.). He is not interested in playing the game by the rules. Having demolished all his predecessors and their methods in his *Protestant Theology in the Nineteenth Century* (Barth, 1972), Barth is not lacking in the theological confidence – or rather bravado – to lay down his own rules. I must admit that I find this difficult to take in Barth. It is not a virtue to be so cavalier with the logic of language. Barth's concern for the integrity of revelation is misplaced. A proper discernment of such genres as metaphor, symbol and myth shows an appropriate respect for the authority of revelation.

Such a careful discernment of genre is the key to an understanding of analogy, one that does not, I believe, invite Barth's strictures on Aquinas or lapse into Barth's own lacunae. A whole series of post-war studies has attempted the justification of analogy both by bringing out its connection with metaphor and by insisting that all knowledge of what is more than merely empirical is actually analogical.

1   Dorothy Emmet, in her work *The Nature of Metaphysical Thinking* (first published in 1945), asserted that metaphysics was an essentially analogical way of thinking about the world and attempted an analysis of various kinds of metaphysical analogy: 'It takes concepts drawn from some form of experience, and extends them either so as to say something about the nature

of "reality", or so as to suggest a possible mode of coordinating other experiences of different types' (Emmet, 1966, p.5).

2   In *The Glass of Vision*, Austin Farrer linked images and analogies in his contention that theology is the analysis and criticism of revealed images and that analogy is only a refinement of appropriate images. He insisted that we cannot bypass thinking by images in order to seize hold of an imageless truth (Farrer, 1948, pp.44, 71, 110). Farrer believed that poetry, scripture and metaphysics (in that order) were united by the fact of working with inspired images, though the inspiration was of differing degrees:

> Poetry and divine inspiration have this in common, that both are pro-
> jected in images which cannot be decoded, but must be allowed to sig-
> nify what they signify of the reality beyond them ... [biblical] inspiration
> stands midway between the free irresponsibility of poetical images, and
> the sober and critical analogies of metaphysical discourse. For meta-
> physics can express its objects in no other way than by images, but it
> pulls its images to pieces and strips them down in the exact endeavour
> to conform to the realities ... The subjective process of inspiration is
> essentially poetical, the content it communicates is metaphysical.
>
> (ibid., p.148)

3   In 1953 Mary Hesse published *Models and Analogies in Science*, in which she explored the role of analogies in scientific exploration. She quoted with approval N.R. Campbell's claim that 'analogies are not "aids" to the establishment of theories; they are an essential part of theories' (Hesse, 1966, p.4). In a later edition, Hesse related analogies to metaphors by including her paper on 'The Explanatory Function of Metaphor' – the provocative combination of 'explanatory' and 'metaphor' already challenges the denigration of metaphor in the analytical tradition of Hobbes and Locke (Hesse, 1966, pp.157ff.).

4   In *Ethics and Christianity* (1970), Keith Ward pointed out that analogy is not unique to theology, but arises out of ordinary language. The difficulties of analysing a theological analogy, such as 'wise' or 'good', into univocal and equivocal meanings applies much more widely. Because language is built of metaphors, almost all uses of language are analogical to some extent. Keith Ward proposes, therefore, that 'it is the terms "univocal" and "equivocal" which are peculiar, and to be defined by contrast with the normal case of the "analogical"'. The vast majority of word-uses in ordinary language, he claims, are analogical 'in that they stress partial resemblances' and these resemblances depend on the associations and connections that are made by speakers and hearers between the various contexts in which the words are used. Analogical discursive concepts are required not just in theology but in the interpretation of all distinctive or unique kinds of human experience (Ward, 1970, pp.103f.).

5   In his work *Analogy and Philosophical Language* (1973), David Burrell admitted the deficiencies of analogy regarded as a formal syllogism or equation (a:b::c:d) and brought out its nature as the rationalisation of an insight – and thus its continuity with the way that we interpret the world spontaneously through the generation of metaphors. Burrell proposes, in essence, that analogy is a formal and reflective expression of that capacity of which metaphor is an informal and unreflective expression. The significance of any given analogy cannot simply be read off by anyone unversed in the Christian ethos: it needs a judgement that has become attuned to its nature through skill in using the analogy (Burrell, 1973, pp.215–67).

6   This insight, drawn from Ward and Burrell, which connects the analogy typical of theological statements with the metaphors that throng all meaningful discourse, has been developed by J.F. Ross in his rigorous analysis *Portraying Analogy* (1981) in the light of Wittgenstein's concept of 'forms of life' which have their own framework of meaning. Ross convincingly asserts that

> the central issues in the dispute about the cognitive content of Judaeo-Christian religious discourse are not peculiar to religion. Metaphysical, ethical, aesthetic, legal and scientific discourse raise generically the same issues. They are all craftbound ... skill in action is necessary for a full grasp of the discourse
>
> (Ross, 1981, p.158)

Particular spheres of discourse generate their own ways of using words which are not transferable. They need to be learned, usually by participating either actually or empathetically in the practice of the craft, whether it be theology or motor mechanics, astronomy or law. As Ross puts it: 'You practice religion as you do law, medicine, or philosophy, through judgements, justified through one's construal of reality, and directed towards action' (ibid., p.168). People who use religious language (especially analogy) are certainly 'cognitivists' and their discourse makes sense within their framework 'even if they talk nonsense'. It is the outsiders to these forms of life, these practices and linguistic conventions, who are actually the non-cognitivists, for they fail to make sense of the world of religion even when what they say is linguistically and logically faultless (ibid., p.177).

My argument here, then, is that there is a continuity between the ambiguities that metaphor imparts to ordinary language and the analogies of Christian theology. When in ordinary speech we want to make significant meaningful assertions, we do so in the form of metaphor. Metaphors can be unravelled into similes or expanded into symbols. Symbols and similes can be elaborated with some philosophical and theological sophistication into analogies. Analogies can be developed into models and these models become the building blocks of theology and doctrine.

Let us take, for example, the biblical idea of the kingdom or kingship of God. 'The LORD reigns!' is the basic, spontaneous metaphor, a triumphant insight into the personal rule of God in the world. Drawn out into a simile, this becomes 'God is like a king', which already implies a theological agenda because it raises the corollary 'How is God not like a king?'. Expanded into a symbol it becomes the theme of the Gospels: 'the kingdom of God'. This symbol both reveals and conceals its meaning, giving rise to a process of reflection, questioning and exploration that never comes to an end. The analogical form of this follows the pattern: 'As an earthly king rules his subjects, so God governs the world.' The analogical form will be developed to include other aspects of the rule of God by analogy with the authority of earthly rulers: protection, provision, compassion, example. This will be scrutinised critically, bringing out the idealised element as far as earthly rulers are concerned and also safeguarding divine perfection by specifying the differences between human and divine government. When this elaboration and refinement take place, we have a theological model – not just a suggestive or heuristic image (the basic metaphor), but an explanatory model with inbuilt self-criticism. This then forms a major component of theological construction and may give rise eventually to a monumental theological achievement that is held together by the theme of the sovereignty of God.

Iris Murdoch has suggested that Christianity is like a great work of art. It holds out to us a mythology, a store of imagery, stories and pictures, together with 'a dominant and attractive central character' (Murdoch, 1993, p.82). The sacred stories of creation and fall, exodus and pilgrimage, exile and return, incarnation and atonement, death and resurrection, second coming and final consummation are rich in metaphor, studded with symbols and bear all the marks of myth.

Does all this become cognitively docetist?
Does JC become something that only 'seemed' real? ie he is a myth that looked human?

* and if you find this central character un-attractive?

It leaves 'the Jews' trapped within the myth: they remain Bultmann's 'reps of unbelief'.

7 Imagination and the adventure of faith

but should not worship tie personalization

Faith is the act of the whole person and has as its object a personal God. Faith cannot be less than personal and personalist categories are required to interpret it. Provided that we remember this, we may speak of the role of various faculties in conducing to faith: reason, conscience and imagination. It is the crucial function of the imagination in the venture of faith that I propose to explore in this chapter. Newman wrote in his Anglican days ('The Tamworth Reading Room', 1841) and quoted himself half a lifetime later in the *Grammar of Assent*: 'The heart is commonly reached, not through the reason, but through the imagination ... Persons influence us, voices melt us, looks subdue us, deeds inflame us' (Newman, 1903, pp.92f.).

Faith is indeed the gift of God, as Ephesians 2.8 suggests, but it operates through human faculties, among which the imagination is pivotal. Belief involves several elements – cognitive, moral and volitional. The *cognitive* element in belief refers to the need to make a judgement on the basis of knowledge, to reflect on the significance of certain facts, normally concerning the Bible, the person and work of Jesus Christ, and the teaching and worship of the Church, together with what our own experience of life tells us, and to assent to the truth of the Christian gospel. The *moral* element is a prime source of motivation; it refers to our sense of spiritual need, of an emptiness that God alone can fill, conviction of our sinfulness, longing for forgiveness and to be made whole. The *volitional* element refers to the act of commitment or decision when we will to believe on the basis of thinking and feeling. However, it is imagination – the *aesthetic* element – that makes the final leap – but it is not an arbitrary one. 'We allow our imaginative assents to be brought into accord with trustworthy testimony and reliable inferences' (Coulson, 1981, p.80).

Beauty, truth and goodness can never be separated. It is questionable whether we can ever know one except in intimate connection with the others. In a potent combination of numinous ideas, the Psalter (at least in the older English translations) exhorted: 'Worship the LORD in the beauty of holiness' and many since have wanted to reverse the expression and speak of the holiness of beauty. There is a truth – a reality, an authenticity – about beauty and goodness. There is a goodness – a wholesomeness, salutariness, a sacredness – about both beauty and truth. There is beauty in truth – in its self-evidence, its simplicity, its transparency – and in goodness, especially in the comeliness of moral character.

Keats wrote that it was only the clear perception of its beauty that made him certain of any truth (Keats, 1954, p.207) and his 'Ode on a Grecian Urn' concludes: 'Beauty is truth, truth beauty' (Palgrave, 1928, p.332). Hegel believed that truth and goodness are intimately related only in beauty (Habermas, 1987, p.89). Von Balthasar suggests, in discussing Dante, that beauty is the expressive form of the good and true (Von Balthasar, 1982–9, vol.3, p.103; Sherry, 1992, p.103). Newman claimed that divine revelation had 'a beauty to satisfy the moral nature' and had the attractiveness of intellectual beauty (Newman, 1895, vol.1, pp.23, 282).

Von Balthasar, who has probably done more than any other theologian to restore beauty to its rightful place in theology, naturally does not overlook the need for the moral and cognitive aspects also (Von Balthasar, 1982–9, vol.1, p.118). Jesus Christ, the revelation of the form of God, is absolute truth, absolute goodness and absolute beauty (ibid., p.607). The beauty of divine revelation, which comes to perfection in the Christ, the centre of the form of revelation, is not given to us for mere aesthetic enjoyment but as a moral and truthful challenge to conversion (ibid., p.209). Beauty, truth and goodness come from God: when we encounter them together the glory (*kabod*) of God is revealed (cf. Harries, 1993, p.54).

Imagination – the holistic faculty – grasps the goal of the venture of faith as a whole, integrating all those elements that relate specifically to the thinking or feeling or willing faculties. Its heuristic power enables imagination to see the end from the beginning and to anticipate what it will be like to arrive at our destination. It is imagination that responds to the invitation in the Psalms: 'O taste, and see, how gracious the Lord is' (Psalm 34.8 BCP). It makes the object of faith real to our inward sight and testifies to our judgement that it is pleasing or desirable. Beauty allures us; because it only exists in this world in embodied form, it generates the desire to possess it or at least to be united with it. Beauty is expressive form: its nature is to communicate itself. It evokes a response, which Burke calls 'love' (Burke, 1834, p.47).

One of the attributes ascribed to beauty in the scholastic tradition is proportion or harmony: when we are receptive to beauty in the world or in art something of that harmony imparts itself to us. Another attribute of beauty is unity or integrity and when we open ourselves to beauty we find ourselves being reintegrated, knit together. Coleridge confessed: 'When I worship let me unify' (Coulson, 1981, p.13, no reference given). The third traditional attribute of beauty is radiance, splendour or clarity, and when we allow beauty to shine upon us we feel ourselves illuminated, elevated and purified. All these come together in Christ, the revealed and embodied form of the beauty of God – the beauty that is God. In him are united proportionate form, wholeness and unity, radiance and glory (for further discussion, see Von Balthasar, 1982–9; Sherry, 1992; Harrison, 1992; Murphy, 1995; Harries, 1993).

Through imagination we indwell the spiritual reality that Christianity postulates for our credence. 'Faith gives substance to our hopes and convinces us of realities we do not see' (Hebrews 11.1, REB). Belief becomes a possibility for the individual when the truths of faith are verified by the imagination. Things 'fall into place' and 'fit together'; they 'make sense' or 'add up'; the 'penny drops' and we see life 'in a new light'. Real assent, in Newman's sense, rises on the wings of the imagination. An aesthetic element belongs to all acts of spiritual perception, as Von Balthasar insists (Von Balthasar, 1982–9, vol.1, p.153). Faith is a theological act of perception (ibid., pp.155, 466). Poetry can effect this assent because it is the voice of imagination. As Coleridge suggests, commenting on Shakespeare, poetry has the power, even by a single word, 'to instil that energy into the mind which compels the imagination to produce the picture' (Hawkes, 1972, p.46). 'The poet,' he says elsewhere, 'brings the whole soul of man into activity' (Coleridge, 1965, p.173). Poetry has the power to suspend disbelief and to invite belief. In 'Dejection' Coleridge calls the imagination (or 'Joy'): 'This beautiful and beauty-making power' (Coleridge, 1969, p.365).

Coleridge's celebrated phrase 'that willing suspension of disbelief ... which constitutes poetic faith' lends itself to this argument, but we should take careful note of the original context. The context in *Biographia Literaria* is a discussion of the innovative method of the *Lyrical Ballads* on which Coleridge and Wordsworth had worked together. Coleridge recalls that in the early days of their collaboration, he and Wordsworth had identified 'the two cardinal points of poetry' as, first, 'the power of exciting the sympathy of the reader by a faithful adherence to the truth of nature' and, second, 'the power of giving the interest of novelty by the modifying colours of imagination' (Coleridge, 1965, p.168). In their respective contributions to *Lyrical Ballads* the two Lakeland poets would attempt to combine both these features. Coleridge's assignment was a 'supernatural, or at least romantic' theme with the aim of transferring 'from our inward nature a human interest and a semblance of truth sufficient to procure for these shadows of imagination that willing suspension of disbelief for the moment, which constitutes poetic faith' (ibid., pp.168f.). Coleridge is saying that it is the infusion of imaginative interest that gives passing credibility to such spectral figures as the Ancient Mariner and Christabel. The poetry that makes them real evokes the sort of credence that Coleridge calls 'poetic faith'. Thanks to Coleridge's poetic gift they cast their spell on us and hold us spellbound just as the Ancient Mariner held the wedding guest riveted with his glittering eye.

Clearly what Coleridge meant by the willing suspension of disbelief that constitutes poetic faith is not immediately transferable to the religious context. Poetic faith is less than religious faith. The objects of religious assent are not 'shadows of imagination' – not spectral, eerie, or occult entities. Yet there is surely an analogy. The imaginative portrayal of religious truth brings aesthetic pleasure even to those who do not yet fully believe. It bypasses our intellectual difficulties and saps our habitual aloofness from religion. It may lead us to admire the beauty of form of religious truth, its sublimity or symmetry. It may even bring us to the point of wistfully wishing that it might all be true after all. Through imagination we are enabled to indwell the world of religious belief and to obtain a glimpse of what it might be like to live as though it were true. As Prickett says: 'Poetry makes religion live in the imagination' (Prickett, 1986, p.48). Noting that for Keble the word 'poetic' takes on many of the qualities that Coleridge had ascribed to the imagination, Prickett quotes Keble's lectures on poetry: 'Poetry lends Religion her wealth of symbols and similes: Religion restores these again to Poetry, clothed with so splendid a radiance that they appear to be no longer symbols, but to partake (I might almost say) of the nature of sacraments' (op. cit.).

Keats' oracular remark in his letter of 1817 sums up the power of the imagination or the poetic to conduce to belief: 'The imagination may be compared to Adam's dream – he awoke and found it truth' (Keats, 1954, p.49). The allusion is to Book VIII of *Paradise Lost* (Milton, 1913, pp.271ff.) where Adam dreams first of the Garden that has been prepared and its trees laden with fruit that evoked within him the desire to pluck and eat:

> whereat I waked, and found
> Before mine eyes all real, as the dream
> Had lively shadowed.
>
> (ibid., ll. 309ff.)

Adam had a second dream in which in imagination he saw Eve fashioned from his rib:

> Mine eyes he closed, but open left the cell
> Of fancy, my internal sight ...
>
> (ibid., ll. 460f.)

> On waking he beholds her
> Such as I saw her in my dream, adorned
> With what all Earth or Heaven could bestow
>   ...
> Grace was in all her steps,
> Heaven in her eye,
> In every gesture dignity and love.
>
> (ibid., ll. 482f.; 488f.)

Keats' dictum that imagination foreshadows reality may be taken as an analogy of religious assent. Poetry – the pleasurable aesthetic – makes religion live to the imagination. And if it lives to the imagination, the battle for belief is more than half over.

"wood between the worlds"
= Khan.

8   Liturgy as literature

The suspicion and hostility of modernity and postmodernity towards the
truth of imagination raises an acute problem for Christian theology because
the language of scripture, theology, belief and liturgy is permeated with
metaphor, symbol and myth. Edit them out and there is little or nothing
left. Christianity is embodied in figurative language and cannot exist in
abstraction from it. The imagination is the matrix of Christian faith. The
language of Christian devotion (that is, of private prayer, meditation and
hymnody) springs from the Christian imagination that is aflame with the
love of God and is therefore incorrigibly figurative – sometimes boldly and
radically so. Let us take a well-known example from the hymn book. In the
eighteenth century, John Newton, in the hymn 'How Sweet the Name of
Jesus Sounds', addresses Christ as

> My Shepherd, Husband, Friend,
> My Prophet, Priest and King,
> My Lord, my life, my Way, my End.

To say this was simply to echo biblical metaphors, especially from Isaiah
and the Psalms, where God is the husband, betrothed or beloved of Israel.
In scripture or traditional hymnody these images seem unexceptionable. Let
us move on to one or two examples that may be a little more provocative.

In the fifteenth century, Julian of Norwich spoke of God as at once
Father, Mother and Spouse and of Jesus as at once Mother, Brother and
Saviour. Her *Revelations of Divine Love* included a 'shewing' of the 'true
motherhood' of Jesus. She sustains and elaborates this maternal metaphor
along the lines of biblical and medieval imagery:

> The mother may give her child suck of her milk, but our precious
> Mother, Jesus, he may feed us with himself, and doeth it full cour-
> teously and full tenderly with the Blessed Sacrament that is precious
> food of my life; and with all the sweet sacraments he sustaineth us full
> mercifully and graciously ... The mother may lay the child tenderly to
> her breast, but our tender Mother, Jesus, he may homely lead us into his

blessed breast, by his sweet open side, and shew therein part of the Godhead and the joys of heaven.

(Julian of Norwich, 1901, pp.149ff.)

The image of God or Jesus as Mother was not new with Julian, but was already found in Anselm of Canterbury, Aelred of Rivaulx, William of St Thierry and Bernard of Clairvaux. Maternal imagery was also applied to male religious authority figures, who represented God to their people: the Apostles, bishops and abbots (Bynum, 1982, pp.110–69).

It is in this tradition that new, non-sexist liturgies pray to God or Christ as 'our beloved', 'our companion', 'our brother', 'our mother', 'our victim', 'our lover', 'our healer' and so on (Morley, 1988). The poet and hymn-writer Brian Wren has reflected on our new freedom to rename God in the innumerable diverse metaphors generated in the intense subjectivity and active sociability of modern religious life. This he sees as something to be celebrated:

Bring many names, beautiful and good;
celebrate, in parable and story,
holiness in glory,
living, loving God.

(Wren, 1989, p.137)

This is, of course, a long overdue reaction against the patriarchy and hierarchy, traditionalism and authoritarianism that maintained a monopoly of naming God. Sexuality has been made a safe area from which to draw images of the divine by long practice by 'respectable' mystics like St Bernard of Clairvaux, St John of the Cross and St Teresa of Avila. At their best, the new metaphors for God and Jesus Christ are drawn from personal relations and reflect the tacit personalism and immanentism of recently emergent theological paradigms. They find their precedent in scripture and tradition. They have their sanction in the doctrines of humanity's creation in the divine image and of the triune nature of God. The struggle for the emancipation and ordination of women in the Church and the celebration of a succession of partial victories has generated enormous creativity in non-sexist spirituality.

However, we also need to think reflectively and self-critically about the scope and limits of the language of prayer, praise and liturgy. The current surge of creativity can help us to understand the dynamics of the creation of metaphor. Is it merely an expression of subjective feeling? Can metaphor be produced at will? Does the 'naming' in metaphor redescribe reality? Do metaphors have a purchase on what is 'out there', transcendent, objective? Are feminist liturgists redesigning the Christian faith? Or are they articulating insights and resources that have always been there, though suppressed?

The language of liturgy

In *Liturgy and Society* (1935), Gabriel Hebert wrote:

> Liturgical tradition is the continuous life of the Church which expresses itself in liturgical forms, and finds in them a meaning that is partly grasped by the intellect, and partly subconscious and unformulated: for that which the forms enshrine is the Christian Mystery and the life of the mystical Body of Christ.
>
> (Hebert, 1935, p.224)

The language of liturgy is poetry rather than prose: it is the product of Christian imagination that has been chastened and shaped by the liturgical and doctrinal tradition. Like any artistic creation, liturgy results from the creative interaction between the imaginative vision of the artist and the disciplined energy of the tradition. The liturgist is above all the servant of the tradition and cannot make free with it. The liturgist is also the servant of the community and must respond to its pastoral needs. This requires a sensitivity to the religious affections of Christians in the Church today. The framing of liturgy therefore demands considerable humility and self-effacement, combined with an intensity of spiritual vision that has been formed both by deep academic study of the tradition and by years of liturgical practice.

It would be stating the obvious to show that the liturgies of the Church are imbued with figurative language. Metaphor, symbol and myth are identifiable as the linguistic types that are characteristic of liturgy. We take these for granted most of the time; when worshipping, we do not pause to ask: 'Is this metaphor, symbol or myth that I am saying?' It is only when the language does not come naturally to our lips, when it is no longer second nature to us, that we stop to analyse what we are doing. Liturgy comes into crisis either when familiar forms lose their power over us and begin to leave us cold or when new liturgies strike us as banal and as bereft of that afflatus of transcendence and mystery that enables liturgy to fulfil its purpose of lifting the hearts and minds of the faithful to God in worship and adoration. This is a function of the figurative language of the liturgy.

In his *Table Talk*, Coleridge in one place defined prose as 'words in their best order' but poetry as 'the best words in the best order'. In another place he defined good prose as 'proper words in their proper places' and good verse as 'the most proper words in their proper places'. Coleridge admitted that the distinction between prose and poetry was not watertight, for some prose (such as oratory) may approximate to verse, and some verse (such as narrative) may approximate to prose. Nevertheless, he suggested that in prose the words are subordinate to the meaning and ought to express it as efficiently as possible without attracting too much attention to themselves, while the words of poetry must be beautiful in themselves, though without detracting from the unity of effect of the whole (Coleridge, 1884, pp.63, 220f.).

In the earlier lectures on Shakespeare and in the *Biographia Literaria*, Coleridge complemented this distinction between prose and poetry by stressing that it is the object of poetry to give pleasure by being beautiful (pleasurability being one of the aspects of the received definition of the beautiful). 'The proper and immediate object of poetry' is not to convey knowledge; it is rather 'the communication of immediate pleasure'. However, Coleridge admits that novels and other prose genres also aim to give pleasure: what is distinctive about poetry? The distinctive characteristic of poetry is found in the experience of intense creativity out of which the poem is born – 'that pleasurable emotion, that peculiar state and degree of excitement, which arises in the poet himself in the act of composition' (Coleridge, 1960, vol.1, pp.147f.).

Coleridge's answer is, of course, typical of the Romantic interpretation of art as essentially the creative expression of the aesthetic experience – the artistic vision – of the individual, whose gift is not under his control. Byron said that poetry is 'the lava of the imagination whose eruption prevents an earthquake' (Abrams, 1953, p.139). In his *Defence of Poetry*, Shelley wrote that: 'Poetry is a sword of lightning, ever unsheathed, which consumes the scabbard that would contain it' (Shelley, 1888, vol.2, p.16). For Keble, poetry acts as a safety-valve for overflowing emotion: the writing and reading of poetry is cathartic and soothes – that is to say steadies or tempers – the spirit suffering the turbulence of passion. In his 'Prospectus' in the preface to 'The Excursion', Wordsworth spoke of the 'soothing' and 'elevating' power of the poetic:

> And I am conscious of affecting thoughts
> And dear remembrances, whose presence soothes
> Or elevates the mind.
> (Wordsworth, 1920, p.755)

Keble dedicated his lectures as Professor of Poetry at the University of Oxford to Wordsworth who, through his poetry, had become 'a minister … of high and sacred truth', for religion and poetry sprang from the same source, that of heightened emotion generated by the imaginative apprehension of transcendent truth. As early as 1814, before Coleridge's *Biographia Literaria*, Keble was describing the imagination as 'creative energy'. In the *Lectures on Poetry*, Keble explained the nature of the poetic in therapeutic, almost religious, terms as 'a kind of medicine, divinely bestowed on man, which gives healing relief to secret mental emotion or overpowering sorrow, yet without detriment to modest reserve, and while giving scope to enthusiasm yet rules it with order and due control' (Beek, 1959, pp.85f., cf. pp.92, 96). In his review of Lockhart's life of Sir Walter Scott, Keble defined poetry as 'the indirect expression in words, most appropriately in metrical words, of some overpowering emotion, or ruling taste, or feeling, the direct indulgence whereof is somehow repressed'. Expression of emotion, 'controuled [*sic*] and modified by a certain reserve' is, for Keble, 'the very soul of poetry' (Keble, 1877, pp.6, 8, 20). It is significant that Keble believed that one purpose of the liturgy (i.e. *The Book of Common Prayer*) also was to soothe and tame our wayward, sinful nature. It is as though liturgy bridged poetry and religion, springing as they did (in Keble's view) from the one source.

In *Biographia Literaria* Coleridge reiterates the pleasure-giving purpose of poetry: it is 'the peculiar business of poetry to impart ... pleasurable interest' (Coleridge, 1965, p.169) – to arrest our attention and convey its meaning by means of its beauty of expression. Coleridge links this aesthetic emphasis – this 'pleasure principle' as we might call it – with what he consistently and frequently asserted about the essence of poetry being the best words in the best order, when he offers the pregnant judgement that 'nothing can permanently please which does not contain in itself the reason why it is so, and not otherwise' (ibid., p.172). A poem is, as we might say, 'just so' – a perfect unity of words, rhythm and meaning. It contains within itself all that it requires to answer its purpose. It relies for its rationale on nothing beyond itself. In communicating its message through beauty of form and expression it has fulfilled its *raison d'être*.

I have mentioned rhythm and Coleridge discusses the role of metre in this connection. Metre is the natural vehicle of that excitement and heightened consciousness – just as we tend to fall into a rhythmic form of utterance, with regular stress, under the power of strong emotion. 'Our language gives to expression a certain measure, and will, in a strong state of passion, admit of scansion from the very mouth' (Coleridge, 1960, vol.2, p.42). In discussing Wordsworth's preface to their joint volume – the *Lyrical Ballads* – in *Biographia Literaria*, Coleridge throws additional light on the distinction between prose and poetry, and does so, on this occasion, by exploring the significance of metre. Wordsworth had asserted that 'there neither is or can be any essential difference between the language of prose and metrical composition' (Coleridge, 1965, pp.203–6).

Coleridge locates the qualitative difference between poetry and prose in the significance of metre, first as to its origins and then as to its effects. Its origin he traces to the mind's innate principle of equilibrium which causes it to regulate the emotions – 'the balance in the mind effected by that spontaneous effort which strives to hold in check the workings of passion'. Coleridge speculates that this 'balance of antagonists' (reason and emotion) became organised into metre by an act of will and judgement which anticipates the pleasure that is derived from rhythm. This in turn supports Coleridge's two contentions that metre should not only appropriately be accompanied by the language of excitement, but that it should show also indications of being subject to control. What is required is 'an interpenetration of passion and of will, of spontaneous impulse and of voluntary purpose'. This is achieved by language that is full of colour and vitality. Figures of speech, which occur with more than ordinary frequency in poetry, combine heightened awareness with intellectual energy. The pleasurable excitement of poetry is due in part to the role of metre in harnessing powerful emotions. For not only is metre produced in the presence of emotional and intellectual excitement, it also perpetuates and enhances it, tending 'to increase the vivacity and susceptibility both of the general feelings and of the attention'. This effect, Coleridge continues, is produced 'by the continued excitement of surprize [*sic*], and by the quick reciprocations of curiosity still gratified and still re-excited' which, though individually imperceptible, have a powerful cumulative effect (Coleridge, 1965, pp.206f.).

Without the above discussion, my contention that liturgy is closer to poetry than to prose might seem merely a truism. The debate among these great Romantics – who were practitioners of both poetry and prose as well as theorists of them – shows that the point needs to be, and has been argued. Liturgy exerts a profound effect on the worshipper by expressing Christian religious affections in a restrained and disciplined form that protects the worshipper from being overwhelmed by an experience of the numinous (just as Keble stressed the importance of reserve, control and order in the expression of powerful poetic emotions). In *The Book of Common Prayer* (1662), this controlled expression of religious emotion is particularly evident in the obliqueness with which God is invoked. It is of the essence of the familiar collect form: 'O God, who didst teach the hearts of thy faithful people ... ', but it is conspicuous in the Prayer of Consecration: 'Almighty God, our heavenly Father, who of thy tender mercy didst give thine only Son Jesus Christ to suffer death upon the Cross for our redemption, who made there (by his one oblation of himself once offered) a full, perfect, and sufficient sacrifice, oblation and satisfaction, for the sins of the whole world ... Hear us ... '. Thoughts that defy expression, emotions that are too strong for human nature to bear, are constrained, contained and made manageable by this obliqueness of address in traditional liturgical forms.

We have the sense in the finest poetry that nothing should – nay, could – be changed. Coleridge as a Blue-coat Boy learned from his headmaster at Christ's Hospital that, in the truly great poets, there was a reason not only for every word but for the position of every word. As a young poet himself, he became convinced that you could as soon dislodge a huge block of stone from one the pyramids as to change a word or the position of a word in the best of Shakespeare or Milton (Coleridge, 1965, pp.3, 12). We feel that there is an almost metaphysical inevitability about those words in that order. You cannot tinker with them or improve on them. In that lies the perfection of the poem. Wittgenstein discussed in the *Philosophical Investigations* the way that some words are unsubstitutable: there is 'something that is expressed by these words in these positions'. He related this, typically cryptically, to understanding a poem (Wittgenstein, 1968, p.144: 531), but the point applies equally to liturgy. Because words in the best poetry and liturgy are unsubstitutable there is an inevitability about them that is not simply the result of frequent repetition. The right words in the right order have authority. It is this authority that gives them their power to articulate worship and to strengthen faith. As we indwell the language empathetically, through participating in the community gathered for worship, we are enabled to believe in the reality of which the words speak.

I have argued that it is not merely familiarity, born of frequent repetition, that gives certain words authority. It is also the aesthetic judgement that they are the entirely appropriate words in the entirely appropriate order. They have a satisfying 'rightness' about them. (This should particularly appeal to Anglicans, for it was Richard Hooker who emphasised the importance of our sense of what is fitting when making judgements about the outward order of the Church.) But to say that, is not to play down the role of familiarity. The words of liturgy or the Bible become deeply ingrained and shape our thinking, believing and praying. They rise to our lips when they are needed – especially in times of crisis. This vital function of religious language is undermined when the words and the order of the words undergo frequent change. The present craze for ever-new Bible translations and for liturgical experiment and revision actually damages the cause of liturgy and Bible knowledge. We need to affirm not only that poetry and liturgy demand the best words in the best order, but also that they demand the same words in the same order.

The need for a stable text is underlined when we consider that one purpose of liturgy is to enable a community of faith to worship together. Common prayer therefore requires a high proportion of the same words in the same order. It belongs to the spirit of the age to diversify, but it belongs to the nature of worship to unify. The marks of our postmodern culture are pluralism, fragmentation, consumer preference, playing with words and doing one's own thing. We should guard against the spirit of the age when it militates against common prayer. Coleridge cries: 'When I worship, let me unify' (Coulson, 1981, p.13, no reference given). The nature of worship is to unify. It unites the worshipper with God, it binds believers together in one body, it knits together our hectic, careworn lives, centres them on the transcendent and refocuses our existence. Worship has an integrative function. Its essence is communion (*koinonia*). As Coleridge above all has taught us, it is the imagination (the 'co-ad-un-ating' faculty) that has the power to bind together many discordant and divergent elements into a unified whole. It does this through metaphor, symbol and myth. Only the truth of imagination has this unifying power. Liturgy is arid and inept without it.

Part III

9 Metaphor

Metaphor has long been under suspicion as a mere embellishment, a rhetorical flourish, a linguistic device, a way of pulling the wool over the eyes of the reader or listener. The dismissive phrase 'a mere metaphor' is indicative. Argument has raged since Aristotle as to whether metaphor is merely ornamental to already existing thoughts or words, or actually creative and constitutive of thoughts and words. Writers in the classical tradition, together with analytic linguistic philosophers, have inclined to the 'ornamental' or 'substitutionary' view of metaphor. The Romantics, followed by many literary critics and some philosophers of science, have held to a 'constitutive' or 'incremental' view. These two schools correspond broadly to what we earlier identified as the 'analytic or naturalistic' and 'synthetic or fiduciary' traditions. Let us examine more closely the argument between these two assessments of metaphor, beginning with some definitions.

Definitions and distinctions

First we note that metaphor itself has become the battleground for these two fundamental views of language. Although there are numerous figures of speech in the grammatical repertoire – hyperbole, metonymy, catachresis, oxymoron, to name but a few – metaphor has tended to absorb the others. Metaphor is no longer one figure among others, but 'the figure of figures' (Culler, 1981, p.189). Metaphor is widely recognised as the operative factor in language. Ricoeur quotes Shelley that language is 'vitally metaphorical' and himself claims that metaphor is the constitutive form of language (Ricoeur, 1978, p.80). The classical scholar Bedell Stanford writes:

> Metaphor is the vital principle in all living languages. It is the verbal expression of the process and products of the imagination with its powers of creative synthesis ... Metaphor is thus the dynamic, synthetic and creative force in language.
>
> (Stanford, 1936, p.100)

Second, metaphor is notoriously difficult to interpret. We are hard put to say how exactly it works. As Bedell Stanford remarks in his study of Greek metaphor, 'a fine metaphor is one of the hardest things in the world to rationalize' – and the problem becomes particularly acute when translating a metaphor from the original language into another. Reflecting on the problems of translation, George Steiner has observed that we cannot fully imagine

> what it must have been like to be the first to compare the colour of the sea with the dark of wine or to see autumn in a man's face. Such figures are new mappings of the world, they reorganise our habitation in reality.
>
> (Steiner, 1975, p.23)

Several writers have emphasised that the meaning of a metaphor depends almost entirely on the immediate context: a metaphor is justified solely by its use (see Searle, 1979; Davidson in Sacks, 1979, p.41; Swinburne, 1992, p.48).

Third, we need to try to clarify the two components that make up a metaphor. Aristotle said that metaphor consists in giving a thing a name that belongs to something else. A basic definition of metaphor, along these lines, is that metaphor describes one thing in terms of another, it joins together two perceptions, an immediate or primary perception and a borrowed or secondary perception. Max Black suggests that metaphor 'selects, emphasizes, suppresses and organizes features of the principal subject by implying statements about it that normally apply to the subsidiary subject' (Black, 1962, p.44). I.A. Richards distinguished between the 'tenor' and 'vehicle' of metaphor, the tenor being the conceptual meaning and the vehicle being the concrete comparison (Richards, 1965, pp.96f.). However, it does seem to me that these terms could be reversed, for the image is often the tenor or substance of the thought and the original occasion for the metaphor simply the vehicle for delivering the insight. These ambiguities suggest to me that it is unhelpful to attempt to decide which of the two components of metaphor is primary and which is secondary. It may suffice to speak of the 'event' of metaphor in which two aspects are fused together instantaneously. If we need to distinguish them conceptually, for the purpose of analysis, we can call them the 'occasion' of the metaphor and the 'image' through which we view the occasion. Together they comprise the total event of metaphor. Let us now try to elucidate these aspects by means of examples.

Shakespeare's paradoxical metaphor 'light thickens' in

> Light thickens, and the crow
> Makes wing to the rooky wood;
> Good things of day begin to droop and drowse,
> While's night's black agents to their preys do rouse.
>
> (*Macbeth* III.ii.50ff.)

comprises the 'occasion' (the perception of the gathering dusk) and the 'image' (the perception of a substance something like porridge that progressively thickens as it settles). There are also sinister overtones: as 'light thickens', so 'the plot thickens' and so also spilt blood coagulates.

To stay with nocturnal metaphors for a moment: Dylan Thomas' night 'starless and Bible-black' in *Under Milk Wood* (Thomas, 1985, p.1) combines the occasion, the physical perception of the night, with the image of the Bible, carrying resonances derived from the child's associations of the family Bible – not only black, but great, heavy, oppressive and awesome. 'Black' is probably the most frequently used adjective in the play and in combination produces a dazzling range of images of night: 'the sloeblack, slow black/crowblack, fishingboat-bobbing sea' (op. cit.); 'the black, dab-filled sea' (ibid., p.2); 'the slow deep salt and silent black, bandaged night' (ibid., p.3).

To move from night to day and from darkness to light: when Louis XIV was called 'le Roi Soleil', the occasion was the perception of the monarch's glory, the image that of the sun in its splendour.

While we are considering metaphors of darkness and light – one of the earliest and most basic insights of human experience – let us look at Blake's tiger, which has already been mentioned as an exceptional example of the pre-Romantic genre of the awe-inspiring 'sublime'.

> Tyger, Tyger, burning bright
> In the forests of the night ...
>
> (Blake, 1977, p.125)

The occasion is not just seeing, but facing or confronting the tiger in the imagination (Blake had seen caged tigers in London, but when he tried to draw a tiger it looked like a rather foolish, friendly pet dog). The beast suddenly manifests itself through the thickets of the jungle. The image is of fire, or rather 'burning': is it two eyes glowing menacingly like red-hot coals? Or are we seeing the animal sideways, with its stripes like flames flickering as its supple muscles ripple along its coat? The tiger burns the more brightly, of course, for being set against the dark backcloth 'the forests of the night' – not just physically dark, but sinister with the impartial cruelty of amoral nature. It is because we already know the second verse that we picture the glowing eyes:

> In what distant deeps or skies
> Burnt the fire of thine eyes!

In the fourth verse the primary metaphor of this poem ('burning bright') is extended, but without losing – it seems to me – its character as metaphor: the 'furnace' is the unfathomable, all-creating, all-consuming mind of its Maker:

What the hammer? What the chain,
In what furnace was thy brain?
What the anvil? What dread grasp,
Dare its deadly terrors clasp?

Blake is here the begetter of one of the most powerfully sustained extended metaphors in literature.

For the Romantics, as we have already noted, the Bible and the natural world were excelled as sources of the sublime by the human mind. The visions and prophecies of scripture became merely the types of the visions that appeared to the Romantic imagination (here Blake surely cannot be denied the name of Romantic). The wonders of natural scenery were simply an analogue of the landscapes of the mind and provided a hermeneutical key to mapping them. Wordsworth and Coleridge conducted a rigorous exploration of the psyche in its heights and depths, not just as they walked the fells but precisely by walking the fells. The Romantics' love–fear relationship with the sea supports this interpretation. Coleridge in 'The Ancient Mariner', Shelley in dicing with death on the fickle waves of the Gulf of Spezia and Byron in swimming the Hellespont, respectively knew by instinct what later depth psychology has abundantly shown: the sea is one of the primary symbols of the unconscious. Coleridge united all three sources of the sublime – the imagery of the Bible, of precipitous nature so enthralling to the Romantics and of the turbulent yet creative psyche – when he said that the poetic mind of Wordsworth was 'a rock with torrents roaring'. Gerard Manley Hopkins receives and is almost overwhelmed by the dark side of Romanticism in his 'Terrible Sonnets', but he needs the imagery of landscape to name the experience of desolation that engulfs him:

O the mind, mind has mountains; cliffs of fall
Frightful, sheer, no-man-fathomed.
Hold them cheap
May who ne'er hung there.
('No worst, there is none'; Hopkins, 1994, p.62)

The occasion, if we must be pedantic, is Hopkins' depression or 'dark night of the soul'; the image that we see is physical, momentous, vertiginous. They are united in the single event that is gifted or inspired metaphor.

Fourth, as will by now hardly need stating, metaphor is a matter not just of words but of thoughts. Metaphor is generated in the drive to understand experience. 'When new, unexploited possibilities of thought crowd in upon the human mind, the poverty of everyday language becomes acute. Apprehension outruns comprehension so far that every phrase ... has a vague aura of further significance' (Langer, 1956, p.149). In fusing together two perceptions, metaphor has a stereoscopic function. Each image carries with it a host of associations which interact and fertilise each other. Metaphor is not just naming one thing in terms of another, but seeing, experiencing and intellectualising one thing in the light of another. To evoke M.H. Abrams' work on the Romantic imagination, metaphor is not just a mirror but a lamp (Abrams, 1953). I.A. Richards suggests that a metaphor is not so much an interaction between words as 'a borrowing between, and intercourse of thoughts', for it is primarily thought that is metaphoric and individual metaphors of language derive from it (Richards, 1965, p.94). Middleton Murray, in *Countries of the Mind* (1937) – the title itself a legacy of the Romantics – supports this interpretation. Metaphors, he says, belong to 'the primary data of consciousness'; they are 'as ultimate as speech itself, and speech as ultimate as thought'. Metaphor is the 'instinctive and necessary' way in which the mind explores reality and orders experience, using intuitive comparisons whereby the less familiar is assimilated to the more familiar and the unknown to the known. Metaphor belongs to 'the genesis of thought' and opens up reality in ways that are 'hazardous, incomplete and thrilling' (Murray, 1937, pp.1f.). It is important that we locate metaphor in this context of knowing. A metaphor is not just a word, not even an image, but a conjunction of discourses, a joining of worlds.

Fifth, though we sometimes loosely say 'image' when we mean 'metaphor', a metaphor is much more than an image. As P.N. Furbank puts it, a picture is not at all the same as a comparison. In metaphor we envisage one thing in terms of another, bringing two images into juxtaposition. An image is somehow static, while a metaphor is 'an invitation to an activity, ending in an impossibility' because the two pictures or images that comprise a metaphor do not mesh: 'Macbeth has murdered Sleep.' Both painting and sculpture deal in images, but in poetic metaphor it is the words, the syntax and the rhythm that do the work (Furbank, 1970, pp.1–12, 23).

Finally, we must clarify the difference between metaphor and simile. Fogelin has suggested that 'similes wear their comparative form on their grammatical sleeves, and metaphors ... differ from similes only in a trivial grammatical way: metaphors are similes with the term of comparison suppressed, they are elliptical similes' (Fogelin, 1988, p.25). But if the grammatical difference between metaphor and simile is 'trivial', the difference of impact or import is great. Metaphor and simile belong to two different psychological worlds. They arise out of different experiences or perceptions; they generate different experiences and perceptions. Fogelin takes up Aristotle's example from *The Iliad* – 'the lion leapt' (metaphor); 'Achilles leapt like a lion' (simile) – and claims that the difference is slight. Analytically it may be slight, but in terms of the perception, the experience and the effect it is considerable. Homer's metaphor presents, virtually simultaneously, two images – Achilles and the lion – and it is hard to say which one is dominant. Translated into simile, however, the dominant image is definitely Achilles, with the lion comparison following rather doubtfully behind. If we return to some of our earlier illustrations of metaphor, centred on the basic images of darkness and light: the differences between these metaphors and the same comparisons in the form of similes is not only the formal elaboration of the thought – the night is getting darker; the night is as black as the Bible; the King of France is resplendent like the sun – but also the loss of immediacy and spontaneity. Wilson Knight, the Shakespearean critic, calls metaphor 'a concrete image ... fused with a spiritual vitality' (Knight, 1933, p.35).

The debate between comparisonists and non-comparisonists is beside the point. There is a comparison involved in metaphor but it has a spontaneity, immediacy and vividness that is absent in simile. Metaphor has been called 'a condensed comparison by which we assert an intuitive and concrete identity' (Ullmann, 1964, p.180). Identity is surely the key to the nature of metaphor. Mallarmé spoke as a true poet when he said: 'I have struck out the word *like* from the dictionary' (ibid., p.181). Ricoeur suggests that metaphor is located not in the word, the sentence or even the discourse, but in what is elided – 'the copula of the verb to be. The metaphorical "is" at once signifies both "is not" and "is like".' Hence, for Ricoeur, metaphors are (equally with symbols) vehicles of 'tensive' truth (Ricoeur, 1978, p.7).

Ornamental or incremental?

I use the terms ornamental and incremental to designate the two main rival traditions in the assessment of metaphor. The first regards it as a rhetorical flourish to increase effect, the second as a source of insight; the former naturally tends to regard it as dispensable, the latter as unsubstitutable. I.A. Richards observes that 'throughout the history of Rhetoric, metaphor has been treated as a sort of happy extra trick with words ... a grace or ornament, or added power of language, not its constitutive form' (Richards, 1965, p.90). It is thanks to the former tradition that metaphor is generally suspect in argument and carries a 'logical taint', as Middleton Murray puts it (Murray, 1937, p.4). We may take Aristotle and Samuel Johnson as representative of this reductionist school of metaphor.

Aristotle is, in effect, the source of the ornamental view of metaphor. While his observations are occasional and therefore fragmentary, they have exerted a profound influence on the assessment of metaphor. In the *Poetics*, he states that metaphor cannot be borrowed from someone else and is an indication of genius, for 'to observe metaphors well is to observe what is like' (Aristotle, 1987, p.28: 59a5). The *Rhetoric* adds little: metaphor is 'in the highest degree instructive' and the most successful simile is one that comes closest to metaphor (Aristotle, 1886, 3.10.11). Bedell Stanford judges Aristotle's statements on the nature of metaphor to be confused and unhelpful (Stanford, 1936, pp.5–12), but the philosopher set the trend for the 'classical', ornamental view of metaphor.

Boswell records Dr Johnson pronouncing that metaphor is 'a great excellence in style, when it is used with propriety, for it gives you two ideas for one; – conveys the meaning more luminously, and generally with a perception of delight' (Boswell, 1953, p.855). In his celebrated *Dictionary*, Johnson defined a metaphor as 'the application of a word to an use to which, in its original import, it cannot be put' and summed it up as 'a simile comprized [*sic*] in a word' (Johnson, 1755, 'Metaphor'). Johnson seems to regard metaphor as a matter of artifice, to be produced when required in order to achieve an intended effect. As we have seen in an earlier chapter, the rationalistic strand of the Enlightenment, influenced by Descartes' insistence of clear and distinct ideas, was suspicious of metaphor. Hobbes and Locke, with their 'counter' theory of language, regarded metaphor as a form of deception.

Romanticism reinstated metaphor as a vehicle of insight; reflection on Romantic literature has given impetus to the constitutive or incremental view. Coleridge's distinction between the contrivances of Fancy and the creative power of Imagination seems to correspond to the difference between simile and metaphor (though Coleridge preferred to discuss the more inclusive concept of symbol).

In his early work *The Birth of Tragedy* and before he had adopted his later jaundiced view of language and its images, Nietzsche recognised the importance of metaphor: 'For the true poet,' he wrote, 'the metaphor is not a rhetorical figure but a representative image that really hovers before him in place of a concept' (Nietzsche, 1993, p.42). The depth psychology of both Freud and Jung revealed the symbolic nature of unconscious thought processes and the determinative role of mental images in shaping our perception of reality.

Philosophers of science, including practitioners such as Einstein and Michael Polanyi, have asserted the heuristic power of metaphor to explore reality and order experience. Leatherdale (1974) provides an overview of the role of metaphor, analogy and models in science, based on a cognitive view of metaphor. Mary Hesse in particular insists that poetic metaphors are cognitive, not just expressive, and intend a 'redescription of reality' (Hesse, 1966, p.176). She affirms a continuity between poetic and scientific metaphors, arguing that 'rationality consists just in the continuous adaptation of our language to our continually expanding world, and metaphor is one of the chief means by which this is accomplished' (ibid., p.164). She points out that acceptance of the view that metaphors are meant to be intelligible implies rejection of all views that make metaphor a wholly non-cognitive, subjective, emotive or stylistic use of language (cf. Hesse, 1988). Hesse is indebted here to Max Black's 'incremental' theory of metaphor.

Black made a notable contribution to the reclaiming of metaphor by developing I.A. Richards' 'interaction' theory into an incremental theory of metaphor which stresses that metaphor is neither decorative of thoughts already chosen nor a substitute for them, but creatively constitutive of new ways of seeing the world. Living metaphors give emphasis and so awaken insight; they give resonance and so invite implicative elaboration (Black, 1962, pp.44f.; Black in Ortony, 1979, pp.19–43).

A similar approach has recently been developed by Kittay whose 'perspectival' theory is broadly equivalent to Black's 'incremental' concept. Kittay insists that metaphor has cognitive value and that this stems not from providing new facts about the world but from a reconceptualisation of the information that is already available to us. In this sense, metaphor actually gives us 'epistemic access' to fresh experience and, to the extent that we have no other linguistic resources to achieve this, metaphor is 'cognitively irreplaceable' (Kittay, 1987, pp.39 [cf. 303], 301). This incremental view of metaphor spans literature, science and theology.

Among theologians, Jüngel is notable for his positive view of metaphor. Jüngel's presupposition is one that could not be held by a theologian in the analytical tradition, that God becomes a reality in the world through language. He shares the incremental view of metaphor that has been promoted among theologians by Ricoeur. Jüngel grounds human transcendence in the capacity for making symbols, culminating in language: the creative freedom evinced in language is the guarantee of ultimate human freedom.

> The metaphorical mode of language has ontological relevance insofar as through it a new context of being is disclosed, grounded in a gain to language. The new (metaphorical) use of a word gives this word a new meaning and with this new meaning new being is brought to speech.
>
> (Webster, 1985, p.261)

Soskice advocates a form of critical realism in which metaphorical description, in science or theology, has cognitive value but is not (of course) claimed to be veridical; as she puts it, it refers and depicts, but does not claim to define. This implies for theology that talk of God, which cannot be abstracted from the world of religious images, can depict reality without claiming to describe it definitively (Soskice, 1985, pp.140f.). Davis has seconded this position, claiming that 'irreducibly metaphorical utterances can themselves state truths about the world'. Inadequate and inaccurate though they may be, they can still successfully refer to reality (Davis, 1989, pp.10, 13; see also Pickstock, 1998, pp.169ff.).

Literal and metaphorical

When we want to say, with emphasis, that something is 'really' true, we sometimes claim that it is 'literally' true. This is perhaps pardonable in common speech, though it is unhelpful and actually meaningless, but in theology, where it is not unknown, it is a classic *faux pas*. Where the metaphors of religious confession are not recognised as such, the qualifier 'literally' produces some interesting biological and cosmological situations with which, I guess, most of us have at some time been regaled by fervent fundamentalists: 'Jesus was literally God's Son. He literally came back to life on the third day. He literally sits at God's right hand. He will literally come again on the clouds.' We will be returning to this problem of misplaced literalism in our final chapters when we consider the implications of metaphor, symbol and myth for the truth of Christian beliefs, but I mention it now to suggest that our approach to metaphor so far leads to a critical re-evaluation of the received distinction between metaphorical and literal language.

There is a danger in exalting metaphor that we forget that not all metaphors are full of spontaneous creativity and open new horizons for human knowing. The language is full of metaphors that are routine, hackneyed or inept. Fogelin makes the point that 'many metaphors are lame, misleading, overblown, inaccurate' and advises: 'It is important to calm down about metaphors. Some are good; some are bad. Some are illuminating; some are obfuscating' (Fogelin, 1988, pp.98f.). Most of our language is composed of 'dead' metaphors (which is a good metaphor in itself) but metaphors they remain. The notion that it is possible to 'translate' a metaphor into 'literal' terms and that this is an advance in understanding is the literalistic fallacy.

The literalistic fallacy is found in some of the most respectable places. The philosopher W.M. Urban, with whom we have frequently made common cause, claims: 'Just as to call all knowledge symbolic without qualification, is to make the notion of symbolism meaningless, so to call all language symbolic is to make unintelligible the distinctively symbolic uses of language.' But Urban concedes that it is impossible to find any use of language that is wholly non-symbolic (Urban, 1939, pp.412, 435). Our likeliest candidate for non-symbolic language is perhaps 'scientific' language of (supposedly) pure description of bare sense-data. But we need to recognise that mere sense-data cannot become the subject of linguistic expression until they have been processed by conceptual thought – a powerfully symbolising event. So Urban admits that 'the only literal or non-symbolic element in scientific knowledge is ... precisely that which is not knowledge at all, namely the mere sense-datum' (ibid., p.544). The best solution, he concludes, is to regard the designations 'literal' and 'symbolic' as relative, as limiting notions, as abstractions. Statements which relate more closely to 'sensuously observable entities' are appropriately labelled 'literal', while statements which relate more closely to interpretative constructions, which have to be translated back into so-called literal statements in order to be verified, are more appropriately called symbolic (ibid., pp.423f., 544).

However, I would go further than this and ask whether the distinction between literal and metaphorical (or symbolic) usage can be rigorously maintained at all. Barfield suggests that literal and metaphorical are relative terms existing in tension and lending meaning to each other. So-called literal language is comprised of metaphors that have lost their living force – dead or extinct metaphors. 'Literal' and 'metaphorical' are merely limit concepts on a sliding scale of imaginative investment – the imaginative investment in so-called literal speech being minimal. It is therefore a fallacy to assume that the original state of language was unremittingly literal and that metaphor represents a deviation from this. A hard and fast distinction 'is based on the premise that literalness of meaning is some kind of unclouded correspondence with a mindless external reality, which was given from the start'. On the contrary, Barfield argues, what we call literalness is a late stage in historical linguistic development. It is impossible to imagine the birth of the first metaphor in a wholly literal world. Metaphor is the primary and inescapable constituent of language as it is of thought. Consciousness and symbolisation (including metaphor) are actually simultaneous and correlative. Literalness, Barfield concludes, is 'a quality which some words have achieved in the course of their history; it is not a quality with which the first words were born' (Barfield in Knights and Cottle, 1960).

Conclusion

Whereas the naturalistic or analytical view of language takes literal truth as its ideal 'speech situation', regarding metaphor and symbol as concealing or distorting the truth, the fiduciary view of language holds that symbolic modes of speech, particularly metaphor, are not a mere adornment to be stripped away in order to reveal the reality underneath, but themselves truly participate in the reality that they seek to convey and induct us into it. The first approach entails the fallacy that reality can be known independently of language, that intuition is separate from expression. The second approach involves a personal commitment to understanding what linguistic symbols are capable of telling us: it is the approach of hermeneutics. Theologians above all need to recognise that any quest for greater and greater degrees of literalness is a wild-goose chase. All the significant assertions of theology are expressed in language that is irreducibly metaphorical.

10 Symbol

What is a symbol?

In a symbol (etymologically speaking) two things, meanings or worlds, are 'thrown together'. Many writers on symbolism offer their own definition of a symbol. Some exercise great ingenuity in distinguishing between symbols and signs, signals, indexes and icons. It will help us to try to reach a working definition straight away. This is possible because there is a broad consensus as to the essential features of symbolism. At its simplest, a symbol means imagining one thing in the form of another. Two aspects of this basic definition – imagining one thing in the form of another – are worth underlining.

First, both when we employ a symbol and when we respond to or 'read' a symbol, we are using our imagination: we are not passive in symbolising, we have to exert our creative, constructive powers. This may seem self-evident applied to creating or generating symbols, but it is equally true of the reception of symbols: to receive what a symbol has to give us, we need to participate in it by imaginative indwelling and that is how we are enabled to participate in the reality of what it symbolises. Imagination is the milieu of symbolism.

Second, form is the key to symbols: we have the ability to abstract the form or essence of a symbol from all its other constituents – the substance from the accidents we might say. Thus we distinguish the fatherly care of the Creator from biological fatherhood; the purity and sacrificial associations of a lamb from the stupidity and herd (flock?) instinct of sheep; the illumination of a candle from the mechanics of combustion; the liturgical significance of vestments from sartorial eccentricity, etc. Susanne Langer, a pioneer of the philosophy of symbolism, says: 'The power of understanding symbols, i.e. of regarding everything about a sense-datum as irrelevant except a certain form that it embodies, is the most characteristic mental trait of mankind' (Langer, 1956, p.72).

The centrality of form in symbolism brings it into close connection with beauty, for philosophers of the aesthetic have generally identified form

(Latin, *species*) as one of the attributes of beauty, along with radiance (*lumen*) and the capacity to give pleasure (*dilectio*). The title of the first volume of Von Balthasar's great work on the theology of beauty suggests immediately the connection between the perception of beauty and its embodiment in the symbol: *Seeing the Form (Schau der Gestalt)* (Von Balthasar, 1982–9, vol.1).

However, as we shall see, these two components of symbolism – imagination and the abstraction of form – lay it open to distortion and manipulation. Symbols clearly have the potential for harm as well as health. They can be hijacked for ulterior purposes. They always serve specific socio-economic interests. They are not ideologically innocent nor are they self-authenticating. Sometimes iconoclasm is precisely what is called for.

Symbol and metaphor

Why are symbols so central to the human world and to theological thinking? It is because through our symbol-making capacity we make sense of the world and find meaning in life. Our capacity for symbolising gives us our characteristic ability to transcend, through imagination, our immediate environment and so envision freedom. The symbolising faculty is the mark of humankind: Susanne Langer claimed that 'the use of signs is the very first manifestation of mind' (Langer, 1956, p.21) and that 'the power of understanding symbols ... is the most characteristic mental trait of mankind' (ibid., p.72). Langer was taking her cue from the massive system of Ernst Cassirer, the *Philosophy of Symbolic Forms* (Cassirer, 1955). Cassirer has taught us to see that symbols are the common denominator (and by no means the lowest!) in all human cultural activities – not just religion, but language, poetry, art, myth, philosophical speculation and even science (Cassirer, 1946a, p.45).

By means of symbols our mental and emotional life is organised and advanced. Symbolisation is at work in basic perception (since, as we have seen, metaphor is a primary mental activity and metaphor is a subdivision of symbol): there is no bare uninterpreted awareness of the world – 'our sense data are primarily symbols' (Langer, 1956, p.21). The symbolising process continues through conceptual thinking, where we organise and deploy the information gained (as raw material) in perception (Price, 1953, pp.145ff.), and on to the higher reaches of overall interpretation of the world through ideas. The driving force of the escalator that promotes us from sensation to perception, from perception to conception, from conception to reflection and from reflection to constructive interpretation is the human power (that humanly mirrors the divine) to create true symbols.

Though I am obviously deeply sympathetic to Ricoeur's approach, I cannot quite agree with the way in which he distinguishes metaphor and symbol. In *Interpretation Theory* (1976), Ricoeur seems to suggest that while metaphor belongs merely to the sphere of words, symbols belong to the realm of reality:

> Metaphor occurs in the already purified universe of the logos, while the symbol hesitates on the dividing line between bios and logos. It [the symbol] testifies to the primordial rootedness of Discourse in Life. It is born where force and form coincide.
>
> (Ricoeur, 1976, p.59)

Ricoeur goes on to claim, very suggestively, that 'symbols are bound within the sacred universe: the symbols only come to language to the extent that the elements of the world themselves become transparent' (ibid., p.61). Metaphor is unconstrained, almost arbitrary ('a free invention of discourse') while symbol is determined by the nature of things ('bound to the cosmos') (op. cit.).

I respond gratefully to the 'symbolic realism' in Ricoeur's statement that 'in the sacred universe the capacity to speak is founded upon the capacity of the cosmos to signify' (ibid., p.62). Such affirmations are a welcome antidote to the Derridean denial of 'presence'. I concur with all that Ricoeur says about the cognitive value of symbol, but I regret his apparent downgrading of metaphor. Metaphor also can reveal reality and evoke presence. A metaphor can be a compressed and condensed symbol; symbols can be enlarged and elaborated metaphors. Both can be the instruments of 'the truth of imagination'.

Language is itself an act of symbolisation through metaphor. In language, meanings are articulated symbolically and shared within a speech community: expression and communication are one (Urban, 1939, p.67). Because language symbolises reality it can be trusted to reveal authentic human meaning – the community's experience of reality. To say this is not to espouse the untenable idealist view that language is the expression of mind which is the ground of the world, but to adopt a fiduciary approach that trusts language to reveal the truly human. From there it is still a great leap to affirmations about the real, and other considerations come into play.

Such fundamental religious images as God the father, Christ the good shepherd, God's grace embodied as it were in bread and wine, God's forgiveness conveyed in cleansing water, are symbols rather than simply metaphors because they have been elaborated through reflection and formal (liturgical) use, leaving behind the original impetus of spontaneous creative insight (on the human side) and revelatory self-communication (on the divine side) to evolve into forms or models that are embedded in tradition.

Symbols, like metaphors, are ubiquitous and may be put to helpful or harmful uses. Just as metaphors are the basic constituents of thought and language, so symbols are the lifeblood of a living faith and the currency of identity formation within the religious community. Symbols (together with myths) sacralise identity and give us, individually and corporately, our orientation to the transcendent. Symbols invest our lives and actions with significance. They thus form one of the primary materials for theological reflection.

Symbol and sign

Though there is always an element of arbitrariness in definitions, symbols should be distinguished from signs. Symbols include signs for they incorporate signification, but symbols transcend mere signs. Symbols are living, dynamic, the product of creative imagination. Symbols effect a connection between the mundane and the transcendent, the particular fact and the universal truth, the present moment and eternity. They cannot be contrived or thought up at will. A sign has no such force. It belongs to the ordinary course of life. It is not dynamic like a symbol. It does not stand for new possibilities: it is not open to the future. Signs are usually conventional and arbitrary: there is no necessary reason why a red light should stand for 'Stop!' – except perhaps some residual symbolic value: red:blood:danger:stop. Symbols cannot be invented or contrived; there is a continuity between the symbol and what is symbolised. For example, the priest's white alb and the bride's white gown are not arbitrary but stand for purity (at least ceremonial purity – that is to say, consecration) – for symbols, but not signs, have the 'capacity to consecrate certain styles of life' (Duncan, 1968, p.22) – whereas the clerical collar is merely a sign, a matter of convention. All symbols are signs, but not all signs are symbols (Urban, 1939, p.405).

Signs point to something on the same level of reality: they are not (as Coleridge would say) translucent, as symbols are. Signs serve to remind us of what we already know; symbols speak to us of things beyond our ken. Signs evoke an instinctive response or conditioned reflex – we automatically stop at a red traffic light – but symbols require some existential involvement. Symbols, unlike signs, have a reference to transcendent reality and themselves participate in that reality, as Coleridge and Tillich emphasised. Their function is to connect us to that salutary reality and they thus have a mediatory purpose. Jung distinguishes sign and symbol by the fact that a symbol always points to a beyond: 'An expression that stands for a known thing always remains a mere sign and is never a symbol. It is, therefore, quite impossible to create a living symbol, i.e. one that is pregnant with meaning, from known associations' (Jacobi, 1959, p.80).

Symbols of transcendence

Ricoeur, interpreting Freud, has argued that the ambiguity of symbolism is not confined to its censoring, reconstructing functions in the unconscious, but is general. Gurvich suggests that this ambiguity is what attracts our participation in the symbols (Gurvich, 1971, p.40). One of the essential characteristics of symbols is that 'they reveal while veiling and veil while revealing, and that while pushing toward participation, they also restrain it' (ibid., p.xv). Symbols are 'tensive' in Ricoeur's sense: they subsist only in tension, they pull both ways. This is important in the theological context because, as Berdyaev points out: 'Symbolism is justified by the fact that God is both knowable and unknowable' (Berdyaev, 1948, p.65). The mediation of symbols between the known and the unknown gives them their orientation to transcendence.

So let us look at some other definitions of symbolism that emphasise their function of referring us to the transcendent. The sociologist Alfred Shutz describes a symbol as an object, fact or event within the reality of our daily lives that refers to an idea or reality that transcends everyday life (Shutz, 1967, vol.1, pp.332f.). Symbols point beyond the mundane: they refer to the ideal or universal; they embody important values. Symbols can reveal new truths, new worlds. Goethe's use of the word 'revelation' in the following statement is not fortuitous: 'True symbolism', Goethe said, 'is where the particular represents the general, not as a dream and a shadow, but as a vivid instantaneous revelation of that which cannot be explored' (ibid., p.356).

Coleridge is our Anglo-Saxon connection with German Romantic thought. Coleridge's way of indicating the potential transcendent import of symbols was to connect them with 'Ideas'. 'An IDEA in the highest sense of the word cannot be conveyed but by a symbol' (Coleridge, 1965, p.85). Ideas, as we have seen in an earlier chapter, represent for Coleridge the inmost essence of something and approach the status of Platonic forms. They are intuitable only by the creative Reason/Imagination (as opposed to the merely associative Understanding/Fancy). The 'living educts of the Imagination' convert ideas into symbolic form, for imagination is

> that reconciling and mediating power, which incorporating the reason in Images of the Sense, and organising (as it were) the flux of the senses by the permanence and self-circling energies of the reason, gives birth to a system of symbols, harmonious in themselves, and consubstantial with the truths, of which they are the conductors.
>
> (Coleridge, 1972, p.29)

Symbols, for Coleridge, are 'the visible tips of an ontological iceberg' (Swiatecka, 1980, p.59).

It belongs to symbols to mediate a reality or meaning that transcends the symbol itself. This need not necessarily be a supernatural reality, the subject of theology, the sphere of divinity. The transcendent realm may be the spirit of a nation, a tradition, a cultural legacy, an ethical or political ideal. But it always carries a value greater than the individual. The crucial point about symbolism is that there is no access to this transcendent realm apart from its symbols. Symbolism (like metaphor) is not an adornment of truth already gained on other grounds: it is itself the path to truth. It is the making present of something absent – something that would remain absent and inaccessible without the symbols. Symbols above all connect. As Tillich often puts it, symbols open up reality to human knowing and open up human knowing to that reality. In symbolism *mimesis* (representation) leads to *methexis* (participation). Symbols have this power because in some sense they participate in the reality that they symbolise. Symbols of the sacred are themselves sacred and are treated as such. We bow to the altar, kneel to receive Holy Communion and do not use Bibles as doorstops. We need to recapture the sense that the ancient world had that symbols participate in and make present the reality that they signify – this is particularly crucial for Christian sacramental theology (see Crockett, 1989, esp. pp.78ff.).

For Coleridge the relation between symbol and reality is that of 'translucence' – especially 'the translucence of the Eternal through and in the Temporal'. A symbol 'always partakes of the reality which it renders intelligible; and while it enunciates the whole, abides itself as a living part in that unity of which it is the representative' (Coleridge, 1972, p.30). For Coleridge, the symbolic is a bridge between God and the world. If this sounds a little too metaphysical and speculative, let us consider the matter from a more specifically theological angle.

Sacramental symbols

Christian theology presupposes and confirms this realist view of symbols. It does this in three ways: first, with regard to the inherent capacity of the creation to reflect and mediate the Creator; second, in connection with the Christian sacraments as means of grace; third, with regard to the Incarnation itself.

1   *Creation*   Christian theology implies a spiritual interpretation of the material world. More correctly, it denies that the world is adequately understood in purely material terms. It points to a transcendent creativity at the heart of the universe and holds that the ultimate ground of all reality is to be perceived in and through the things that have been made. It speaks of a sacramental universe (e.g. William Temple) and affirms the spiritual potentiality of matter. The Fathers held that all created things, and particularly the human psyche created in the divine image, could become symbols of divine truth. Augustine found his inner life lit up as though by a floodlight of divine illumination and postulated various psychological analogies to the unity-in-relation of the Holy Trinity, such as memory, understanding and will. In the Anglican tradition, it is above all John Keble who endorses this. The Keble of *The Christian Year* had learned from the Fathers and from Bishop Butler's *Analogy of Religion, Natural and Revealed* to see spiritual significance in everything. This was naturally congenial to Keble's Romantic outlook. It has been claimed for Keble that 'beyond any doubt' he 'founded his symbolic apprehension of

natural reality on the distinction between Fancy and Imagination'. As early as 1814, before Coleridge's theories were fully developed, Keble, though only a poet of Fancy rather than Imagination (in Coleridge's terminology), was speaking of the imagination as 'creative energy' (Beek, 1959, pp.91f.).

Incidentally, we cannot claim Newman in support of the sacramental universe. The *Apologia* reveals a sense of the absence of God from the world at large, though certainly not from Newman's own consciousness and conscience:

> Starting then with the being of a God, (which ... is as certain to me as the certainty of my own existence ...) I look out of myself into the world of men, and there I see a sight which fills me with unspeakable distress. The world simply seems to give the lie to that great truth, of which my whole being is so full; and the effect upon me is, in consequence, as a matter of necessity, as confusing as if I denied that I am in existence myself. If I looked into a mirror, and did not see my face, I should have the sort of feeling which actually comes upon me, when I look into the living busy world, and see no reflection of its Creator ... The sight of the world is nothing else than the prophet's scroll, full of 'lamentations, and mourning, and woe.'
>
> (Newman, 1959, pp.277f.)

Newman points to an analogy, rather than a symbolic identity and communion, between God and the world. A comparative study of symbolism in early nineteenth-century religious thinkers concludes:

> The 'analogy' between God and the world which Newman maintained, and which was the basis of his 'sacramental principle', did not, then, involve such an affirmation of the presence of God within the world, as would enhance its own proper being, making it a 'symbol' translucent [Coleridge's key word] to that presence.
>
> (Swiatecka, 1980, pp.114f.)

Goethe's *Faust: Part II*, ends with the famous words: 'All things corruptible [or terrestrial] are but a parable' (Goethe, 1959, p.288). Elsewhere Goethe says: 'All that happens is symbol, and as it represents itself perfectly, it points to the rest' (Kaufman, 1968, p.121). Here we have a vision of a world of symbols in which the whole is contained in the part and the part inheres in the whole. Goethe is not a Christian thinker, so let us hear Coleridge, our greatest Anglican lay theologian:

> For all that meets the bodily sense I deem
> Symbolical, one mighty alphabet.
>
> ('The Destiny of Nations', ll. 18f.; Coleridge, 1969, p.132)

Rocking the cradle of his infant son in 'Frost at Midnight', he writes (echoing it seems Psalm 19 – 'Their speech is gone out into all the world'):

> so shalt thou see and hear
> The lovely shapes and sounds intelligible
> Of that eternal language, which thy God
> Utters, who from eternity doth teach
> Himself in all, and all things in himself.
>
> ('Frost at Midnight', ll. 58ff.; ibid., p.242)

2   *Sacrament* The sacramental life of the Church rests on a realist understanding of symbolism. It is because there is a real complicity of God with created matter – which is, moreover, inherently good – that God can make his presence known through material signs. Because we are not Platonic dualists God can be found in, with and under the material form. William R. Crockett has developed this systematically in *Eucharist: Symbol of Transformation*, where he asserts that 'the Christ who meets us in the eucharist meets us in and through the real structures of historical existence – matter, time, space, language, community, culture, and social, economic, and political relationships' (Crockett, 1989, p.261). Article 25 of the Thirty-nine Articles of the Church of England describes the sacraments as 'not only badges or tokens ... but ... effectual signs of grace ... by the which he [God] doth work invisibly in us'. And Hooker insists that the sacraments 'really give what they promise, and are what they signify' because the work of the Holy Spirit, 'the necessary inward cause' of grace, is by divine institution inseparable from 'the necessary outward mean', the sacrament (Hooker, 1845, V.lx.1):

> For we take not baptism nor the eucharist for bare resemblances or memorials of things absent, neither for naked signs and testimonies assuring us of grace received before, but (as they are indeed and in verity) for means effectual whereby God when we take the sacraments delivereth into our hands that grace available unto eternal life, which grace the sacraments represent or signify.
>
> (ibid., V.lvii.5)

In receiving the sacraments of the Gospel we receive Christ; symbols of the sacred are themselves sacred because they participate in what they represent.

3   *Incarnation* The Incarnation itself is the ultimate validation for a realist understanding of symbols. It is one of the great merits of Karl Rahner's theology that his understanding of Christology, ecclesiology and sacramental theology is unified by a grasp of the symbolic character of all created reality. As rational beings we are inescapably symbolic beings, Rahner

asserts, because we are compelled to express or project ourselves in order to attain our true nature. Rahner affirms that the symbol is united with the thing symbolised, 'since the latter constitutes the former as its own self-realisation'. This is the fundamental structure of all Christianity (Rahner, 1965–92, vol.4, pp.24, 152). Rahner favours the term *signum efficax* for an efficacious sign or real symbol (ibid., vol.21, p.250). Thus Christ is the *signum efficax* of God and the Church is the *signum efficax* of Christ. In the Christian scheme of things, symbols are ordered hierarchically so that lower symbols point to higher, human to divine, the world to God, the Church to Christ and he to God.

Whether or not it is appropriate to speak of the Incarnation as myth (we will discuss that question shortly), it certainly seems right to speak of Jesus Christ as the metaphor and symbol of God incarnate and there is nothing necessarily reductionist about that (though Hick, 1993, does deploy it in a reductionist way). Wilson Knight believed that 'the process which is at the heart of metaphor is exactly the most important thing in Christianity. The Incarnation is itself one gigantic metaphor whereby the divine Logos is married to a human form' (Knight, 1933, p.46). Using David Lodge's summary of Jakobson's study of the difference between metonymy (which is association by continuity, coherence within a single world of discourse) and metaphor (the combination of different worlds), Ruth Etchells brings out the metaphoric identity between Jesus and God on the cross.

> The metonymy of destruction and dereliction is built up powerfully for us in the events between Palm Sunday and Good Friday: but when we see him on the Cross as the metaphor of God we begin to conceive how a coherent world picture, detail by detail, has been cut across by the conjunction of disparate worlds, the divine and the human, at the point where similitude is total ... A plurality of worlds is joined, each interpreted in terms of the other. The metaphoric mode of the Gospel here totally alters the cumulative effect of that coherent and suffocating metonymic world of plotters whispering, thirty pieces of silver, armed guard at night, law court, splintering wood of the Cross, and agonising fleshly pain.
>
> (Etchells, 1983, pp.101f.)

I would add that the whole person and destiny of Jesus Christ, from Bethlehem to the Ascension, constitutes the metaphor of God and the conjunction of divine and human worlds, in identity and difference, not only Jesus on the cross – though this remains the climax and paradigm of Christology.

Implications for doctrine

The implications of symbolism for Christian theology will be fully explored in Part IV, but for the moment it may be helpful to make brief mention of some issues that immediately suggest themselves.

1   Modern theology (especially Protestant theology, but with the exception of Tillich) has dangerously neglected symbolism and the modern Church tends to be symbolically insensitive and illiterate. We need to learn a new respect for our sacred symbols and a deeper understanding of them. The work of Hans Urs Von Balthasar on theological aesthetics can help us here.

2   Doctrines have their symbolic equivalents in the repertoire of humanity's symbolic inheritance, as Jung has shown. For example, the symbols of new birth, spiritual marriage and wholeness run parallel in the Christian doctrine of salvation and in Jungian psychotherapy. This suggests that it is possible to make fruitful connections between the Christian symbols of salvation and the spiritual needs and aspirations of human culture beyond the boundaries of the Church (a method of correlation, essential in evangelism and apologetics). The Church's sacramental ministry, through the so-called rites of passage (baptism, confirmation, marriage, funerals), is the pivotal point at which the connections are made.

3   The symbolic construction of Christian doctrines is not a unique case on which we need to be sensitive in this scientistic age, but an instance of the evident truth that all claims (in ethics, metaphysics and cosmology) that go beyond the here and now and attempt to make broad affirmations about a realm that is not open to empirical inspection, must be made in a symbolic mode.

4   The realist intention of figurative statements will be thoroughly aired in the next section, but for the present it is enough to note that religious symbols are intended to make informative assertions about reality. As Soskice puts it:

> A model in religious language may evoke an emotional, moral or spiritual response, but this does not mean that the model has no cognitive or explanatory function. In fact the reverse is true; the model can only be effective because it is taken as explanatory ... The cognitive function is primary.
>
> (Soskice, 1985, p.109)

5   Finally, we should be alert to the emergence of new or recovered symbols of the sacred, informed by Christian commitments, that can help Christian doctrine to address the needs and aspirations of our

generation. Among these, two stand out: the immanental and holistic models of God's relation to the world and the personal, relational, social models of salvation in feminist theology (they are connected of course).

11 Myth

Myth is probably the greatest casualty of our contemporary suspicion of figurative language and imagistic thinking. Myth is now synonymous with fallacy – a fallacy got up, decked out and doing the rounds. Myths are equated with ignorance, illusion and error. 'It's just a myth!' is the ultimate dismissal, sufficient to consign a story, a theory, an idea, a vision to oblivion. The mass media and common speech resort to it habitually and compulsively, in a way that suggests that we are all trying to deny something important. Common usage rubbishes the genre of myth, obscures the fact that even today we live in and by our myths, and makes it more difficult to take seriously the ideas that motivate people, even when they are mistaken, and thus damages mutual understanding by stereotyping positions and devaluing those who hold them. Informed argument succumbs to the same usage, witness a topical example: *The Islamic Threat: Myth or Reality?* (1992). And yet, willy-nilly, the denigration of 'myths' pays reluctant tribute to the power inherent in them. For there is something wistfully appealing about a myth even when it has been 'exploded'. A myth retains an aura of transcendence and the numinous, even when it has been debunked. An exposed myth has shock value.

Perhaps that is why authors and publishers of theological books, who should know better, go for titles containing the word myth; I spare the authors and publishers their blushes:

The Myth of Christian Beginnings   The fallacy exposed here is not that Christianity had a beginning – like everything else, it had to start somewhere – but that these origins were uniform, tidy and providential, as portrayed in the Acts of the Apostles. Actually Christian beginnings were sporadic, *ad hoc*, confused and experimental, just like life, surprisingly!

The Myth of God Incarnate   Jesus Christ was not God incarnate, for God cannot become incarnate; the idea does not make logical sense. Please don't ask us how we know what seems logical to God.

The Myth of Christian Uniqueness   Christianity is one of a plurality of valid paths to the divine. But don't expect us to deny the uniqueness of other major world faiths: we would not be so impertinent. On second thoughts, we don't mean 'uniqueness' but 'exclusiveness', but that doesn't have quite the same ring about it, and we'd have to admit that, after Vatican II, it is rather a man of straw anyway.

The Myth of the Empty Church The fallacy exposed here is not that most churches are not more empty than full – we know they are – but the assumption that this is a recent decline. By making the mistake of building more, and larger, churches than were required by the numbers attending, the churches revealed the tenuousness of their grip on the loyalty of the population. Furthermore, it would now be counter-productive to close many of these over-spacious buildings. With its connotations of community meanings embodied in public narrative, this thesis is not inappropriately termed a myth. But the title is a brilliant *double entendre* because we subconsciously expect to hear not 'empty church' but 'empty tomb': there are connections that are both theological and psychological between tomb, womb and church.

This publishing gimmick has surely exhausted itself now: 'myth' titles are beginning to sound like a parody. Great fictional myths like *The Lord of the Rings* have an immense popularity that shows that we still yearn for myths and that myths fulfil a need. Nowadays we like to indulge in myths: we enjoy creating and elaborating them, but we do not believe in them. They are a function of nostalgia, of escapism, of the overriding demand to shape life by narrative, and they embody enduring moral values of good and evil, courage and heroism. Schelling claimed that each truly creative individual must invent a mythology for themselves. But modern fictional or science-fictional myths are not on a par with the religious and cosmological myths of old for the simple reason that our modern myths are acknowledged from the beginning to be myths. They have been summarily demoted to the land of make-believe. We can, as it were, hold them at arm's length and name them for what they are. That constitutes a fundamental change in the rules of the game. Meanwhile, however, the real modern myths that we inhabit, that form part of our mental furniture, pass unrecognised. Real myths, the ones that people live by rather than the ones they fantasise with or escape to, are not known to be myths. When they are so identified, they immediately lose their privileged status, becoming demythologised or at least reconstructed.

   In this supposed 'new age', myths are once again promoted and protected – but at a price. These myths belong in the context of cultural nostalgia or leisure activities: in both these ways they are trivialised. My treatment will offer no incentives to anyone with a private fascination for mythology as such. My subject is the myths by which Christians live and die, and my target is the problem that arises when we know them to be myths for the first time. In this chapter it is not at all my intention to glorify myth or to privilege myth as some Gnostic source of esoteric truths. I deplore all mystification in the realm of myth. I will not be invoking some nebulous realm that is protected from critical scrutiny. On the contrary, I hope to subject the category of myth to some rigorous analysis, employing the tools and insights of the social sciences and of the great theorists of myth and symbol, myth and ritual. My ultimate aim, having clarified the whole area for the purposes of theology, is to ask whether myth can be the vehicle of truth – the truth of divine revelation and of human discovery.

Locating myth

There is no agreed definition of myth but a wide variety of approaches prevails (see, for example, Cohen, 1969). There are anthropological, sociological, psychological, cosmological and theological theories of myth. However, it would be widely agreed that myth is a literary genre in which numinous symbols are constellated in narrative form. Myth is marked by fantasy, complexity and idealisation. Myth typically deals with origins and destiny, change, transition and becoming ('liminality' in Van Gennep, 1960, and Turner, 1968). The *dramatis personae* of myths are superhuman figures who lived on the earth when life was different or who will come in the future to bring about great changes.

Myths tend to dehistoricise – relating eternal truths or cycles of repetition – but the historical religions also have their myths which are symbolic narratives bringing out the theological significance of historical events, even though they also serve to obscure the exact historical lineaments of those events. Thus myths are only indirectly historically informative – they cannot be exchanged for any empirical cash-value – but they are theologically significant and indispensable. There can be a cognitive and realist concept of myth, that sees myth as setting out to be explanatory of the way the world is. This approach recognises that the biblical myths reflect a genuine encounter with divine revelation (though it could not of course be claimed that all myths are veridical, in the sense of corresponding exactly to an objective reality, since they are sometimes conflicting). 'Myth embodies the nearest approach to absolute truth that can be stated in words' (Coomaraswamy).

Rationalist notions of myth (such as that of Frazer's *The Golden Bough*) took it to be primitive science, just as they took legend to be primitive history. There is an element of truth in this, as myths often contain cosmological conjectures and aetiological features (why do snakes go on their bellies?). But this misses the essential point that myth interprets transactions in the realm of the sacred, the dialogue between God and humanity. This need not be taken in the primitive sense of the anthropomorphic antics of the Greek pantheon.

D.F. Strauss, in his seminal interpretation of the Bible as myth, rightly pointed out that the Old and New Testaments are not mythological in the sense of being histories of the gods. Strauss believed that he was providing an antidote to the rationalistic approach to the Bible. Though the gospel history was not an account of the facts, neither was it deliberate fabrication; it was the product of theological ideas. Those ideas retained their validity as myth, but in a reductionist sense as symbols of an interior spiritual dynamic, not in the realist sense for which we are striving in this book. Thus Strauss states in the preface to the first German edition (1835):

> The author is aware that the essence of Christian faith is perfectly independent of his criticism. The supernatural birth of Christ, his miracles, his resurrection and ascension, remain eternal truths, whatever doubts may be cast upon their reality as historical facts ... The dogmatic significance of the life of Jesus remains inviolate.
>
> (Strauss, 1972, p.lii; cf. ibid., pp.77, 80, 86)

Bultmann's view contains echoes of the rationalist approach in that he identifies myth as anthropomorphic and unscientific (he famously asked: how can we believe biblical myths of spirits and miracles in the age of radio and electric light?). But, like Strauss, Bultmann certainly insists that myth is the vehicle of religious truth which, however, needs to be translated into meaningful existential terms (see the later discussion of Bultmann and demythologising).

Religion is not constituted by straight myth, but (as Tillich argued) by myth refined by philosophical criticism, ethical prophecy and scientific information. Myth, thus refined, goes towards the making of dogma, in combination with a metaphysical worldview and in the context of worship. For while myths are the symbolic stories of a community, rituals (including worship) are the symbolic actions of a community. Lévi-Strauss has highlighted the role of myths in reconciling opposites, containing conflicts and integrating energies. Cassirer has stressed that, to be believed and lived in, myths cannot be known to be myths. We are not aware of our myths as such. It is only when a myth no longer fits the needs and situation of a community, through changes in its structure or environment, that critical reflection on the myth emerges and it becomes known as myth. Critical consciousness discriminates between reality and its representation. At this stage a myth may be refined or superseded, being replaced by other myths.

Symbol as myth

The cryptic title 'Symbol as myth' means that I am implying that myths are a product of the same innate human faculty of symbolisation that gives rise to metaphors, symbolism (verbal, visual and ritual) and, in science, interpretative models. In the early eighteenth century, the *New Science* of Giambattista Vico challenged emerging rationalistic concepts of the origins of human discourse with the theory that the human race was an inveterately symbol-making species. Language, poetry, myth, religion, law and social structures had been born out of humanity's imaginative response to the universe, not out of the calculated progress of discursive, prosaic reason. For Vico, poetry came before prose, arising spontaneously out of the inarticulate cries and rhythmic utterances of early man. Thinking poetically was the primary activity of the human mind; prose was secondary, derivative and somewhat artificial. In the Cartesian intellectual climate of the early Enlightenment – hostile to metaphor – Vico claimed that metaphor was the basic form of rationality and gave insight into reality. 'The first nations thought in poetic characters, spoke in fables and wrote in hiero-glyphs' (Vico, 1961, p.139, para.429). Vico was a cautious, conforming Catholic in Inquisitorial Italy and did not allow himself to speculate in print about the origins of the Christian religion. But as far as Gentile religion was concerned, Vico believed that it emerged from the mythopoeic response of humans to the numinous phenomena of nature.

> The first theological poets created the first divine fable [myth], the greatest they ever created: that of Jove, king and father of men and gods, in the act of hurling the lightning bolt; an image so popular, disturbing and instructive that its creators themselves believed in it and feared, revered and worshipped it in frightful religions.
>
> (ibid., p.118, para.379)

Myth, for Vico, also dealt with momentous occurrences in the gradual socialisation of humanity, especially the institution of marriage, the establishment of families and the practice of solemn burial (cf. Avis, 1986b, pp.147ff.).

The most important modern exponent of what we might call the Vichean tradition, is Ernst Cassirer who believed that language, metaphor and myth emerge inseparably, both in the history of the race and in the development of the individual. 'Language and myth stand in an original and indissoluble correlation with one another,' he claims. 'They are two diverse shoots from the same parent stem, the same impulse of symbolic formation, springing from the same mental activity' (Cassirer, 1946b, p.88). Cassirer points out that for 'mythic thinking' metaphor represents a real identification, not a mere substitution or decorative figure of speech (ibid., p.94). As our analytical and critical faculties develop, however, this identification breaks down and language, art and religion become demythologised. We learn to discriminate between reality and representation. While that liberates us from bondage to primeval psychic forces, there is a price to be paid – that of imaginative impoverishment. For Cassirer, this split is healed in art where the unity of thought and image reveal the mind to itself (ibid., pp.97ff.). Cassirer's is an idealist rather than a realist philosophy of symbolism: the highest office of the symbolic is to reveal the mind, not of God, but of the thinker or artist.

Myth and dream

Mircea Eliade has claimed that 'there is no mythic motive or scenario of initiation which is not also presented, in one way or another, in dreams and in the working of the imagination' (Eliade, 1968, p.16). He points out, however, that dreams lack the 'constitutive' quality of myths: they are not exemplary, laying down a pattern of life, nor are they universal, conveying a revelation of reality, but myth and dream share a sacred aura (ibid., pp.18, 23). Jung is in no doubt that these similarities arise from the universal archetypes of the collective unconscious as they make themselves known in the symbols of myth and dream. We do not need to subscribe to that Jungian doctrine to acknowledge the correspondences between myth and dream: the common fund of symbols, the shared aura of the numinous, the aesthetic completeness and the narrative unity.

Poets and novelists have made the connection between myths and dreams. Sometimes the dream-like quality of existence is invoked to suggest its unreality, but equally it may support its aesthetic unity. Perhaps Edgar Allen Poe had both these in mind when he wrote:

> All that we see or seem
> Is but a dream within a dream.
> ('A Dream within a Dream')

George MacDonald intended to affirm both the reality and the symbolic coherence of life when in his two fantasias of the unconscious – a myth within a dream – *Phantastes* and *Lilith*, he evoked the world of dreams. 'There is one heart ... whose very dreams are lives', we learn (MacDonald, 1964, p.206). He recalls the biblical valuation of dreams when he suggests that there are dreams that are given by God through the imagination to show us a better, truer world. 'When a man dreams his own dream, he is the sport of his dream; when Another gives it him, that Other is able to fulfil it' (ibid., pp.419f.). 'When I wake at last into the life which, as a mother her child, carries this life in its bosom, I shall know that I awake, and shall doubt no more' (ibid., p.420). I quoted these words in the postscript to my study of the great reductionist thinkers, from Feuerbach to Freud, who held that the human spiritual vision is a gigantic exercise in wish-fulfilment. I pointed out that because a thing is wanted that does not make it wrong; the fact of longing is not in itself an index of illusion. I quoted MacDonald's closing words from *Phantastes*: 'Novalis says, "Our life is no dream, but it should and will perhaps become one". ' (ibid., p.420; Avis, 1995, p.122). That must mean that our lives may acquire something of the wholeness, integrity and significance of dream and myth through a deeper understanding of both.

In *The Unbearable Lightness of Being*, Milan Kundera twice calls the dream 'an intelligible lie, concealing an unintelligible truth'. Here he is reflecting the Freudian view of dreams as the symbolic emergence into consciousness of unacceptable desires. The aesthetic aspect is muted in Freud's theory, with its wearisome repetition of umbrellas, purses and other bourgeois appurtenances (Freud, 1954). It has taken Jung to bring home the beauty of dreams: like *mandalas* they are complex, ornate and tell a story (Jung, 1982). Altogether they are beautiful works of art. A passage in Kundera's novel owes more to Jung than to Freud:

> The dreams were eloquent, but they were also beautiful. That aspect seems to have escaped Freud in his theory of dreams. Dreaming is not merely an act of communication (or coded communication, if you like); it is also an aesthetic activity, a game of the imagination, a game that is a value in itself. Our dreams prove that to imagine – to dream about things that have not happened – is one of mankind's deepest needs ... If dreams were not beautiful, they would quickly be forgotten.
>
> (Kundera, 1984, p.59)

Nietzsche explored the significance of dreams, applying the scalpel of his mordant cynicism under the searchlight of his radiant mind. Before the advent of depth psychology, Nietzsche knew that the psyche was 'a Milky Way', a glowing vortex of worlds into which we found ourselves drawn in our dreams (Nietzsche, 1910, p.249, para.322). In his first major work, *The Birth of Tragedy*, he suggests that we are merely the dreams – or projections – of God and that our dreams are, therefore, 'the illusion of illusion'. To dream belongs merely to Apollonian measure but 'intoxication' is the fruit of Dionysian frenzy, the source of insight and creativity (Nietzsche, 1993, pp.25, 32, 14). In his essay on 'Truth and Falsity', in which Nietzsche first developed his reductionist method, that of 'baseless suspicion', he claimed (a generation before Freud) that 'dreams lie to us every night of our lives'. Dreams open up a pitiless world: traversing a night of dreams is like riding on the back of a tiger. Myth and art are assimilated to dreams – so much the worse for myth and art, we might think, but at least the connection is made (Nietzsche, 1873, pp.175f., 188). This is developed in later writings where Nietzsche postulates that dreams are the origin of metaphysics (he abominates metaphysics for its dualism) and suggests that 'in sleep and dreams we repeat once again the curriculum of earlier mankind', though even in dreams we do not enjoy the vivid, visionary experience which earlier peoples beheld while awake (Nietzsche, 1986, pp.14, 17, 113). Nietzsche rather unconvincingly asserts that we no longer live in fear of our dreams (Nietzsche, 1982, pp.9, para.5), but in *Thus Spake Zarathustra* it is Zarathustra's nightmares that lead to his renunciation of God (Nietzsche, 1961, pp.156f., 167f.).

Analytical psychology reinforces the connection between myths, symbols and unconscious psychic processes. Von Franz sees all myths as straight expressions of psychic processes (Von Franz, 1980, pp.78f.). Jung quotes Karl Abraham's assertion that: 'The myth is a fragment of the superseded infantile psychic life of the race and dreams are the myths of the mind' (Jung, 1956, p.24). Both myths and dreams are produced by the unconscious and exhibit common features that suggest to Jung the existence of a corporate fund of images that is drawn upon in both myth-making and dreaming. Jung suggests that dreams liberate the resources of the unconscious to counter-balance the excesses and one-sidedness of the conscious mind, prone as it is to foreclose the possibilities of experience, being characterised by 'concentration, limitation and exclusion' (Jung, 1985, p.96). The symbols that emerge from the unconscious are not necessarily, as Freud would have it, coded expressions of unacceptable, shameful desires, but may contain resources conducive to greater wholeness and integration. They not only reveal psychic conflicts, but also have the power to reconcile and resolve them. Hans Mol has suggested that what the dream does for personal identity, myth does for social identity (Mol, 1976, p.258). Myths too, therefore, may have a reconciling, integrating function. They may combine opposites, contain conflicts and unify divergent energies. They 'relativise discordance through emotional sublimation' (ibid., p.252). In this connection it is perhaps significant that Lévi-Strauss maintains that mythical thought, in the anthropological context, operates by mediating, reconciling and resolving binary oppositions.

In line with the suggestion that myths are the dreams of mankind, Berdyaev attributes the birth of mythology to a time when the consciousness of humanity was 'not yet fully awake'. His evocation of this supposed epoch is strikingly Vichean:

> Mythology had its origin in the dawn of human consciousness when spirit was enveloped in nature, when the natural world had not yet become a rigid system, and when the frontiers between the two worlds had not been clearly defined ... The core of man's being was still unconscious, and it is to his subconsciousness that mythological creation owes its origin.
>
> (Berdyaev, 1948, p.72)

Berdyaev disowned any intention of offering a purely expressive, non-realist account of mythic and symbolic thought (ibid., p.75). However, recent developments in the study of primitive societies have brought into question the stage of pre-logical thinking that Vico and Berdyaev postulated – of the so-called 'savage mind'. Lévi-Strauss has insisted that the 'primitive' mind was (or is) capable of disinterested thinking and that it aimed at a total grasp of the world. It is certainly difficult to see how primitive humans could have mastered their environment with the aid of tools, social organisation and deductions from experience if their thinking took place purely at an unconscious level. Happily, no such fiction as the 'primitive mind' is implied when we speak of the intuitive, subconscious origins of myth. Epistemologists such as Polanyi and Lonergan have taught us to beware of a crude dichotomy between discursive (logical) and intuitive (imaginative) thinking. In the 'tacit dimension' (Polanyi, 1967), subliminal but real ratiocination goes on. We cannot see all the steps, but we cannot deny the outcome. In spite of – or perhaps because of – its origins, myth does have a drive towards the truth of human life, it does express insight derived from the collective experience of humanity. As Langer has put it: the purpose of myth is always, so to speak, philosophical: mythology is the primitive phase of metaphysical thought, the first embodiment of general ideas (Langer, 1956, p.201).

The discernment of genre

If I pick up a book and read: 'Take so much sulphur, so much saltpetre and so much charcoal and mix together', I am not consulting a cookery book about what to get for my meal – I am perusing a volume on explosives or fireworks and it is telling me how to make gunpowder. If, on the other hand, I pick up a book and read: 'Mix so much flour, so much milk, so much butter and so many eggs', I am probably this time checking how to make a *soufflé* for supper, and I then have to decide whether it shall be cheese, fish or whatever; it is more likely to implode than explode! But if I pick up a book and read a passage with a rather different list of ingredients – one secret garden, one talking snake, one magic fruit, two figures named Man and Woman, and a divine person taking a stroll in the evening breeze – I know immediately that the document is neither an elementary science textbook nor a book of recipes but a myth of human beginnings. It is, of course, the myth of Genesis 1–3.

Just as we instinctively know the difference – a fundamental difference of type, or genre – between a text that states the components of gunpowder and a text that states the ingredients of a recipe, so too we need to be sensitive to the genres of the Bible. They tend to differ in relation to four typical elements: structure, vocabulary, setting and function (Coats, 1985, pp.11ff.). But how easy – and how disastrous – it is to be oblivious to these major differences. If I attempt to treat Gospel like Epistle, parable like miracle, apocalyptic like Wisdom literature, or Jonah like Chronicles, I will soon realise my mistake. Similarly, if I interpret myth as history, I will badly miss the point. If there is myth in the Old Testament – and we all know that there is – we should not be coy about it. If there is myth in the New Testament – and some of us are troubled by the thought – let us prepare the appropriate tools to interpret it. If there is myth in the creed and Christian doctrine – and this is a question left disturbingly unresolved by some recent discussions – let us make a rigorous attempt to deal with it constructively.

We are accustomed to say, uncontroversially, that biblical texts should not be taken out of context, that scripture should interpret scripture and that the analogy of faith (*analogia fidei*) should be our guide. We are not so well used to extending this salutary principle to take in broader ranges of context (cf. Swinburne, 1992, pp.64f.).

1   There is the deep cultural context: the relation of a text to the cultural, intellectual tradition in which it stands, to the inheritance of learning of which it is the particular expression, and this deep cultural context carries a freight of what Collingwood called 'absolute presuppositions', assumptions about what makes sense, what is possible, what is plausible, how things hang together: in other words, a worldview (Collingwood, 1939, p.66). It was precisely the worldview implications of a text that so concerned Bultmann and led to his proposals for 'demythologisation' of the New Testament message.

2   Then there is the social context: the immediate social environment of a text, its potential audience or readership – with the economic, class and educational structures, differences and conflicts within that audience, the constraints that these exert on what can be said and heard and done in response; in other words a context that is inescapably ideological. Therefore we need to be suspicious of the text and to ask: why is this being said? Who stands to benefit? Whom is it designed to silence or marginalise? What vested interests does this text (symbol, narrative, myth) defend? (Regrettably, the ideological critique of narrative traditions is a topic that will have to be reserved for another occasion.)

3   Finally, there is the literary context of a text: the relation of a text to the literary unit to which it belongs, to the sentences in which it is set, to the 'form' in which it is embedded, to the whole work or part work that gives it its overall significance. This literary context is where the question of genre becomes pressing. As Swinburne has put it, just as the context provided by the sentence is crucial for understanding the sense of any particular word in it, so the context provided by the work as a whole is crucial for understanding the meaning of a sentence (Swinburne, 1992, p.55). That context concerns – critically, but not exclusively – the literary genre. Let us explore 'genre' a little further.

In its broadest sense, genre includes all the multifarious forms in which language may be articulated in discourse. The difference between poetry and prose is an example of a fundamental difference of genre. The difference between iambic hexameters and blank verse is a narrower distinction. That between legend, saga, myth and history is of rather more importance to theology, as it determines how not only Genesis 1–11 but also the Four Gospels are to be read. Genre, then, indicates how a text – a portion of writing – is to be taken as a whole. The importance of genre has been stressed notably by Northrop Frye (Frye, 1957), who discerns four major genres: drama, epic, lyric and 'fiction' (the latter in an idiosyncratic sense), and by E.D. Hirsch, though he does not discuss the distinctions between legend, myth and history nor apply genre discernment to the Bible. Hirsch points out that 'an interpreter's preliminary generic conception of a text is constitutive of everything that he subsequently understands ... All understanding of verbal meaning is necessarily genre-bound' (Hirsch, 1967, pp.74, 76; Fowler, 1982, has provided a substantial, detailed, technical and wide-ranging exposition of the matter of genre).

Frye and others have stressed that genre is set up by – and itself sets up, when understood – a basic understanding between the author and the reader/hearer. 'The genre is determined by the conditions established between the poet and his public', writes Frye (1957, p.247). It is, says Dubrow, like a code of behaviour agreed between them, setting the parameters, guiding expectations (Dubrow, 1982). Todorov insists that genres exist as objective institutions and as such determine both the reader's 'horizon of expectation' and the author's 'model of writing' (Todorov, 1990, p.18). All this suggests that, just as social occasions can prove disastrous when one has made the wrong assumptions – taken one's hostess to be the waitress, or vice versa; worn a pullover when the evening was 'black tie', or vice versa – so too a mistake over genre can be disastrous for biblical and theological interpretation.

Myth is a genre subdivision of a broader genre, that of narrative. Resisting the temptation to elaborate on the characteristics of narrative or to plunge into the pros and cons of narrative theology, let us simply agree that numinous symbols in narrative sequence approximate to myth. Within the world of narratives it is, above all, the kind of narrative we call myth that is the bearer of moral meaning and sacred vision.

Myths and legends

Although 'myths and legends' are thrown together on the shelves of our bookshops they make uncongenial bedfellows. Among anthropologists there seems to be a consensus about what distinguishes myth from legend and folklore.

1   *Folktales*   Folktales need not detain us long. They are secular, fictitious and serve no serious social or 'metaphysical' function. There are folktales in the Old Testament – in Judges and the Elijah–Elisha saga – but I do not know of any theologians who have managed to discover any revelatory significance in them.

2   *Legends* (German: *Sagen*)   Legends may be sacred or secular and are believed to be factual. They take place in our recognisable human world but in the recent, not the remote past. The characters in legends, though often extraordinary and gifted with outstanding powers, are indubitably human, 'of like passions with ourselves'. Legends retain and retrieve the past of a people, they belong to tradition and may be said to be a primitive form of historical record. For rationalists like J.G. Frazer, legends were failed history:

> By legends I understand traditions, whether oral or written, which relate the fortunes of real people in the past, or which describe events, not necessarily [entirely] human, that are said to have occurred at real places. Such legends contain a mixture of truth and falsehood, for were they wholly true, they would not be legends but histories.
>
> (Dundes, 1984, p.26)

Frazer's assumption that historical writing is completely true and objective is extraordinarily naive.

It may be useful to distinguish between legend and saga. Saga is a term that belongs to literary theory rather than to the philosophy of history. It is used to refer to a body of narrative literature whose origins lie in oral prose composition and which extends over a number of episodes fairly loosely strung together. There is little in the way of editorial connecting material: it is the action that carries the story. Some regard the Abraham stories of Genesis 12–25 as saga. The distinction between legend and saga is complicated by the tendency to translate the German *Sagen* by the English 'legend(s)'. The Latin *legenda* means simply things to be read and refers to stories of holy men and women which would be read on that saint's day. Legends of this kind are honed down to 'a virtue embodied in a deed' and are recounted to encourage imitation. When the element of literary artifice is pronounced, as in the Joseph story or the book of Esther, we may speak of a 'novella' (Coats, 1985, pp.25, 49, 96). Legend certainly has overtones of historical exaggeration, embellishment and elaboration that saga, as a literary-critical term, does not have.

There is clearly an abundance of legendary material in the Bible: the Joseph cycle of stories, Elijah and Elisha, aspects of the histories of Saul, David and Solomon, the more blatantly embroidered aspects of the Gospels, elements of the Acts of the Apostles. To be specific, I would tend to designate the Noah story as myth and the Joseph story as legend; Elijah's ascent in a whirlwind as myth but David's slaying of Goliath as legend; the nativity stories of Matthew and Luke as myth and the story of the boy Jesus in the Temple as legend; the phenomena of the Day of Pentecost as myth, the details of Paul's shipwreck as legend. The criteria will, I hope, become apparent if we turn finally to myth itself.

3   *Myth*   In contrast to folktales and legends (sagas), myths are always sacred and have an air of the numinous. Myths constellate sacred symbolism in narrative sequence. They are set in sacred time – the beginning (creation) or a new beginning (the resurrection) – and sacred space – the Garden of Eden, the Garden of Gethsemane, the New Jerusalem. The actors in myths are great representative figures – Adam or the Last Adam – not ordinary, puny mortals. Myth tells of divine–human interaction (the Incarnation), of origins and destiny (eschatology), of transformations and

transactions (the Fall, the atonement) that explain our present lot and our future hopes.

Some scholars hold that myth is by definition incompatible with the central Christian beliefs, because it tells only of universal truths and cannot accommodate particular historical events. It is perfectly true that myth has a drive towards the universal and away from the particular, towards the timeless, away from the historical. Roberto Calasso prefaces his account of the Greek myths with the words of Sallust in *Of Gods and of the World*: 'These things never happened, but are always' (Calasso, 1994). But let us not forget that religions contain not unadulterated, raw myths but broken myths, myths that have passed through a process of deconstruction and have become infused with prophetic ethical vision and with something of a metaphysical worldview. If Christian belief has anything in common with myth, it will be myth that has been subject to this profound refinement. It is the symbolic, the mythic that gives particular, 'one off' historical events the capacity to be of universal relevance. There are no uninterpreted events. Myth may provide the interpretation, the vehicle that gives universal, timeless significance to an historical event.

Myth is a particular literary genre with recognisable features and as such carries no freight of historical scepticism. But it is also a category in philosophy of history and as such raises acute questions of historicity, fact and truth. The literary and the philosophical aspects of myth should be clearly distinguished. The question ultimately facing us in this book is whether a frank recognition of the elements of myth in the Bible and Christian beliefs is compatible with a full-blooded, orthodox faith.

Theories of myth

G.S. Kirk has warned against all simplistic and exclusive definitions of myth. There are always exceptions to every definition of this elusive phenomenon. 'There is no one definition of myth, no Platonic form of a myth against which all actual instances can be measured. Myths ... differ enormously in their morphology and their social function' (Kirk, 1971, p.7). Not all myths are stories about the gods; myths are not necessarily connected with ritual; they cannot always be clearly distinguished from legend and folklore; not all have a cognitive, explanatory function (as Malinowski would have it – see below). Their characteristics of fantasy, complexity and an ability to generate further developments, together with their irrationality and unpredictability (their 'strange dislocations') give them an affinity with dreams and tend to substantiate the view of Rank, Abraham, Freud, Jane Harrison and Jung that myths are the dreams of the human race (Kirk, 1971, pp.9–13, 25, 269f.; cf. Kirk in Dundes, 1984). Let us now turn to three main groups of theories.

1   *Scientistic cognitivism*   The overtones of falsehood that 'myth' carries in popular speech harks back to the rationalistic view of myth that emerged in the Enlightenment and received its most extreme expression at the hands of J.G. Frazer (1854–1941). For Frazer, myth was false science just as legend was false history. In *The Golden Bough* and his voluminous other writings, Frazer assumed that primitive people perceived the world as a series of intellectual problems and attempted to produce theories to solve them. Their mythical theories are false while our scientific theories are true (Ackerman, 1987, p.65). Frazer was excessively inconsistent in his theoretical basis: his biographer comments that one can find, strewn throughout the three great editions and the ultimately seventeen volumes of *The Golden Bough*, several mutually incompatible theories of myth (ibid., p.231), though the cognitive theory is particularly associated with Frazer:

> By myths I understand mistaken explanations of phenomena, whether of human life or of external nature. Such explanations originate in that instinctive curiosity concerning the causes of things which at a more advanced state of knowledge seeks satisfaction in philosophy and science, but being founded on ignorance and misapprehension they are always false, for were they true, they would cease to be myths.
>
> (Dundes, 1984, p.26)

Frazer continues: 'Myth has its source in reason, legend in memory, and folk tale in imagination ... The three riper products of the human mind which correspond to these its crude creations are science, history and romance' (op. cit.). For Max Muller, myth represented a linguistic breakdown, a 'disease of language' (Ackerman, 1987, p.76).

It is well known that Frazer's heavy-handed interpretations of 'primitive' myth and ritual as though they were early attempts at scientific explanation or action incurred the disgust of Wittgenstein. He was offended that Frazer had reduced profound expressions of religious feeling to shallow technological manipulations:

> Frazer cannot imagine a priest who is not basically an English parson of our times with all his stupidity and feebleness [*sic!*] ... Frazer is much more savage than most of his savages, for these savages will not be so far from any understanding of spiritual matters as an Englishman of the twentieth century. His explanations of the observances are much cruder than the sense of the observances themselves.
>
> (Monk, 1991, p.310)

2   *Social functionalism*   In contrast to what we might call Frazer's scientific theory of myth, we have Malinowski's social theory. In his *Myth in Primitive Psychology* of 1926, Malinowski gave an interpretation of the myths of the Tobriand Islanders of Melanesia. Myth is not merely 'a story

told but a reality lived'. It cannot simply be gathered from texts but must be seen in its context of social organisation, morals, customs and rituals. Myth is 'a narrative resurrection of a primeval reality, told in satisfaction of deep religious wants, moral cravings, social submissions, assertions, even practical requirements'. Myths are not crude intellectual explanations, or attempts to make abstract ideas intelligible, but to justify, validate and legitimate the traditional social order. Myths are, therefore, 'a special class of stories, regarded as sacred, embodied in ritual, morals and social organisation, and which form an integral and active part of primitive culture'. They are 'a statement of a primeval, greater, and more relevant reality by which the present life, fates and activities of mankind are determined'. Myth plays its crucial part when the social fabric is put under strain – when profound changes are taking place, when there are stresses related to differences of rank, power and precedence, when subordination is challenged. Altogether, Malinowski believes, the function of myth 'is to strengthen tradition and endow it with a greater value and prestige by tracing it back to a higher, better, more supernatural reality' (Malinowski, 1971, pp.18f., 30ff., 58, 91f.).

3 *Structuralism* Lévi-Strauss' structuralist approach to myth has something in common with Frazer's cognitivism because it assumes that the so-called primitive mind is impelled to try to understand the world. It differs from Frazer's rationalism in broadening the scope of primitive thinking: it is not crude scientific explanation that myth is attempting, but a grasp of the totality of experience, a view of the meaning of existence, and understanding of both nature and society. But Lévi-Strauss lines up with Frazer in holding that the cognitive achievement of myth is illusory: 'Myth ... gives man ... the illusion that he can understand the universe and that he does understand the universe. It is, of course, only an illusion' (Lévi-Strauss, 1978, p.17). He shares with Malinowski, on the other hand, the view that myth has a function in relation to tradition, to ensure social stability and to perpetuate received ways of doing things: 'For societies without writing and without archives the aim of mythology is to ensure that as closely as possible ... the future will remain faithful to the present and the past' (ibid., p.43).

Lévi-Strauss' distinctive contribution is to emphasise the structure of mythic thinking: it arises from awareness of a contradiction in experience and progresses through numerous polarities towards a resolution. 'The purpose of myth is to provide a logical model capable of overcoming a contradiction (an impossible achievement if, as it happens, the contradiction is real) ... Thus myth grows, spiral-wise, until the intellectual impulse which has produced it is exhausted. Its growth is a continuous process, whereas its structure remains discontinuous' (Lévi-Strauss, 1968, p.229). The meaning of a myth resides not in its discrete elements, but in the way they are combined, in the structure as a whole. As long as that structure persists, through innumerable elaborations, permutations and translations, the myth will survive. A myth retains its power for its readers anywhere in the world. While a myth always refers to events alleged to have happened long ago, the pattern of those events, the structure of the myth, is timeless and sheds light on the present and the future as well as on the past (ibid., pp.209f.).

I want to carry forward a number of insights from the three classical theories of myth that we have glanced at: from Frazer, the insight that myth is intended to be explanatory; from Malinowski, the truth that myth is bound up with tradition and has a social, legitimating function; from Lévi-Strauss, the perception that the motive force of myth is the attempt to reconcile contradictions in experience and that this is expressed in an enduring structure, pattern or form.

The nature of myth

The young Nietzsche said that myth is 'the concentrated image of the world' (Nietzsche, 1993, p.109). If so, it is certainly not a orderly world, with clearly defined boundaries, a world that follows the logic of spatio-temporal reality. For myth is illogical, confused, repetitive, circular, diverse, contradictory and inimical to clear analysis. Lévi-Strauss writes: 'It would seem that in the course of a myth anything is likely to happen. There is no logic, no continuity. Any characteristic can be attributed to any subject; every conceivable relation can be found. With myths everything becomes possible' (Lévi-Strauss, 1968, p.208). In his enthralling retelling of the Greek myths, *The Marriage of Cadmus and Harmony*, Roberto Calasso comments that 'myths are made up of actions that include their opposites within themselves'. The hero slays the monster, but as the story continues we find that the monster encompasses the death of the hero; the hero carries off and rescues the princess, but we go on to learn that the hero deserts the princess (Calasso, 1994, pp.280f.). There is always a variant that twists the story into the opposite of what it seemed to set out to tell. These variants are not accidental or disposable by-products of myth, but essential: 'they keep the mythical blood in circulation' (ibid., p.281). Calasso elaborates:

> The mythographer lives in a permanent state of chronological vertigo, which he pretends to want to resolve. But while on the one table he puts generations and dynasties in order, like some old butler who knows the family history better than his masters, you can be sure that on another table the muddle is getting worse and the threads ever more entangled. No mythographer has ever managed to put his material together in a consistent sequence, yet all set out to impose order ... The mythical gesture is a wave which, as it breaks, assumes a shape, the way dice form a number when we toss them. But as the wave withdraws, the unvanquished complications swell in the undertow, and

likewise the muddle and the disorder from which the next mythical gesture will be formed.

(ibid., p.282)

In contrast to Robert Graves' reduction of the Greek myths to some kind of logical order, with all their variants harmonised as far as possible and everything cut and dried in numbered sequence (Graves, 1960), the secret of Calasso's success in his retelling is that he allows the irreducible variety and complexity of the mythology to carry his story forward, for example, introducing each variant of the first encounters of gods and humans with the refrain: 'But how did it all begin?'.

In the Bible, the book of Genesis is well known to have two creation narratives which fundamentally differ and underlying these several sources can be detected. In the mythic proto-history of Genesis 1–11 there are numerous permutations of genealogy and several inconsistent accounts of Noah and the flood. Turning to the New Testament: if, for the sake of argument, we may allow that the Gospels bear some of the marks of myth as a literary genre (without at present jumping to any conclusions about their historicity or truth-value), the diversity and inconsistency of the resurrection appearance narratives would be a prime piece of evidence to bear this out.

In the light of the chronic tendency of myth towards diversification and complexification, it would seem more correct to say, not (with Nietzsche) that myth contains the concentrated image of the world, but that myth reflects the deepest human experience of the world. The world is a unity, but experience is infinitely varied. The world is what it is, but experience is filled with deception. The world is inexhaustible in its depths of meaning, but human experience can only scratch the surface. In my interpretation of the nature of myth, I am discriminating delicately between extremes, walking a tightrope. I am insisting that myths are cognitive: they embody thought and arise from attempts to interpret and explain the world; they are not arbitrary functions of psychological states or group consciousness. But I am not advocating any simplistic view that myths are true: it does not follow that, because the myths are cognitive, they approximate to reality. I will not talk carelessly about 'true myth'. There are grossly inadequate myths, illusory myths and downright destructive myths. In other words, I am suggesting that myths are informative but not definitive, descriptive but not veridical. This is a critically realist concept of myth; it entails that in our experience of the world (expressed partly in myths) we are in touch with reality; but it acknowledges that as subjects we play a part in constructing our perception of reality and that, therefore, perceptions have to be checked, the deliverances of experience require to be scrutinised by all available means, interpreted, evaluated and criticised in the light of all our relevant knowledge.

Myth and reality

Exponents of the theory of myth insist with one voice that myths are always held by their adherents to be 'historically' true. It is absolutely integral to the function of myth that the events it describes are believed to have really happened. Cassirer, referring to Kant's contention that pure aesthetic contemplation is 'entirely indifferent to the existence or non-existence of its object', points out that such indifference is completely alien to the mythic imagination: 'In mythical imagination there is always implied an act of belief' (Cassirer, 1944, p.75). Genuine myth is not known to be myth, but is held to be real (Cassirer, 1946a, p.47). Eliade, likewise, insists that myth is always regarded as 'true history', dealing with realities (Eliade, 1964, pp.6, 8f.). Myth, he writes, expresses 'absolute truth because it narrates a sacred history' (Eliade, 1968, p.23).

The crucial function of myth is to make that sacred history, those primordial events, live contemporaneously and to incorporate devotees into them. Myth takes place in what Eliade calls 'the Great Time at the beginning' (op. cit.) and are of exemplary authority, requiring to be repeated and imitated. Without prejudging what we may wish to say about the extent to which myth impinges on the Gospel history, it is clear that, phenomenologically, the Christian liturgy has the function of incorporating believers into the death and resurrection of Christ as the salvation history is rehearsed in the eucharistic prayer. This fact leads Eliade to suggest that Christianity is essentially mythic because it incorporates its members into liturgical time and reunites them with those primal events (ibid., p.30).

But no myth is sacrosanct. All myths are constantly undergoing a process of evocation, elaboration and fixation, followed by interrogation, modification and reinterpretation – or dissolution. Myths decay and lose their sacred power. Myths undergo a crisis when they are 'unmasked' and seen for the first time to be myths. This may come about through advances in knowledge that challenge the cognitive function of myth (e.g. the Genesis story after Darwin), or socio-economic changes that undermine the social legitimation function of myth (e.g. biblical patriarchy after the emancipation of women), or through profound psychic changes (not unrelated, to be sure, to the advances in knowledge and the socio-economic shifts) that render the structure, pattern or form of myth somehow inappropriate. What happens when a myth is challenged? To function effectively, a myth needs to be completely taken for granted. What Jung says about symbols in general applies to myths in particular:

A symbol loses its magical or, if you prefer, its redeeming power as soon as its liability to dissolve is recognised. To be effective, a symbol must be by its very nature unassailable. It must be the best possible expression of the prevailing worldview, an unsurpassed container of meaning; it must also be sufficiently remote from comprehension to resist all attempts of the critical intellect to break it down; and finally, its aesthetic form must

appeal so convincingly to our feelings that no argument can be raised
against it on that score.

(Jung, n.d., p.21)

All these factors – worldviews, meanings, feelings – are obviously vari-
ables. When they begin to change, a myth is in imminent danger. Langer
writes: 'The first enquiry as to the literal truth of a myth marks the change
from poetic to discursive thinking. As soon as the interest in the factual
values awakes, the mythical mode ... is on the wane' (Langer, 1956, p.202;
see also Lévi-Strauss on 'How Myths Die', in Lévi-Strauss, 1977, pp.256ff.).
Cassirer points out that religion, with its abhorrence of idolatry, cannot
escape the tension between its images or myths and the objects that they
purport to represent. For him, however, this is not a problem, for idealism is
content to contemplate images as purely immanental expressions of artistic
creativity (Cassirer, 1955, pp.260f.). For Cassirer – as for Tillich – religious
consciousness is not identical with mythic consciousness, but marks a
further stage of development. Myth at first is not conscious of itself as myth;
there is no separation between the ideal and the real, between meaning and
existence. The principle of identity reigns supreme. But the breakdown of
this identity constitutes the beginning of the specifically religious consciousness. Religion exists in tension and contains an inherent dilemma: on the
one hand, it cannot destroy its myths without destroying itself; on the other,
it can never absolutise them but must carry on a continual prophetic critique
of idolatry (ibid., pp.238f.). This of course raises the crucial question of
demythologisation, made notorious by Bultmann: we shall examine it in our
final main section.

Conclusions and agenda

1   In common use the term 'myth' has been debased and become equivalent
to 'worthless fiction'. It carries a freight of popular misconception and it is a
moot point whether it is usable in a theology that hopes to reach a broad
audience. On the other hand, in learned discourse 'myth' is indispensable
and it is a nettle that theologians should grasp. In the Doctrine Commission
report *Believing in the Church* (Doctrine Commission, 1981), Anthony
Thiselton argued that the term 'myth' was best avoided and should be
replaced by the word 'story'. But what sort of story: history? legend? myth?
pure fiction? Paul Tillich rightly insisted that theology should discriminate
between these and that this would affect our theological conclusions. The
term 'myth' is certainly in the public domain. More damage may be done by
the Church's conveying the impression that it expects all biblical narratives
and credal statements to be taken 'literally' (i.e. as though they were
scientific or historical statements and at face value), than by risking
deployment of 'myth' and making clear what is meant by it.

2   Myths are essentially narratives that embody numinous symbols. They speak of origins, transformations and destiny, the interaction and commerce of God and humanity, heaven and earth. Myths are set in a different timeframe, 'the Great Time' (Eliade, 1968, p.23) when the world was different. Their characters, though not always gods, are superhuman. Dundes defines a myth as 'a sacred narrative explaining how the world and man came to be in their present form' (Dundes, 1984, p.1). Every component of this definition carries significance. Myths are sacred; they are narratives; they have an explanatory function – not scientifically but metaphysically explanatory; they deal with becoming; they speak of totalities – humankind and the world. Myths are the earliest and remain the most vivid forms of reflection on the truth of existence. Even Plato, who believed that ultimate reality was beyond all images, used myths. In myth, the sacred or supernatural effects a breakthrough into the ordinary world (Eliade, 1964, p.6).

3   Victor Turner (Turner, 1968, pp.576–82) has drawn attention to the role of myth in 'liminal' situations, times of transition and transformation, of 'betwixt and between'. On the macro scale, myths tell of world transformations: how chaos became cosmos, how immortals became mortal, how androgynous beings became men and women. On the micro scale, Turner follows Van Gennep's celebrated work on *The Rites of Passage* (English translation, 1909) in pointing to the role of myths at times of initiation, which are periods of structural impoverishment (when the individual leaves behind one stage of life or social attachment) and of symbolic enrichment (when the person is fortified and sanctified for a new phase of their life through contact with primordial and archetypal events). In the Christian Church we are already familiar with the application of Van Gennep's notion of liminality and rites of passage to the sacramental journey that we make from baptism, through confirmation, to marriage and finally burial.

4   To accept the mythic status of some biblical narratives is now uncontroversial. The stories in Genesis 1–11 (from creation to Babel) would be accepted as myth by all but the most benighted fundamentalists. The mythic status of biblical eschatology would also be widely accepted with few attempting to take the myths and symbols of the book of Revelation literally. Creation and fall, on the one hand, and eschatology, on the other, are urgently in need of meaningful restatement which can only be done in a symbolic or mythic mode. Christological myths are more controversial: the narratives of the virginal conception and the resurrection, descent into Hades and ascension of Jesus contain evident mythic components. To recognise this is simply to acknowledge the literary genre that we are dealing with and carries no hidden agenda as to what 'actually happened'. However, it does imply that the narratives are not straight history, and that the actual events are probably irretrievable. At the same time, this

acknowledgement privileges these narratives as sacred, numinous and authoritative; their givenness is reinforced.

5   If there is no escape from the mythic and if any demythologising needs to be followed by remythologising, this still leaves Bonhoeffer's question awaiting an answer: who is Jesus Christ for us today? Are new Christological symbols and myths emerging which will make the person and work of Jesus Christ live anew for our age?

Part IV

12 Critical realism

Symbols and doctrine

Not all theologians would accept the argument that it is the figurative or imaginative mode of expression alone that is appropriate to speaking about the ineffable God. The report of the Church of England's Doctrine Commission *We Believe in God* seems to suggest that alongside symbolic language about God, there is available to us a non-symbolic, literal truth about God, against which the former, symbolic language can be checked and controlled (Doctrine Commission, 1987, pp.42f.). Without this privileged, literal route, the Commission suggests, 'we seem, as it were, to be trapped within a circle of images from which there is no escape' (op. cit.). The metaphors 'trapped' and 'escape' in this statement are plainly tendentious. The term 'circle of images' speaks to me not of the futility of symbolic theology – as though the theologian paces fretfully round and round the cage of images, longing to break out and to return to the wide plains of literal speech – but rather of the sheer gratuitous givenness of divine revelation and the human response to it through believing communities and their traditions filled with symbols and myths. Symbols are not stifling and constricting, but – as we have learned above all from Jung – full of liberating, quickening virtue. So if there is a circle of images, it is certainly a virtuous circle. The truth of Christian theology cannot be understood from outside the circle, but only by committing oneself in praxis to the symbolic process. In theology there is no fixed point. Theology speaks of the relation of a personal God with personal, created beings. The classical doctrine of analogy presupposes that. Analogy is not a form of literal predication (as the Doctrine Commission appears to suggest, op. cit.), but a mode of personalist symbolism which testifies to the fiduciary character of all significant human discourse (see Chapter 6 of this book). There are no guaranteed gambits, no assured fall-back positions in such personal transactions. Newman was right: *Cor ad cor loquitur*: let heart speak to heart – or not at all.

Tillich provides a corrective to the hankering after literal speech of God as a sort of safety-blanket that undertakes for the risks of theological tightrope-walking. In the first volume of his *Systematic Theology*, Tillich laid it down that nothing can be said about God that is not symbolic – with one exception: 'The statement that God is being-itself is a non-symbolic statement' (Tillich, 1968, vol.1, p.264). But by the time that he came to write the second volume of his *magnum opus*, Tillich was insisting that everything without exception that religion says about God is symbolic and that 'if we make one non-symbolic assertion about God, his ecstatic transcendent character seems to be endangered' (ibid., vol.2, p.10). For Tillich, it is not just the spontaneous language of religion, but also the reflective language of theology that is symbolic.

The statement 'God is being-itself' is certainly not the normal language of prayer, worship or preaching. Christian doctrine (Tillich refers to 'dogma') is a combination of 'direct religious language, with its fragmented religious symbols, and rational metaphysical language with its fragmented mythical concepts'. Doctrine is the product of myth that has undergone a rigorous critique at the hands of prophetic religion (cf. Tillich's celebrated 'Protestant principle'), philosophical analysis and scientific reductionism, and has become fused with metaphysics – which itself contains a basic mythological impulse and history – to give it a universal validity. According to Tillich, the Christological dogma (of the appearance of the New Being in Jesus as the Christ as our ultimate concern) is mythical. By this, Tillich does not of course mean that it is the product of fantasy, of mere human projection, or of unreconstructed primitive instinctive impulses. The mythical character of the Christological dogma means that it is not historically verifiable: historical research cannot affect it, either to demonstrate its truth or to undermine its claims. Tillich believes that the Christian religious consciousness testifies to the fact that the New Being has appeared in history, but that religious consciousness cannot give historical information about him. The Christological dogma is simply given: it is the ultimate revelatory and redemptive symbol (Tillich, 1968, vol.2, pp. 112–35; cf. Avis, 1986c, pp.192ff.).

In his posthumously published Gifford Lectures, *God Beyond Knowledge*, H.A. Hodges argues for the personal and existential nature of theological statements. They do not give us information about the make-up of the world, as scientific statements do, and so cannot be dignified with the label 'knowledge' as that is normally understood (Hodges, 1979, p.14). In Hodges' view, Christian theism 'makes reality-assertions in order to house a life-pattern' embodied in myths (ibid., p. 153). The Christian commitment of faith is an existential leap on the basis of inadequate evidence. Charles Davis has advocated an approach that is broadly comparable. In faith we inhabit a world of sacred symbols which are sufficient to inform our praxis but which do not claim to be descriptive of reality. Knowledge is not foundational; it is entailed within the circle of praxis. The Christian faith does not provide a worldview and does not give informative answers to speculative questions. It assures us of the ultimate reality of transcendent love, manifested definitively in Jesus Christ and communicated to us in symbolic and mythic forms (Davis, 1986). Both Hodges and Davis, for all their difference of background, develop an essentially apophatic theology, in which God remains ineffable mystery, and a world of revelatory symbols mediates between that mystery and the commitment of faith to life and practice. To this extent they – and Tillich – have the heart of the matter in them. As Edwyn Bevan pointed out in one of the earliest modern discussions of our theme, *Symbolism and Belief* (first published in 1938), symbolism presupposes the ineffability of the divine and the transcendence of God – that 'essential infinite unannullable difference' between God and creatures (Bevan, 1962, p. 60). The great question to be resolved is: what is the truth-value of the symbols?

First of all, let us consider the possibility that the rationality of Christian beliefs can be corroborated by setting them in the light of 'archetypal' symbols. We will want to bear in mind that, however vital it may be to insist on the irreducible historical particularity of the central events of salvation, they only find a universal appeal and relevance by means of commonly accessible symbols. I suggest that Christian doctrines are derived from symbols of revelatory experience, embodied in the narratives of the faith community, which are then translated and refined into discursive propositional statements. As symbols of revelation these symbols are anchored in historical particularities; as symbols of revelatory experience they have a universal credibility and speak a language that rings bells with people of all times and cultures. The symbols liberate, as it were, divine revelation from the confines of historical particularity and make it universally available. For example, revelation in the particularity of the historical man Jesus of Nazareth unfolds into a gospel for the whole of humanity through the symbol of the Christ, a corporate, androgynous persona (see Avis, 1989, ch.5). Because doctrines retain substantial elements of their narrative and symbolic provenance, they speak a universal language. Jung writes:

> The dogmatically formulated truths of the Christian Church express, almost perfectly, the nature of psychic experience. They are the repositories of the secrets of the soul, and this matchless knowledge is set forth in grand symbolical images. The unconscious thus possesses a natural affinity with the spiritual values of the Church, particularly in their dogmatic form.
>
> (Jung, 1983b, p.29)

As Jung also puts it: 'The archetypes of the unconscious can be shown empirically to be the equivalents of religious dogmas' (Jung, 1953, p.17).

Jung believed that the very process of increasing differentiation of ritual and dogma, which precisely served to perpetuate and communicate these revelatory symbols, also had the effect of alienating the religious consciousness from its natural roots in the unconscious (Jung, 1983a, p.283). So, for Jung, the creeds remain lifeless until reinterpreted back into those symbols. People speak of the death of God when creeds have become dead forms and the symbols no longer speak through them. Then the creeds (according to Jung) need to be superseded and fresh channels need to be discovered for the revelatory symbols of the eternal archetypes (Jung, 1958, pp.9, 90; Jung, 1956, p.435)

The revelatory symbols that are codified in creeds and doctrines are transmitted from generation to generation and from one act of worship to another in narrative enactment, the Christian story of salvation. To be more precise, revelatory symbols, which are inseparable from the story of their reception in the events of revelation, are constellated in myth. Jung insists that only myth is adequate to convey ultimate mysteries. 'What we are to our inward vision, and what man appears to be *sub specie aeternitatis*, can only be expressed by way of myth.' Christianity, like other mythologies, is an expression of the ineffable. Jung points out, importantly, that it is not that 'God' is reducible to a myth, but that myth is required to articulate the divine life in man (Jung, 1983c, pp.17, 373). We do not need to subscribe to Jung's more speculative theories and we should be wary of his interpretation of Christianity (for further discussion, see Avis, 1995, ch.6), but we should heed his testimony with regard to the consonance of doctrines and symbols of the unconscious.

The suggestion that theological doctrines are distillations of revelatory-redemptive symbols expressed in narrative form into discursive grammatical propositions is not meant to be reductionist, to undermine the authoritative role of Church teaching, of doctrines. So let me try to state how I understand the relation between symbols and doctrines.

1   The provenance of doctrines in symbolism does not in any way imply that doctrines are trivial and to be taken less than seriously. On the contrary, no one who has learned from depth psychology (and particularly from Jung) would presume to treat the great religious symbols with other than the utmost respect and even reverence – which they surely demand as vehicles of the numinous. In Jung's view, doctrines (dogmas) are not our servants, but we are theirs. They are not at our disposal by any means. They represent transcendent truths that emerge of their own accord from the collective unconscious in response to human spiritual conflicts. 'Dogma is like a dream, reflecting the spontaneous and autonomous activity of the objective psyche, the unconscious', asserts Jung (1958, p.46). If Jung is right, his claim supports the assumption of Christian theology that doctrine is not speculative, arbitrary and contrived – as extreme liberals would have it – but is certainly related (how, we shall enquire shortly) to reality and fulfils perennial human needs.

2   The symbolic complexion of doctrine does not imply, either, that doctrines are essentially relative – infinitely variable, unstable, ephemeral, 'a nose of wax'. The revelatory symbols of the Christian sacred are authoritative: the central symbols have the status of dogma. They point to the actuality of divine revelation, though that is not directly and unmediatedly accessible to us now. The Christian doctrines have this status because the symbols in which the reception of revelation was expressed belong within a community of faith and practice where they have become conformed to an existing tradition whilst at the same time exerting a critical influence on it. The symbols have authority because they are sacred symbols: they induct us into a transcendent realm, they convey God.

3   The approach that I am advocating, that brings out the symmetry between doctrines and archetypal symbols, does not mean that doctrinal statements – propositions and formulae – are not important. Doctrinal statements are the means whereby the Church appropriates and deploys the resources of its corporate experience of the Christian sacred realm. As crystallisations (critical crystallisations, we should say) of the symbols of the sacred, doctrinal formulae are a kind of shorthand and as such are obviously useful in a number of ways – for theological education, ecumenical dialogue, and the criticism and reconstruction of faith and practice. But they remain human constructions, vehicles not only of the sacred but also of ideological distortion. This view has implications for the propositional character of doctrines. It excludes, first, the traditional notion that revelation itself (in the original and primal sense) is given and received propositionally, and, second, the claim of the Roman Catholic Church that doctrines defined by the magisterium on the basis of original revelation are themselves revealed by God through the Church. Furthermore, it militates against the assumption found in elements of the Roman Catholic tradition (currently favoured by the magisterium) that the Church's pilgrimage in truth is to be understood as their progressively deepening grasp of propositional revelation, with its corollary, the ability and authority to apply this bindingly to doctrinal, ethical and pastoral problems. On the contrary, I would suggest that the Church's apprehension of truth is primarily given, not in the realm of theory but in the realm of praxis – 'not through steadily more precise and accurate interpretations of its doctrinal formulae, but through its life of worship, prayer, fellowship, service and suffering' (Avis, 1986a, p.43).

4   The approach that seeks illumination of the nature of doctrine by setting it in the light of archetypal symbols, does not entail that propositional elaboration of beliefs is superfluous. A proposition is often loosely taken to be a written or spoken statement, expressed according to the laws of grammar, essentially a form of words. But, as G.E. Moore has argued, a proposition is really what is meant by a given form of words: what the words express, what we understand when we read or hear them. Interpreted

in this way, it is clear that propositions can be, and often are, apprehended without words – that is to say, symbolically, in images, and even (instantaneously and subliminally) without a defined image (Moore, 1953, pp.57–60). A proposition, according to Moore, is a constellation of meaning, commonly but not invariably expressed in a whole sentence, apprehended as a whole in which the parts – not apprehended all at once – subsist (ibid., pp.61f., 68). This chimes in with Polanyi's teaching that we apprehend whole meanings through subsidiary indwelling of the clues which are the components of the whole. Taking my cue from Moore and Polanyi, I would want to say that doctrinal statements or propositions are derivative of and dependent on the constellations of symbolic meaning which they attempt to articulate and elucidate. The truth transcends our attempts to express it. We have an intuitive grasp of the Christian mystery as a whole. Our assent and commitment to this truth is rather to its symbolic subsistence than to a human form of words that inevitably fails to measure up to it. The more impersonal, objective, clinical and precise doctrinal formulae become, the further removed they are from that personal reality – whose heart is love and who can be known only in passion and praxis – which propositions, necessary as they are, exist to serve (Avis, 1986a, pp.38ff.).

5   The theory of the symbolic complexion of doctrines does not mean that doctrines are not true. They are as true as they can be (the oxymoron is intentional), given the ineffability of God, the unverifiability of revelatory experiences in history, the hermeneutical gap between the primary witnesses to revelation and ourselves, and the limitations inherent in human intellectual and linguistic competence. A personalist, dynamic conception of truth enables us to speak of an approach to truth, an approximation to truth, a tentative grasp of truth – where truth is understood as an apprehension of, and participation in, a transcendent reality that constitutes the ultimate goal of our quest (cf. Avis, 1986a, pp.6ff.). Truth is a stronger term than knowledge. Truth includes knowledge but transcends it. Knowledge impinges on truth but falls short of it. When we speak of knowledge, the emphasis is on the subjective pole of the subjective–objective continuum. When we speak of truth, the stress falls on the objective pole. It is not without reason that both Hodges and I have reflected on the elusiveness of doctrine. Doctrine is elusive, not only because of the problems bound up with the notion of revelation and its reception, not only because it is humanly and ideologically conditioned, not only because it is contested between the churches, but because, though it has a purchase on truth, it is not identifiable *tout court* with the truth of God.

6   The central Christian doctrines of creation, providence, revelation, redemption, sanctification and consummation or eschatology are symbolic because the language in which they are articulated cannot be – is not intended to be – taken literally. These doctrines burst the bounds of mundane discursive concepts. They are not empirically cashable. You

cannot point to the realities that they represent. You cannot see or (even in theory) describe revelation or redemption as they happen. Bultmann would say that they are not objectifiable. The concepts express meaning, but meaning is a human construction/discovery evoked in response to what we encounter from beyond ourselves. The essential affirmations of Christian theology are postulated by faith as the ultimate explanation of the things we can see – the things that are empirically verifiable: the world around us, the history of the human race, the character and destiny of Jesus of Nazareth, the Church and its sacramental life, the hope and vision of Christians for the present and for the future. 'His eternal power and divine nature, invisible though they are, have been understood and seen through the things he has made' (Romans 1.20). We cannot pin down what lies behind these phenomena; we can only affirm its reality in faith. Our faith statements refer but do not describe, they point but do not define, they gesture but do not grasp. The faith that affirms, refers and points is not, however, a contentless faith; it is a cognitive faith that expresses its content in symbolic form. The symbols are handed down in tradition and are already heavy with meaning.

7   The suggestion of the symbolic provenance of doctrine is, then, intended to refresh doctrine by restoring the connection between it and the revelatory experiences, conveyed to us symbolically, which are the ultimate justification and *raison d'être* of doctrine. What are the consequences for Christian theology? Does our approach put paid to Christian truth-claims? Not at all, because the same analysis applies to every area of intellectual endeavour that attempts to go beyond supposedly 'literal' description of empirical phenomena and to enter the realm of significant, meaningful general affirmations. As John Macquarrie has well said: 'As soon as we cease to speak of sticks and stones we must begin to use symbols and metaphors' (Macquarrie, 1973, p.165). The symbolic realm, with its contributory ingredients of metaphor or analogy and its elaboration in narrative form which produces myth, precedes and undergirds all the conscious constructions of human intellectual endeavour. Wherever we move out from the relatively safe intellectual activities of collating and interpreting the results of empirical investigation, into the speculative realm of constructing an overall interpretation or explanation of reality, where we are not in a position to verify our theories as verification is normally understood, and we have to seek instead for the most adequate total interpretation – as in cosmology, anthropology, depth psychology, metaphysics and theology – we are compelled to resort to figurative language, to metaphor, symbol and myth.

8   However, the position defended here does have implications for theology and for ecclesiology. If doctrines are distillations of Christian experience mediated by symbols and shaped by the political, social and economic pressures at work in a community and its tradition, it follows that the criteria of clarity, distinctness, precision and objectivity are not appropriately

applied to doctrines. Textual interpretation rather than conceptual analysis is the appropriate method to bring to doctrines. The analysis and critique of doctrines, leading to their restatement and reconstruction, remains vital, but it ought to be preceded by an exercise of interpretation that seeks to understand doctrines in their historical and communal contexts. They need to be evaluated in personalist, symbolic terms, as pioneered by Karl Rahner.

Varieties of realism

Can we speak the truth about God? Can we even speak the truth about the world? We have been arguing, in a cumulative fashion, throughout this book that, when we employ figurative language with the intention of making significant statements, that language is not merely expressive but cognitive: it conveys something meaningful about the world as we have experienced it. A symbol in literature or religion, in poetry or liturgy, certainly evokes an emotional, moral or spiritual response, but it does not follow from the fact that it has an evocative function, that it has no invocative function. In fact the reverse is the case: the symbol is only effective because it is held to have a purchase on reality. I have earlier argued that what is true of the primary language of faith is also true of the secondary language of theological reflection: it too discourses in metaphor, symbol and myth, though refined by criticism and mediated through a conceptuality of analogy. Our claim for the cognitive (that is interpretative or, in the weak sense, explanatory) import of symbolic language raises the question of theological realism: how far are theological statements adequate accounts of a sacred, transcendent reality?

In both the physical sciences and theology there is a continuing debate about the adequacy of our descriptions to the entities that they purport to describe – whether those entities are, for example, subatomic particles in all their apparently bizarre behaviour, or the attributes and acts of God. At one extreme, literalism in science – the position known as 'naive realism' – is matched by literalism in theology – fundamentalism. At the other end of the spectrum, instrumentalism in science corresponds to the most relativistic and pragmatic theology, such as that of Don Cupitt. Between the two is the position known as 'critical realism', and this too has its advocates in both science and theology. Let us look at these three approaches in turn.

1 *Naive realism* Realists of all shades hold that 'scientific theories are true or false as the case may be in virtue of how the world is, independently of ourselves' (Newton-Smith, 1981, p.43). Hacking describes realism as the view that 'the entities, states and processes described by correct theories really do exist. Protons, photons, fields of force and black holes are as real as toe-nails, turbines, eddies in a stream and volcanoes' (Hacking, 1983,

p.21). Roy Bhaskar (Collier, 1994, pp.6f.) suggests that realism involves four claims for knowledge:

(a) *Objectivity*: what is known would be real whether it became an object of knowledge to us or not.
(b) *Fallibility*: knowledge claims are always open to modification or refutation by more information about the real world.
(c) *Transphenomenality*: knowledge goes beyond appearances to the underlying structures (this is 'depth' realism, as opposed to 'shallow' realism which confines itself to superficial states of affairs).
(d) *Counterphenomenality*: knowledge of the deep structure of something may not only explain appearances by going beyond them, but may also contradict appearances, correcting our perceptions.

Realism becomes 'naive' or crude realism when it claims that not only do these occult entities exist, but also that they exist just as our theories describe them. All realism entails that there are real entities 'out there', but naive realism seems to involve a reification of our knowledge of these entities. Naive realism blithely ignores the fact that our knowledge is mediated through social as well as psychological structures.

I imagine that it would be difficult to find paid-up naive realists in the scientific community. The branches of science to which Hacking alludes – particle physics and radio astronomy – are engaged in the study of entities that, either in principle or in practice, are unobservable. Thus Hacking's own realism is confirmed not by the accumulation of observations (which are not available in many cases), but by the fact that unobserved but postulated entities can be made to work for us in experimental situations. The theory proves its value: the entity that the theory postulates thereby demonstrates its reality.

> Experimental work provides the strongest evidence for scientific realism. This is not because we test hypotheses about entities. It is because entities that in principle cannot be 'observed' are regularly manipulated to produce a new phenomena [*sic*] and to investigate other aspects of nature. They are tools, instruments not for thinking but for doing.
>
> (Hacking, 1983, p.262)

It would also be difficult to find defenders of crude or naive realism among theologians. Christian theology has consistently protested against taking God-language literally. The doctrine of analogy of classical Christian theism is an attempt to break out of the dilemma that if talk about God is meant univocally (in the identical sense) then it would be blasphemous, and if meant equivocally (in an entirely different sense) it would be agnostic. Karl Barth's view of theological language is strongly realist: as we have seen (in Chapter 6 of this book), he holds that human speech cannot attain to

God until in divine condescension God adopts it for his revelatory purposes. But Barth is preserved from the worst excesses of naive realism by his dominant conviction of the transcendence of God, the Kierkegaardian 'infinite qualitative distinction' between God and man, infinite and finite, eternity and time. Richard Swinburne is accused by Don Cupitt of 'designer realism' – presumably because Swinburne notoriously has everything cut and dried with no blurred edges, murky depths or loose ends – every question has its answer (Cupitt, 1986, ch.5).

Generally speaking, it is not theology that is guilty of naive realism but unreflective popular faith and preaching. C.A. Campbell commented in his Gifford Lectures, given in the mid-1950s:

> The note struck in Tersteegen's dictum that 'a God comprehended is no God' has seldom been absent for long from the course of theistic theology ... What is lacking, in my opinion, is sufficient ruthlessness and candour in following out its implications in the system of doctrine that rational theists elaborate and present to the religious public as entitled to acceptance.
>
> (Campbell, 1957, p.347)

Naive realism is incompatible with the Christian tradition of apophatic theology.

2   *Crude instrumentalism*   In science this is the view that theories are simply useful fictions constructed for certain purposes. Any correspondence that they may have to ultimate reality is fortuitous and is not the concern of the scientist. 'A law of physics', claimed Duhem revealingly, 'is, properly speaking, neither true nor false, but approximate.' It is simply 'something more or less well selected to stand for the reality it represents, and pictures that reality in a more or less precise, a more or less detailed manner' (Duhem, 1954, p.168). Duhem stressed that a physical theory was not an explanation but a simplified representation of experimental laws. The physicist must not allow himself to be seduced by the fancy that his experimental laws may actually conform to the true nature of reality; he must confine himself to the data of observation (ibid., pp.26f.). In his book *To Save the Phenomena* (first published in 1908), Duhem frankly stated that 'the hypotheses of physics are mere mathematical contrivances devised for the purpose of saving the phenomena' (Duhem, 1969, p.117).

A corollary of the instrumental approach is the doctrine of the incommensurability of scientific theories. Different theories cannot be evaluated by the same criteria. They belong to different worlds and speak different languages. There can be no continuous transition from one to another. Duhem, for example, asserted that 'if we confine ourselves to considerations of pure logic, we cannot prevent a physicist from representing by several incompatible theories diverse groups of laws: we cannot condemn incoherence in physical theory' (Duhem, 1954, pp.100f.). The current debate on incommensurability takes its rise, of course, from Thomas Kuhn's account of 'paradigm shifts' from a social-science point of view in *The Structure of Scientific Revolutions* (1962), where theories are shown to belong to a complete worldview which, in turn, is related to a specific set of historical-social-economic conditions. Fortunately, we do not need here to become involved in this debate, which has been pursued by Popper, Lakatos, Toulmin, Laudan and many others.

Kuhn's incommensurability thesis has been taken to its logical (or perhaps illogical) conclusion by Paul Feyerabend, a self-styled epistemological anarchist. In *Against Method*, he writes:

> Knowledge ... is not a series of self-consistent theories that converges towards an ideal view; it is not a gradual approach to the truth. It is rather an ever-increasing ocean of mutually incompatible (and perhaps even incommensurable) alternatives, each single theory, each fairy tale, each myth that is part of the collection forcing the others into greater articulation and all of them contributing, via this process of competition, to the development of our consciousness.
>
> (Feyerabend, 1975, p.30)

Feyerabend concludes: 'Nothing is ever settled; no view can ever be omitted from a comprehensive account' (op. cit.). In writing on theological method myself (Avis, 1986c, p.202), I have deployed Feyerabend as a salutary check on all forms of methodological absolutism – but that is the limit of my sympathy with his approach. I agree with Bhaskar that, like an undercover agent working both sides of the fence, Feyerabend plays the game of reason to undermine the authority of reason (Collier, 1994, p.95).

The instrumentalist view of science, and with it the strong doctrine of the incommensurability of theories, seems to have had its day. It militates against any claim that science is a form of knowledge. However, that has not prevented theological non-realists from appealing to scientific instrumentalism and the supposed death of scientific realism in support of their own theological instrumentalism. Thus Cupitt invokes the instrumental view of scientific theories, which sees them as 'tools', not 'replicas of objectively existing cosmic structures' – as though there were no *via media* for the status for theories between the extremes of 'tools' and 'replicas' (Cupitt, 1986, p.103).

Theological instrumentalism is the belief that 'religious language provides a useful, even uniquely useful system of symbols which is action-guiding for the believer but not to be taken as making reference to a cosmos-transcending being in the traditional sense' (Soskice in Abraham and Holtzer, 1987, p.108). This approach takes existential and ethical forms.

(a) *Existential theological instrumentalism* finds the meaning of God within the (Wittgensteinian) Christian language-game within the believing community (form of life). It is informed as a theory by linguistic positivism and metaphysical scepticism: it does not believe that we are in a position to make claims about the nature of ultimate reality. Faith statements are appropriated from the tradition in which we find ourselves in order to express an attitude towards life and its meaning, but they are not intended to be descriptive, explanatory or interpretative of a transcendent reality that they ostensibly address or to which they purport to refer. D.Z. Phillips is the most distinguished exponent of this approach.

(b) *Ethical theological instrumentalism* is associated in modern philosophy of religion with R.B. Braithewaite and is expounded by Stewart Sutherland for whom 'God' symbolises a personal commitment to certain ethical values of which Christian theism, historically, has been the vehicle (Sutherland, 1984). This approach is ultimately as reductionist as the language-game version of theological instrumentalism, but it is objective in a way that is not true of the linguistic view, in that it holds that the universe is so constituted as really to sustain those values – though not the theological doctrines to which they have been attached in the tradition. Unlike the linguistic gambit, ethical instrumentalism is not dependent on corporate believing but can serve as a philosophy for the individual in their solitariness. Its motive is not so much the epistemological one of the veto of critical philosophy on metaphysical assertions (though in Sutherland the Kantian limits of knowledge are assumed), as the moral one that takes the problem of evil with radical seriousness and finds theological apologetic on this issue morally repugnant.

There is something to be said for the approach that claims to 'see through' the imagery of religion – so often grandiose, melodramatic or bizarre – and yet wants to hold on to its values. Iris Murdoch's sifting of the religious worldview with the searchlight of moral seriousness is deeply impressive. She wants to remain religious but without belief in a personal God. She wants to keep meditation though not intercession. She values the Gospels while discarding their Christology. Part of her motive is clearly moral, but another part is alienation from the symbolism which she believes she would be required to accept dogmatically and literally. This remains unelaborated in *Metaphysics as a Guide to Morals*; it is merely asserted (Murdoch, 1993).

There is a strange paradox in Murdoch's position. She is a robust realist in epistemology, morals and art, but an expressivist when it comes to religious belief, articulated in theology. Her realism in the realm of knowledge of the world (epistemology) is actually grounded in a realism about morals. Moral choices are not arbitrary, existential episodes of self-expression – 'not a grandiose leaping about unimpeded at important moments' (Kerr, 1997, p.71) – for the moral life is nothing less than a continuous serious engagement with objective moral truth. 'There exists a moral reality, a real though infinitely distant standard ... ', she asserts, and continues in the same words that Polanyi uses: 'Where virtue is concerned we often apprehend more than we clearly understand and grow by looking' (ibid., p.80). Moral realism contains within it a realism about art, about beauty. When we perceive beauty, we are drawn out of our self-centred concerns into the orbit of a transcendent object. Goodness and beauty are not opposed: both Plato and Kant (Murdoch reminds us) saw the beautiful as an aspect of the good. The pursuit of both art and morals is a striving to see reality justly, as it is in truth. The key to this is the imagination. 'We have not been driven out of a brightly coloured mythical world which now belongs to a false illusioned past. ... We still live in the old familiar mysterious world and explain and clarify and celebrate it in the old endlessly fertile and inventive modes of speech. We enjoy the freedom of a moral imagination' (Murdoch, 1993, p.455).

We note that Murdoch speaks of a *moral* not a theological imagination and makes it clear that we should substitute Good for God (op. cit.). When it comes to religious truth, Murdoch believes that our relationship to 'God' cannot be stated in terms of what we know. For her, theological language is not descriptive (critical realists do not claim it is that), or even capable of bearing a critically or symbolically realist relation to reality, but merely expressive. Murdoch does not apparently see the immediate relevance to religious belief of her championing of imagination as a way of grasping the deeper dimension of reality in art and morals. Her repugnance for literalistic interpretation by religious people erects a barrier to deeper insight into the truth-bearing potential of religious language appropriately interpreted.

Murdoch is certainly not alone in her aversion to crude literalism in religion. In so far as the attitude of the reductionists (such as Cupitt, Phillips and Sutherland, as well as Murdoch herself) evinces a revulsion from the cruder and more literalistic forms of religious expression – the brashness of the fundamentalist evangelist, the fanaticism of the bigot, the petty certainties of the literalist and the inveterate tendency of all religion to domesticate the transcendent – it must surely have our sympathy. As Adorno put it in one of the less obscure of the aphorisms in *Negative Dialectics*: 'Religion *à la lettre* would be like science fiction' (Adorno, 1973, p.399).

However, there is an alternative. The more excellent way is to attempt to show that there can be a realist and cognitive view of metaphor, symbol and myth, which holds that these linguistic and conceptual forms are not crude, primitive and inferior, to be patronisingly set aside, but are significant, creative and – though not to be taken literally – the vehicles of truth about the world and its transcendent ground.

3   *Qualified realism*   This middle way is widely favoured by both philosophers of science and philosophers of religion. Barbour, Bowker and

Soskice speak of critical realism, and Bhaskar develops a socially critical realism. Tillich and Bellah advocate symbolic realism and Berdyaev 'realist symbolism'. Peacocke writes about sceptical, qualified or critical realism and Newton-Smith proposes 'temperate rationalism'. Barbour writes:

> Like the naive realist (and unlike the instrumentalist), the critical realist takes theories to be representations of the world. He holds that valid theories are true as well as useful. To him, science is discovery and exploration as well as construction and invention.
>
> (Barbour, 1974, p.36)

Like the instrumentalist, but unlike the naive realist, the critical realist recognises the role of the imagination and the place of symbols – the subjective component – in knowledge.

In the light of the sociology of knowledge, our critical realism should be socially qualified. For our knowledge is not acquired apart from the social, economic and political conditions in which we work at it. Bhaskar asserts: 'Science is produced by the imaginative and disciplined work of men on what is given to them. But the instruments of the imagination are themselves provided by knowledge. Thus knowledge is produced by means of knowledge' (Bhaskar, 1978, p.185). This recognition leads him to propose that knowledge should be viewed as a socially produced means of production and science as an ongoing social activity. The aim of science is, therefore, 'the production of the knowledge of the mechanisms of the production of phenomena in nature' (ibid., p.17). This stress on the social conditions of scientific knowledge does not prevent Bhaskar espousing a strong version of realism which he calls 'transcendental realism' – the view that

> the objects of science are neither phenomena (as in empiricism) nor human constructs imposed upon the phenomena (idealism), but real structures which endure and operate independently of our knowledge, our experience and the conditions that allow us access to them.
>
> (ibid., p.25)

Cassirer takes it for granted that science fully recognises that its theoretical constructions are symbols and he points out that this is what distinguishes it from poetry, myth and religion.

> What distinguishes science from the other forms of cultural life is not that it requires no mediation of signs and symbols and confronts the unveiled truth of 'things in themselves', but that, differently and more profoundly than is possible for the other forms, it knows that the symbols it employs are symbols and comprehends them as such.
>
> (Cassirer, 1955, p.26)

The Jungian exponent M.-L. Von Franz claims that: 'There is not one essential scientific idea that is not in the end rooted in primordial archetypal structures' (Von Franz, 1980, p.72). Scientists might baulk at the suggestion that what they imagined they were constructing to fit the data already existed deep in the unconscious! But critical realism certainly acknowledges that our understanding of the universe comes about through the interaction of a creative human imagination reaching out, by means of symbolic forms that are produced by the mind, with whatever it is that is already out there to be known. Barbour writes:

> The critical realist thus tries to acknowledge both the creativity of man's mind and the existence of patterns in events not created by man's mind. Descriptions of nature are human constructions but nature is such as to bear description in some ways and not others.
>
> (Barbour, 1974, p.37)

13 Symbolic realism

We have arrived at some form of qualified realism, but this position still leaves much work to be done. Qualified realism may be 'critical', 'symbolic' or even 'mythic'. It seems to me that the term critical realism – though really meant in the Kantian sense of the contribution made to our knowledge by the inherent structures of the mind – could appear to imply that the path to truth is primarily discursive, analytical and prosaic. The term symbolic realism, on the other hand, brings out the vital imaginative and creative factor in our significant knowledge, both of the world and of God (the possibility of mythic realism will be explored in the next chapter). As we have seen in sufficient measure, I trust, and without making pretentious and inordinate claims, imaginative insight expressed in metaphor, symbol and myth has the capacity to convey the truth about the world and God. But neither critical nor symbolic realism (and the difference is simply a nuance) claims that such knowledge embodies a definitive and exhaustive account of its object. Realism is critical or symbolic precisely because our object is transcendent.

This has important implications for theology. C.A. Campbell – like Kant and others before him – exposes the problems of literal or 'rational' theism and argues persuasively that the alternative is not merely a critical but a 'supra-rational', that is to say symbolic, theism:

> a theism which proclaims that the nature of God is in principle incapable of being conceived in terms of rational concepts in their literal significance, but that certain of these concepts are validly applicable to God when understood not as literal portrayals, but as appropriate symbols, of the divine nature.
>
> (Campbell, 1957, p.345)

I would qualify Campbell's position, which is still ultimately propositional (he speaks explicitly of 'concepts'), by a personalist form of symbolism which sees aspects of human life and creativity as the most indicative symbols of God.

A test case: symbolic Christology

We are examining the hypothesis that the rationality of Christian beliefs is strengthened when we look at them in the light of archetypal symbols. Let us take Christology as a test case. Modern theologians have often spoken of the person of Christ in terms of myth or symbol. The mythological road of Christology seems – rightly or wrongly – to arrive at mainly negative and reductionist conclusions, from Strauss to the contributors to *The Myth of God Incarnate* (Hick, 1978) – we shall see what can be made of mythic realism shortly. Meanwhile, the symbolic approach appears to be more immediately fruitful. Rahner, Schillebeeckx and Von Balthasar are the most notable exponents of a symbolic Christology. Let us glance at their views before returning to Jung.

Rahner has shown how the Incarnation belongs within the pattern of God's self-communication in which God becomes present through symbols. It is what the symbol signifies – the presence of God in revelation and redemption – that constitutes it as a symbol. Thus Jesus is the symbol of God and makes God present to humanity because it is God who makes Jesus who he is (Rahner, 1965–92, vol.4, pp.221ff.). There is nothing reductionist about Rahner's attempt here to see Christology as the supreme effective symbol.

In his early book *Christ the Sacrament of the Encounter with God*, Schillebeeckx speaks of Christology in terms of sacrament rather than of symbol. He defines a sacrament as 'a divine bestowal of salvation in an outwardly perceptible form which makes the bestowal manifest; a bestowal of salvation in historical visibility' (Schillebeeckx, 1963, p.15). In this sense, Jesus himself is the ultimate sacrament:

> The man Jesus, as the personal visible realisation of the divine grace of redemption, is the sacrament, the primordial sacrament, because this man, the Son of God himself, is intended by the Father to be in his humanity the only way to the actuality of redemption ... Human encounter with Jesus is therefore the sacrament of the encounter with God.

> (op. cit.)

In his later work, *Jesus: An Experiment in Christology*, Schillebeeckx favours the term parable rather than sacrament. 'Jesus himself – his person, his stories and his actions – is a parable ... In the care he shows for man and his record of suffering ... Jesus is the living parable of God.' But the principle of symbolic identity is the same whether Schillebeeckx is speaking of sacrament or parable. Jesus conveys and makes present as a reality all that he stands for and proclaims. His gospel and ministry constitute an offer of salvation in themselves. His presence among humanity was 'a concrete tender of salvation then and there ... where he appears he brings salvation and becomes God's rule already realised'. 'Jesus proclaims the salvation to come and at the same time by his conduct he makes it present' (Schillebeeckx, 1979, pp.158f., 306, 311, 152). Jesus' whole life was open to God and became, as it were, transparent to the divine presence. His self-consecration to God's redemptive purpose made him (if I may put it like this) a highly efficient symbol, offering minimum resistance to God's self-communication through him.

Von Balthasar does not develop a theory of symbolism as such, but his view of Christ as the centre of the form of revelation has a close affinity with the symbolic Christologies that we have been considering. For Von Balthasar the unfolding of salvation history constitutes a unity that with the eyes of faith we can perceive as a whole or as a 'form' by means of a spiritual perception that is analogous to aesthetic or artistic contemplation. The Gospel too, as the essential message of salvation history, is such a form. It points to Christ who is the inner reality of the form of revelation, its content and configuration. 'Jesus is the Word, the Image, the Expression and the Exegesis of God' (Von Balthasar, 1982–9, vol.1, p.29). Just as in all aesthetic experience there is a conjunction of the concrete artistic or natural image and an awareness of universal significance, so in Jesus Christ his historical particularity is united to universal salvific significance (ibid., p.234). The radiance of God's beauty breaks forth from within the form of Christ to illuminate the world (ibid., p.151).

For Jung, the Christ-figure is one of the symbols that the archetype of wholeness in the collective unconscious takes when it emerges into conscious thought in the Western cultural tradition shaped by Christianity. The archetype of wholeness also produces the symbols of the divine and of the self. There is thus a gratifying symmetry in this Trinitarian symbolism of God–Christ–self (cf. Avis, 1995, ch.6). Like Tillich, Jung believes that the 'New Being' or Christ had to be identified with an historical person, but it did not have to be Jesus of Nazareth. 'If Christ means anything to me,' Jung wrote to A. Keller in 1951, 'it is only as a symbol. As an historical figure he could just as well have been called Pythagoras, Lao-Tse, Zarathustra, etc.' (Jung, 1973–6, vol.2, p.10). But an historical connection was essential for Jung as for Tillich: 'That the Christological projection remained attached to the "historical" man Jesus is of the greatest symbolical significance,' Jung wrote to another correspondent at this time, 'otherwise the Incarnation of God – most important! – could never have come about' (ibid., p.6).

Jung's symbolic Christology sits loose to history – the vital historical link seems arbitrary – and Rahner typically operates in the realm of the a priori, but Schillebeeckx is drawing inferences from the narrative of the Gospels. What is the relation between a symbolic Christology and history? Is such a Christology freestanding, independent of what actually happened in the life and destiny of Jesus of Nazareth? If not, how is it constrained by the history of that figure? (For a brave attempt to reinterpret the historical-critical method of biblical study in the light of a critical-realist epistemology – in this case the cognitional theory and methodology of Bernard Lonergan – see Meyer, 1989.)

When Jung takes off into the archetypes of the collective unconscious, the theologically trained reader experiences a mild attack of vertigo. Are we not getting the Jesus of history and the Christ of faith shockingly confused? Jung's reply – and I believe that he has something to teach us here – is that the historical Jesus and the Christ of Christian faith are now effectively abstractions. The historical and the ideal components in the symbolic figure of Jesus Christ cannot be separated any more. Even in the Gospels they are inextricable. As Jung says:

> In the gospels themselves factual reports, legends and myths are woven into a whole. This is precisely what constitutes the meaning of the gospels, and they would immediately lose their character of wholeness if one tried to separate the individual from the archetypal with a critical scalpel.
>
> (Jung, 1958, p.88)

If Jesus of Nazareth had not been such a person as to evoke and generate faith in himself as the Christ of God – if he had not been a supremely symbolic human being who created immediate rapport with the numinous images emerging from the unconscious of his disciples – there would have been no Christian faith. The fact that he evidently was such a person means that he can no longer be distinguished – except notionally – as an actual historical person from all the symbolic meanings that he attracted to himself by means of the projections of believers. At an early stage 'the real Christ vanished behind the emotions and projections that swarmed about him from far and near; immediately and almost without trace he was absorbed into the surrounding religious systems and moulded into their archetypal exponent' (ibid., p.154).

Jung's colleague M.-L. Von Franz elaborates this idea, suggesting that in Jesus as the Christ the historical and the ideal have become one:

> With the coming of Christianity [she writes] there occurred something completely unprecedented ... the doctrine of the historically real Christ figure. It is as if the whole mythical heaven full of gods had come down into one human being and as if the Gnostic pleroma, the primordial mythical world, had now been incarnated on earth. It was concentrated in the one man, Christ, in whom it took historical shape. Christ clothed himself, as it were, in all the earlier images and assimilated them into his own image.
>
> (Von Franz, 1980, p.41)

Jung and his exponent have a point but they grossly overstate it. Schillebeeckx is a good antidote and that is why I have juxtaposed Jung's and

Schillebeeckx's symbolic Christologies. The historical Jesus has not been absorbed into the projections of his followers. By painstaking work on the text of the New Testament (such as Schillebeeckx's own *Jesus*) we can reconstruct the ministry, teaching and identity of Jesus of Nazareth – though much remains conjectural. We must also allow, in a way that Jung does not, for the power of Jesus' own self-understanding, drawn from the Old Testament figures of the Servant, the Son of Man, the Mosaic Prophet, the Davidic King and the Messiah, to discipline and correct the more free-wheeling fantasies of his modern followers.

Jung emphatically refused to draw reductionist conclusions from the theory of projection. He definitely left the door open to the possibility of a real objective correlative to psychic images of the divine. As he wrote in a letter in 1951:

> Psychology as a natural science must reserve the right to treat all assertions that cannot be verified empirically as projections. This epistemological restriction says nothing either for or against the possibility of a transcendent Being. Projection is an unavoidable instrument of cognition.
>
> (Jung, 1973–6, vol.2, p.6)

The fact that Jesus exerted a magnetic attraction on all the hopes, dreams and ideals of humankind does not mean that there was and is no real Jesus Christ. On the contrary, it makes sense to postulate such a figure who was all that Christians believe him to be, precisely on the evidence of his symbolic power and influence. There is no symbolic meaning without an actual symbolic fact to serve as its vehicle.

The positive point that Jung is making has been also made by Tillich: without his people who believe in him, Jesus could not be the Christ. The fact is interpreted within a context of meaning. Together they constitute the appearance of the New Being in Jesus as the Christ as our ultimate concern. Fact and interpretation are fused. The symbol participates in what it symbolises. Christ and his people are one. That way of stating the matter seems to me to be profoundly congruent with the Christian revelation which is given by a God who is the creative artist *par excellence* for the appropriation of humans whose symbolising capacity and imaginative grasp of truth is not the least part of their affinity with God.

Emotions? Hate? Resentment?

Concluding reflection

It is reassuring to find that it is not just Jung but such solid theologians as Rahner, Schillebeeckx and Von Balthasar who are advocating a symbolic Christology. But a symbolic Christology – a realist symbolic Christology – is only possible within the context of a theology of symbolic forms which sees the beauty of God radiating from every created form of beauty; that believes

He has failed to take a/c of Xian origins

that the values of truth and goodness cannot be divorced from aesthetic value; that holds to the symbol-forming power of the human imagination as the key to knowledge, and maintains the correspondence between the symbolic structure of the mind and the symbolic structure of the world and human life. The subjectivity of faith lives by indwelling the objectively given revelatory symbols, among which that of Jesus Christ is supreme. (For a sophisticated attempt to unite the movements of human creative imagination and of divine self-revelation in the event of Jesus Christ, see Milbank, 1997, pp.123–44: 'A Christological Poetics'.)

The question of realism is inescapable in religion as it is in science. Scientific practice, in the laboratory and the observatory, takes realism for granted. It is the philosophy of science that asks whether that realist assumption is justified and how it needs to be qualified. Religion too takes realism for granted. Most worship is probably unreflective and uncritical: it is content to assume that the objects it evokes (divine beings, angels, miracles, prophecies, historical revelations, eschatology) reside precisely as described out there in the sacred realm. It is the task of theology, and specifically of that branch of theology known as Fundamental Theology, to ask whether that realist assumption is justified and how it needs to be qualified.

Cassirer was right to claim that science is distinguished from religion because it knows that its symbols are symbols, provided that he included the philosophy of science within 'science'. But religion is not the same thing as theology, though it can be imbued with it to a greater or lesser extent. Theology also knows that its symbols are symbols. It recognises their limitations, but believes that the symbolic imagination is the best guide to truth. It may wish to make more scope for reverent agnosticism than popular religion would be comfortable with, but it performs an essential service to religion in guarding it from the spiritual inflation that comes from taking the symbols all too literally. A theology of symbolic forms knows that there is a vital difference between a literal statement and a true statement. It has learned from St Augustine that God is a poet and from William Blake that God is an artist too. What do you have to do to get on the wavelength of a poet or artist? You attune your spirit to beauty, you listen intently to the imagination, you reach out to form, you turn towards the radiance of the inspired word, you open your being to the aesthetic vision.

14 Mythic realism

Myth is the constellation of numinous or sacred symbols in narrative form. It is the literary genre that is unavoidable when communities speak of the origins or destiny of their history, the great transformations that it has undergone and the involvement of divine beings in it. That is entirely without prejudice to the real existence of such divine beings and their actual involvement in a history that has a divinely-given source and a divinely-intended destiny. Myth is a symbolic language and unless we are alive to the role of symbols in sustaining the dimension of depth in human life – unless we can read this language – we will misunderstand it. Myth presupposes that human existence, individually and corporately, is constituted by narrative; it is one form of such narrative – a sacred form, a form that evokes ultimate identity, a form that sets humankind *coram Deo*, before the face of God. The paradox of myth is that it is the only way in which the most significant aspects of human history can be presented to us, while at the same time it conceals from our gaze what actually – empirically – happened. The Bible is shot through with myth – transfigured though it is by the objectivity of the revelation of which it is a primary form. Christian credal beliefs are couched in mythic form, for they are a narrated unfolding of the sacred symbols of the Christian revelation.

To assert the mythic character of some biblical and credal material is not, I want to emphasise again, to prejudge the question of its truth and relevance. It is simply to identify the character and type of certain biblical statements. It is merely to settle the preliminary question of genre. We need to know the genre of a text before we begin the business of interpretation. While the genre of Genesis 1 may be uncontroversially recognised as myth, the genre of the infancy narratives and the resurrection appearances in the Gospels is more open to question. The Christian interpreter does not doubt that there is a real event of divine–human encounter lying behind these narratives. Christian faith postulates the reality of a certain personal life which, mediated through the response of the disciples and through all the cultural and religious influences that bore upon them, produced the picture of Jesus as the Christ in the New Testament (as Tillich would put it), the form of the beauty of God embodied in Christ (as Von Balthasar would say). Whether with Tillich we embrace the historico-critical method or with Von Balthasar we spurn it, we tend all the same to postulate a correspondence, symmetry, isomorphism or *analogia imaginis* between the picture or form of Jesus Christ in the Gospels and the actual historical life that gave rise to it.

Myth and history

Tillich is right to insist on the importance of distinguishing between historical, legendary and mythical elements in the Bible. He is surely also correct to claim that, of the three, it is the mythical that is most important for the Christian faith (Tillich, 1968, vol.2, pp.123f.), for it is the archetypally symbolic quality of myth that gives universal significance to its message. To provoke reflection, let us glance at two extreme versions of the claim that it is the myth that counts.

In the late nineteenth century – after Darwin and evolution, Strauss and biblical myth, Wellhausen and 'higher criticism' – Matthew Arnold advocated abandoning the quest for historical foundations for faith and embracing instead the mythic or poetic expression of religious meaning.

> There is not a creed which is not shaken, not an accredited dogma which is not shown to be questionable, not a received tradition which does not threaten to dissolve. Our religion has materialized itself in the fact, in the supposed fact; it has attached its emotion to the fact, and now the fact is failing it. But for poetry the idea is everything ... the idea is the fact.
>
> (Arnold, 'The Study of Poetry', cited in Coulson, 1981, p.97)

Nearly a hundred years later, Northrop Frye wrote: 'It has been obvious for at least a century that "mythical accretions" are what the Bible is: it is the bits of credible history that are expendable, however many of them there may be.'

> If the historical element in the Bible were a conscientious, inaccurate, imperfect history like the Anglo-Saxon Chronicle, we could understand how important it would be to make a further reconstruction of the history. But when it shows such an exuberant repudiation of everything we are accustomed to think of as historical evidence, perhaps we should be looking for different categories and criteria altogether.
>
> (Frye, 1982, p.42)

Frye therefore suggests that it is in keeping with the actual nature of the Bible that its myths should be read poetically, that is to say with an aesthetic intention, for 'certainly, the poetic parts of the Bible are genuinely poetic in a way that the historical parts are not historical' (ibid., p.46).

Unfortunately it is not as simple as that. It is true that the historical, factual, basis of biblical revelation is almost irretrievable and is both conveyed to us and concealed from us by the mythical tenor of much biblical material. It is undeniable that realities beyond our ken – creation, prehistory, divine intervention, eschatology – must be depicted in symbol and myth or not at all. It is also correct that part of our response to biblical narrative is aesthetic: we respond to it as we do to poetry, its beauty of form captivates us. But for the Christian believer and the Christian theologian a further, deeper response is required: a theological judgement regarding the divine revelation that lies behind and within the mythic, poetic forms – and we can never allow ourselves to forget that that revelation is given in salvation-history, which is at least history, even though it may be very much more.

Following Wilson Knight (1933, p.76), we might suggest that, as far as the relation between myth and history is concerned, we can distinguish three orders of event.

1   The sort of trivial event that is factually or historically true, but imaginatively insignificant: yesterday I went for a walk; today I made a cup of tea; tomorrow the postman will call. Though there have been novelists and poets who have ascribed deep poetic significance to the trivia of diurnal routine – and though to the eyes of faith the most ordinary action may reflect the glory of God – such commonplace happenings are too frequent to be memorable or significant.

2   The event that, though factually untrue, is symbolically or morally highly significant: *King Lear* never happened in real life, but its significance is immense. It remains within the sphere of the imagination – though we should not overlook the fact that *Lear* is an artefact, having been incarnated (as it were) in the material world and written by a material person, William Shakespeare, at a particular time, in a particular place, on material paper, with a material quill pen, and performed by material actors in a material theatre. Though the story did not happen, the imaginative creation is embedded in history. It seems to be along these lines that Arnold and Frye want us to interpret the Bible.

3   The event that is true to fact and at the same time imaginatively and spiritually significant: the history of Israel, the life and destiny of Jesus Christ, the mission of the Christian Church. The Incarnation is the paradigm of an event that is grounded in history, yet by its transcendent significance, expressed in symbol and myth, hides that history from us. Wilson Knight suggests that in myth 'fact and value are reintegrated, and an immediate, unfalsified reality created'. The New Testament, he claims, is neither pure poetry nor straight history but a marriage or fusing of the two. Often it reads like a work of art, yet reality is so stamped upon it that we are convinced that this is no fiction (Wilson Knight, 1933, pp.70, 83). With this third position we go beyond Arnold

and Frye and attempt to do justice to the salvation-history character of the Bible.

Demythologisation?

We need to explore carefully the relationship between the meaning, significance or message of scripture and the literary vehicle, strongly mythic, through which it is conveyed. Bultmann's solution – demythologisation – was to abandon the mythic vehicle in order to save the essential message for an age to which myth was alien. First we need to ask: what does Bultmann mean by 'myth'?

1   For Bultmann, myth is essentially *anthropomorphic*. 'Myth speaks of gods in the same way as of men, of their actions as human actions' (Bultmann in Bartsch, 1953, p.183). Myth 'conceives of the gods as endowed with superhuman power and of their actions as incalculable, as capable of breaking the normal, ordinary order of events' (Bultmann, 1960, p.19). All talk of God 'acting' in the world is mythological because it is anthropomorphic. Bultmann himself prefers the verb 'objectivize' to the adjective 'anthropomorphic'. To objectivize God in myth is to make divine action visible to the eye of the beholder and thus demonstrable and even controllable (Schmithals, 1968, p.272). Myth objectifies by introducing other-worldly causality into the chain of cause and effect in this world (Bultmann in Bartsch, 1953, p.183).

As far as his fear of anthropomorphism is concerned, Bultmann is in the company of the Old Testament prophets when they rebuked the people for thinking of Yahweh as like one of themselves. The critique of myth in this sense is part of the constant battle of theology to refine our concepts of God. With regard to divine intervention, Bultmann is surely right to insist that the divine action is always hidden: the acts of God are always ambiguous because they are not demonstrable. But neither of these points so far departs from the theological consensus and justifies demythologising.

2   For Bultmann myth is *unscientific*. As he famously said – the reference to electric light and the wireless sounds quaint now – 'it is impossible to use electric light and the wireless and to avail ourselves of modern medical and surgical discoveries, and at the same time to believe in the New Testament world of spirits and miracles' (ibid., p.5). Myth embodies a primitive and discredited worldview. The message of Jesus in the Gospels is bound up with such mythological notions as the three-decker universe, spirit-possession as the explanation of various medical conditions and the expectation of the imminent catastrophic end of the world (Bultmann, 1960, pp.14f.).

Bultmann's presuppositions show through clearly here, but I cannot see that they are controversial. No one holds the biblical cosmology today. Some believe in demon-possession, but that does not stop them calling in the doctor when they fall ill. Belief in the imminent catastrophic end of the world (as Bultmann has it) has been made difficult by the passing of time: how long can something remain 'imminent'? 'The course of history has refuted mythology' (ibid., p.14). Nor do I think that Bultmann is open to objection for insisting that the modern worldview is the criterion for the interpretation of scripture (Schmithals, 1968, p.259; Bultmann, 1960, p.35). As Bultmann says, everyone approaches scripture with presuppositions. There is no alternative to the modern scientific worldview which provides us with our presuppositions for the rest of life. No one claims that first-century cosmology, psychology and eschatology are still binding on Christians. 'To demythologise is to deny that the message of scripture and of the church is bound to an ancient worldview which is obsolete' (ibid., p.36).

However, Bultmann uses myth as a blanket concept and, as a result, indiscriminately identifies belief in a pre-scientific cosmology, demon-possession and the end of the world with myth as such. Changing world-views are not identical with myth, though they may draw on myth or lend themselves to myth. Our own cosmology, psychology and expectations for the future of the world have changed drastically in the past century: does that make them mythological? Like the contributors to *The Myth of God Incarnate*, Bultmann is operating with a defective concept of myth. He is confusing presuppositions about worldview with myth as a genre. This is because myth is an all-embracing category for Bultmann. He reduces all realist talk about God, in the New Testament and in theology, to myth. He fails to differentiate between authoritative theological models such as incarnation and atonement, on the one hand, and their culturally condi-tioned vehicles, such as cosmology and demonology, on the other.

3   For Bultmann, myth is the vehicle of *religious truth*. This truth is eschatological in that it reveals the fulfilment of God's purpose beyond the present age; it is an invitation, a summons to authentic existence. All myth expresses humanity's understanding of itself in the world. The biblical myths, therefore, express the biblical understanding of humanity's true existence (Bultmann in Bartsch, 1953, pp.10f.). For Bultmann this is to be found in the response of faith to the encounter with God through God's word. The Christian message (*kerygma*) is contained in the myth, but is also detachable from it. The myth must be stripped away so that the message stands out clearly (ibid., pp.3f.). Bultmann says:

> Christian preaching is *kerygma*, that is, a proclamation addressed not to the theoretical reason, but to the hearer as a self ... Demythologising will make clear this function of preaching as a personal message, and in doing so it will eliminate a false stumbling block and bring into sharp focus the real stumbling block, the word of the cross.
>
> (Bultmann, 1960, p.36)

Clearly, Bultmann does not have a reductionist view of myth. He gives it a high status as the embodiment of God's word. But for him there is no intrinsic connection between the biblical myths and that word: they are, it seems, the disposable container of the message. This seems to me to evince a lack of respect for the givenness of the historical forms of divine revelation. They were, presumably, chosen by God in God's freedom in order to mediate revelation. It would appear to follow that they should have normative value for Christian theology. However much we may wish to interpret, apply and expound them, we are not at liberty to discard them.

Bultmann protested that his purpose in the programme of demythologising was not the reductionist one of making 'religion more acceptable to modern man by trimming the traditional biblical texts, but to make clearer to modern man what the Christian faith is' (Bultmann in Bartsch, 1962, p.183). This seems to me to be nothing less than is demanded by any Christian apologetic; Bultmann's mistake may have been to think that he knew better than the Bible how to do this.

The difficulties in Bultmann's concept of demythologising lie deeper than his deficient understanding of myth – in the corollaries that demythologising has in his theology: his historical scepticism, his non-interventionism, his abandonment of the narrative character of faith, his lack of image and form, and his attenuated grasp of the *kerygma*. These deserve fuller treatment than would be appropriate here, but they are worth mentioning as they have consequences for Bultmann's treatment of the category of myth and help to explain his motives.

1 *Historical scepticism* Bultmann believes that it is enough for the *kerygma* for us to know of Jesus that he lived and died. But here we must distinguish between what is the minimum necessary for there to be a Christian proclamation and what historical research can achieve in practice. Bultmann's own historical reconstructions of the Gospels, though tending to the minimal, went well beyond the bare datum that Jesus lived and died. It is worth comparing Tillich here. For Tillich, faith needs to know that the New Being has appeared in a particular person. Indeed, faith carries the assurance that it did. But the certitude of faith does not entail certainty about the conclusions of historical research. It cannot even guarantee that the name of this person was Jesus. Moreover, this does not matter! (Tillich, 1968, vol.2, pp.123, 125, 131). Bultmann and Tillich are right to point out that it is not the amount of assured information that we have about Jesus that is theologically significant; it is the myth that carries the message. Bultmann wanted to strip away the myth to bring out the power of the message for salvation (authentic existence); Tillich reinterpreted the myth to create a new myth or symbol, that of the New Being appearing under the conditions of existence in the person of Jesus as the Christ. The less reliable historical information we have about Jesus, the greater freedom we enjoy to handle what we do have, namely the myths. Bultmann is in the same boat as

Jung in this connection: both see the historical Jesus as swamped and obscured by the expectations and myths of the first century. Both fail to make sufficient allowance for the corrective, normative impact of Jesus of Nazareth on those expectations. Utterly implausibly, they make Jesus a cipher.

2   *Non-interventionism*   Bultmann has a firmly non-interventionist concept of divine action. He rejects any idea of God intervening in the causal nexus of events to make things happen that would otherwise not happen, or to prevent things happening once the causal nexus is set in train. Bultmann's reasons are not, as we might suppose, connected with the question of theodicy: why does not God step in to heal the sick, end wars, destroy concentration camps, prevent accidents and natural disasters? He was actually unmoved, as far as his faith was concerned, by either the First or the Second World War (Jones, 1991, p.18). Bultmann's motive in his non-interventionism was his modern scientific worldview. God does not manipulate the elements but works through the human heart. To speak of God acting in the world is mythological unless it refers to the individual's experience of divine grace. But of course myth typically depicts divine interaction with the world; it is the only means we have of doing so.

3   *Non-narrativity*   As we have seen, narrative is one of the essential components of myth. Sacred symbols, constellated in narrative form comprise myth. Bultmann not only demythologises the *kerygma* but denarrativises it. His existentialist interpretation finds the encounter of God and man in the eschatological moment. Bultmann's is a theological actualism with a vengeance. Because statements of faith are abstracted from the world and its history, they become statements of a timeless reality. Bultmann makes this explicit in his reply to his critics:

> If the revelation of God becomes effective only on specific occasions in the 'now' of existence [*Dasein*] (as an eschatological event), and if onto-logical analysis points us to the temporality in which we have to exist, an aspect of existence is thereby exposed which faith, but only faith, understands as the relatedness of man to God.
>
> (Jones, 1991, p.132)

Narrative and myth stand or fall together.

4   *Lack of image and form*   In dispensing with myth, Bultmann disposes not only of narrative but also of image or symbol, for myth comprises the constellation of numinous symbols in narrative form. Bultmann thus abandons symbol and form. Von Balthasar claims that Bultmann's deep seriousness about Christ is 'full of anguish because of its total lack of imagery and form' and constitutes 'a real dead end for Protestantism'. Von Balthasar contrasts this approach with that of Barth who saved Protestant

theology from shipwreck by a dogmatics that was creative in both imagery and form. Once again the glory of God was allowed to shine forth in Protestant doctrinal theology (Von Balthasar, 1982–9, vol.1, pp.52f.).

5 *Attenuated kerygma* Bultmann's understanding of the Christian message is individualistic, private, internal and highly verbalised. The message has a purely subjective application. He rules out any claims about God's action in the world, say in creation or atonement. No wonder he found mythology uncongenial, for its *raison d'être* is to depict the relation between God and the world, God and history, God and the community. Myth is antithetical to the privatisation and interiorisation of religion.

Finally, in a study that has drawn on depth psychology among a range of non-theological disciplines, it is worth noting the insight that Jung brought to the question of demythologising. In a letter of 1951, Jung deplored Bultmann's agenda as a consequence of 'Protestant rationalism' and forecast that it would lead to a progressive impoverishment of symbolism. This would threaten the psychological equilibrium of Protestantism: 'What is left over does not suffice to express the prodigal (and dangerous) world of the unconscious, to join it to consciousness or, as the case may be, to hold it in check' (Jung, 1973–6, vol.1, p.7). Tillich, who took the unconscious seriously and whose systematic theology is structured by symbolism, claimed that 'complete demythologisation is not possible when speaking about the divine' (Tillich, 1968, vol.2, p.33).

Demythologisation or deliteralisation?

There is a respectable precedent for declining to take biblical and credal myth literally in Calvin's reinterpretation of Christ's descent into hell (mentioned in the creeds and the New Testament: 1 Peter 3.19) as his bearing of the wrath of God on the cross (Calvin, n.d., II.xvi.8–12). But there is still resistance among more conservative theologians to the mere recognition of the presence of myth in the Bible and Christian beliefs. In his contribution to the Church of England Doctrine Commission's report *Believing in the Church* (Doctrine Commission, 1981, pp.70ff.), Anthony Thiselton argues that 'myth' is an unsuitable and unhelpful category for interpreting the Christian faith. He believes that it endangers the 'irreducible paradigms' of biblical Christianity on three counts:

1   Myth tends to be associated with a worldview which is primitive, uncritical and pre-scientific. This is unjust and patronising towards the Bible.
2   Myth suggests that language is some kind of opaque wrapping which needs to be detached from the thought which it both expresses and obscures. Biblical truth is inseparable from its linguistic vehicle.

3   Myth does not lend itself to realist claims (however that realism may
     need to be qualified) for its message, but is often employed in a subjec-
     tivist and pragmatic way that fails to anchor it in objective reality.

I believe that Thiselton is being unnecessarily timid about myth here. It is
true that 'myth' is open to misunderstanding, but one of the greatest
stumbling blocks (as Bultmann liked to put it) to Christian belief in the
modern world is the gross literalism with which those both inside and
outside the Church take the Bible and Christian doctrine – with the result
that neither is taken seriously. In my view the task of apologetics, at a fairly
sophisticated level, among the intelligentsia, would be helped by a sensible
deployment of 'myth'. And if apologetics and Fundamental Theology are
unified, as Rahner advocates convincingly, myth must become a topic of
Fundamental Theology. Hence this book! At a more popular level, however,
Thiselton is, I am sure, right to urge caution: the word 'myth' has become
incorrigibly debased in general currency and means merely falsehood and
illusion. But if we cannot use the name in preaching and the media, we can
certainly use the thing. We must make it clear that 'parable' and 'symbolic
story' play a part in the Bible and Christian beliefs. Now to reply specifically
to Thiselton's points:

1   Though an age of science and technology, such as ours, undoubtedly
     has its own myths, in the case of the Bible we are dealing precisely with
     a worldview that is uncritical and unscientific. Those adjectives are not
     intended in a disparaging, patronising sense, but in a neutral, descriptive
     sense. We do not honour the Bible for its outdated cosmology but for
     other reasons.
2   Though Thiselton is right to protest against the illusion that language is
     like a wrapping that can be removed to reveal thoughts of abiding
     value, we are not so much concerned with the language of the Bible as
     with whole symbols and symbolic narratives. There is no reason to
     suppose that the 'canonical' expressions of the Bible are the only ones
     that we are permitted to use. Obviously the Church has never thought
     itself bound in this way. We are free to 'translate' biblical statements
     into secondary forms more immediately intelligible to our present cul-
     ture (but without denying the normative authority of the primary scrip-
     tural expressions).
3   Though Thiselton is absolutely right to warn of the tendency to use
     'myth' in a non-realist sense, the same danger applies to all figurative
     modes, including metaphor and symbol: are they to be out of bounds
     too? Our earlier discussion of symbolic realism holds out the promise of
     an alternative approach. If there can be symbolic realism, why not
     mythic realism? That question will occupy us immediately.

If 'myth' is unhelpful, according to Thiselton and the Doctrine Commission, it is not clear to me what the alternative should be. Thiselton himself speaks simply of the Christian 'story', but the question remains: what sort of story – history, legend, myth? I stand with Tillich on the importance of distinguishing between these. The greater danger, it seems to me, is that, if 'myth' is eschewed altogether in theological work and its equivalents 'parable' and 'symbolic narrative' are shirked in more popular presentations, we shall find ourselves falling back into a literalistic interpretation of the Christian 'story'. Nothing could be more unhelpful.

The debate about the mythic status of the Incarnation has been bedevilled by the use of the word 'literal' on both sides of the argument (see Hick, 1978, pp.34, 171, 201f.; Goulder, 1979, p.4). Hick himself is a notorious offender (see Hick, 1973, pp.167, 176f.). In his recent interpretation of the Incarnation, Hick argues that it is best understood not as myth but as metaphor: 'the idea of divine incarnation is better understood as metaphorical than as literal' (Hick, 1993, p.ix). The Christian idea of the Incarnation, he suggests, 'has never been given a satisfactory literal sense; but ... it makes excellent metaphorical sense' (ibid., p.12). 'The dogma of Jesus' deity' is not 'a literal claim with universal implications' but metaphorical discourse that makes sense within the Christian community (ibid., p.88). Much hangs on what Hick means by 'literal' and 'metaphorical'.

Literal use of language is defined by Hick as 'simply standard use within a given linguistic community', conveying agreed meanings. The literal sense of a word is its publicly understood – universalisable – sense which may be verified by recourse to a dictionary (ibid., p.99). The metaphorical use of language breaks away from this consensus, using words in a private, non-standard sense which cannot be accommodated by a dictionary with its fixed meanings. Through frequent use, metaphors lose their novelty, becoming 'dead metaphors' and tantamount to literal speech (ibid., pp.99–101). What does this imply for the Incarnation? It means (as Hick has suggested before; see Hick, 1973, pp.176f.) that 'Jesus embodied, or incarnated, the ideal of human life lived in faithful response to God, so that God was able to act through him, and he accordingly embodied a love which is a human reflection of the divine love' (Hick, 1993, p.ix).

Here Hick is clearly employing what Lindbeck calls the cultural-linguistic model of Christian doctrine (Lindbeck, 1980): 'The son of God metaphor is part of the private, idiosyncratic family speech of this community. But it should not be turned into a metaphysical dogma which is supposed to have objective and universal truth' (Hick, 1993, p.79). But there are also overtones of Lindbeck's 'expressive' view of doctrines in which they function to articulate the subjective religiosity of the believer – the Christian religious affections expressed in speech, as Schleiermacher classically put it. In terms of the approach we have been developing in the present study, Hick's interpretation of the Incarnation falls short in three respects:

1   Its understanding of the difference between metaphorical and literal
    speech is misconceived. As we have argued earlier, metaphorical not
    literal meaning is the norm for significant discourse. Metaphor is pri-
    mary and embodies insight into the real world. It is not metaphor that is
    the private language – it is in touch with reality – but literal speech,
    which is lazy, uninspired and unproductive. With regard to the Incarna-
    tion, of course the term is a metaphor (just as Hick's favoured term
    'embodied' is): the central Christian doctrine of the unique identity of
    God and a human individual cannot be reduced to the image of
    'enfleshment' which is what 'incarnation' means. But, as we have seen,
    metaphors like this are pointers, windows, arrows to the truth to which
    they testify. So Hick is right to say that the Incarnation is a metaphor,
    but wrong to draw his reductionist conclusions from that.

2   The cultural-linguistic model of doctrine that Hick borrows from
    Lindbeck, is itself inadequate to the import of Christian beliefs. Doc-
    trines do indeed have a cultural-linguistic function, but they only have
    that because they have a primary and determinative cognitive function.
    It is because they are believed to be true that they are important to the
    community and its identity. So once again, Hick is right to assert the
    cultural-linguistic provenance of a doctrine such as the Incarnation, but
    wrong in the reductionist consequences that he deduces from that.

3   In so far as Hick approximates to the expressive theory of doctrine (of
    which Schleiermacher is the greatest exponent), as articulating an in-
    ward disposition and intention to follow a way of life commensurate
    with those beliefs, he fails to do justice to the aesthetic aspect which was
    important to Schleiermacher as a Romantic. This religious subjectivity
    is quickened by the imagination, not as fantasy or even Fancy, but as a
    real reaching out to its object apprehended in the image or form. So,
    once again, Hick is not wrong to imply an expressive origin for doc-
    trines, but he really fails to see the point that this depends on 'the truth
    of the imagination', for 'what the imagination seizes as Beauty must be
    truth' (Keats, 1954, p.48). There is a real cognitive intent even in aes-
    thetic expressivism.

The protagonists of *The Myth of God Incarnate* reject a 'literal' Incarnation;
their critics, the advocates of incarnational orthodoxy, sometimes seem to
suggest that to believe in the Incarnation one must take it 'literally'.
Nicholas Lash has astutely pointed out that 'running through several of the
contributions to *The Myth of God Incarnate* there is an assumption that
"literal" discourse is "objective", fact-asserting, whereas imaginative,
metaphorical, symbolic or mythological discourse is "subjective", expressive
of attitudes' – and that this entails the further assumption that there is a
clear and straightforward distinction between literal and metaphorical
language (Lash in Goulder, 1979, pp.21, 24). However, there is evidence that
defenders of incarnational orthodoxy are also prone to make these

assumptions. Then, indeed, 'ignorant armies clash by night' (Arnold, 'Dover Beach', in Palgrave, 1928, p.461). The fault on both sides is extenuated by the fact that these assumptions are endemic in modern theology because they are endemic in modern culture. If only we could acknowledge the metaphorical, symbolic and mythological status of the language of faith without letting go of the point that such language can be believed with a good conscience through an act of imaginative assent!

Three test cases

1 *Eschatology* Eschatology is an avowedly symbolic area of doctrine. Few would wish to deny that the doctrine of the 'last things' can only be stated in the form of metaphor, symbol and myth. In the Bible certain numinous eschatological symbols recur: the darkening of the sun and moon, the falling of the stars, earthquakes, the powers of primeval chaos (symbolised by the sea) let loose upon the world, clouds and trumpets. These themes are prosecuted from the Psalms and prophets of the Old Testament to the Gospels, Epistles and Revelation in the New. This is not the place to attempt to interpret this repertoire of symbols, but they are familiar to all readers or hearers of the scriptures.

> There will be signs in the sun, the moon and the stars, and on the earth distress among nations confused by the roaring of the sea and the waves ... For the powers of the heavens will be shaken. Then they will see the Son of Man coming in a cloud with power and great glory ... your redemption is drawing near.
>
> (Luke 21.25–8)

If myth deals with remote origins and distant destiny (as well as with divine–human encounter on the earth), we would expect eschatology to be expressed in mythic terms – that is to say, in symbols constelled in narrative form. But of course much hangs on one's definition of myth. In the late 1950s a discussion took place in the journal *Vetus Testamentum* with regard to eschatology and myth. S.B. Frost had argued that 'myth is opposed to eschatology by its very nature'. Myth is static whereas eschatology is dynamic. Myth presents eternal truths or cyclical events, but eschatology moves to a particular definitive conclusion according to the purpose of God. While apocalyptic combines eschatology and myth, a non-mythical eschatology is found in the prophets Amos, Isaiah, Zephaniah and possibly Micah (Frost, 1952).

Some years later, James Barr responded – not only to Frost but also to Bultmann. Against the latter Barr argued that the Old Testament – not New Testament cosmology (as Bultmann had asserted, with his famous references to the three-decker universe) – should be determinative of the meaning of myth in biblical studies. Mythological thinking should be seen as a totality because it represents a striving to achieve a complete worldview. For Barr, myth is not properly symbolic knowledge and not all symbolism is myth. The character of myth lies above all in its doctrine of correspondences, of hidden harmony in the cosmos, society and individual life. But this unreconstructed conception of myth is shattered by the salvation-history theme of ancient Israel. Barr believes that the central position in Israelite thought is occupied by history rather than by myth and that 'such survivals of myth as exist are controlled by the historical sense'. Barr rejects Frost's claim that apocalyptic represents the fusion of eschatology and mythology, and regards apocalyptic as a kind of symbolic philosophy of history (Barr, 1959).

The fact that apocalyptic is a genre of eschatology – one particularly rich in symbol and myth – reinforces the argument that eschatology is intrinsically symbolic-mythical. G.B. Caird asserts that mythological language forms the exact counterpart to eschatological language (Caird, 1994, p.249). If, as we have claimed, realist symbolism refers but does not define, gestures but does not grasp, how much more true is this of eschatology which deals with mysteries hidden in the counsels of God for the fulfilment of God's purpose for the world?

The Niceno-Constantinopolitan creed holds out eschatological beliefs for us to affirm: 'He will come again in glory to judge the living and the dead, and his Kingdom will have no end ... We look for the resurrection of the dead and the life of the world to come.' Though the figurative element here is muted and the statements are spare and sober, the clauses of the creed that touch on the last things are expressed as narrative bearing numinous symbols – that is to say, as myth. The 1938 report of the Archbishops' Doctrine Commission was not at all coy about this aspect of eschatology: 'Inasmuch as eschatological beliefs and doctrines are concerned, of necessity, with matters in respect of which "eye hath not seen nor ear heard", these beliefs are inevitably expressed in symbolical language.' The Commission went on to be outspokenly specific: 'We ought to reject quite frankly the literalistic belief in a future resurrection of the actual physical frame which is laid in the tomb' (Doctrine Commission, 1938, pp.203, 209).

We have been arguing throughout this book that there is a vital aesthetic component in all belief: we see the beauty of the form of truth presented to us by divine revelation in scripture or by the Church in its liturgies and creeds. It has persuasive and convincing power to win our assent. We have been careful to note that the aesthetic is insufficient and even dangerous without the cognitive and the moral – but its importance, often overlooked, remains. It seems that in eschatology the aesthetic element in assent is particularly pronounced. How do we believe in such elusively expressed doctrines as the coming again of Christ (the *parousia*), the resurrection of the body, the final judgement and the vision of God enjoyed by the blessed, except by an intuitive, almost aesthetic assent to the symbolism and by allowing ourselves to be caught up into the self-involving narrative in which those powerful symbols are embedded?

Perhaps nothing evokes the awesome immediate presence of God or the soul's sense of utter unworthiness to enter that presence more powerfully than the combination of Elgar's music of 1900 and Newman's poem of 1865–6, *The Dream of Gerontius* (Newman, 1908):

> Take me away, and in the lowest deep
> There let me be,
> And there in hope the lone night-watches keep,
> Told out for me.
> There, motionless and happy in my pain,
> Lone, not forlorn –
> There will I sing my sad perpetual strain,
> Until the morn,
> There will I sing and soothe my stricken breast,
> Which ne'er can cease
> To throb, and pine, and languish, till possest
> Of its Sole Peace.

Quite apart from any difficulties that one may have about the doctrine of purgatory, the hints of masochism in this are disturbing – 'happy in my pain' – and demand to be set beside the verse of 'Praise to the Holiest in the Height' that is never sung, with its brutal Platonic dualism of soul and body and violent images of purgation:

> Glory to Him who evermore
> By truth and justice reigns;
> Who tears the soul from out its case,
> And burns away its stains!

But, making a willing suspension of disbelief as far as the literal sense is concerned, we readily assent to what Newman is saying symbolically about our total dependence on the mercy of God, the need for a process of purification and education to prepare us to see God, and the progressive nature of our journey after death, ever nearer to the heart of God's love.

When we hear Berlioz's overpowering setting of the *Dies Irae* in his Requiem Mass, with its mighty fanfares of brass, seemingly coming from the four points of the compass, giving way to thunderous drummings as the choral basses announce the Last Trump, we believe more strongly – though not more 'literally' – in the truth that 'we must all stand before the judgement seat of Christ' (2 Corinthians 5.10):

> *Tuba mirum spargens sonum*
> *Per sepulchra regionum*

Coget omnes ante thronum.
Mors stupebit et natura
Cum resurget creatura
Judicandi responsura.
Liber scriptus proferetur
In quo totum continetur
Unde mundus judicetur.

A trumpet, spreading a wondrous sound
Through the graves of all lands,
Will drive everyone before the throne.
Death and nature shall be astonished
When all creation rises again
To answer to the Judge.
A book, written in, will be brought forth
In which is contained all that is,
Out of which the world shall be judged.

Only a philistine would ask: what will actually happen? We do not need to question the literal truth of the trumpet, the book and the bodies rising from their graves. We give our assent to the meanings (in Moore's sense, the propositions) that they represent. It could all be put in the more prosaic, less evocative language of human accountability, the continuity of the person after death, the vindication of God's just purposes, and so on – but what would that achieve? It is not the language of Zion, but it is appropriate to theological enquiry where pre-reflective symbol and myth, together with previous interpretations of these, come under critical scrutiny.

2   *The resurrection of Jesus*   If we recall for a moment Bultmann's three criteria of mythology – that it is anthropomorphic (picturing God at work in human terms), unscientific (belonging to an obsolete worldview) and at the same time the vehicle of religious truth (embodying the *kerygma*) – we can, I think, agree that eschatology fits this description. But no one is likely to want to go to the stake for their eschatology alone. What of the more sensitive and central topic of the resurrection of Jesus Christ? It belongs to eschatology, for the resurrection of Jesus is the inauguration – if not the actual fulfilment – of eschatology, yet it also impinges on the Incarnation and the doctrine of the person of Christ, which is the very touchstone of orthodoxy.

The biblical resurrection narratives certainly correspond to myth taken simply as a literary genre. They tell of divine–human interaction. They are anthropomorphic in their deployment of angelic figures to interpret what is going on. They attempt to describe events that transcend our framework of space and time – especially when, as so often in the New Testament, the resurrection is inseparably linked to the ascension and glorification of Jesus. Then these narratives are actually bursting with symbolism: they have been creatively crafted around certain key symbols. The early morning visit to the tomb by the women suggests the ancient belief (found frequently in Dante) that a dream just before daybreak has a visionary quality and can disclose the profoundest truth. The elemental special effects in Matthew (earthquake and lightning) indicate cosmic significance as well as being recognisable eschatological stage props. Men and women hovering on the edge of the open tomb, the place of revelation and new life, suggests Nicodemus' question to Jesus in John 3: 'Can a man enter again his mother's womb and be born?'. The symbolic (eucharistic) feeding of the disciples, when the risen Christ was made known to them in the breaking of the bread, structures several of the narratives.

The resurrection stories, as symbol-bearing narratives, meet the criteria for myth. But that does not begin to settle the question of 'what really happened'. It does not rule out a physical resurrection or resuscitation if that is what the evidence points to. It does not establish that the resurrection appearances were either objective or subjective visions. However, recognising the story as belonging to the genre of myth does have implications for the theological interpretation of the story or event. It entails, first, that we cannot know with any certainty what did happen; second, that something momentous enough to generate interpretations at the mythic level certainly did take place, and, third, that the symbols (mostly eschatological, especially in Mark and Matthew) that stud the narrative are the surest guide to what the evangelists are attempting to convey (cf. Avis, 1993).

3 *The Incarnation* Finally we come to the crux of mythic realism, the Incarnation of God in Jesus Christ. The symposium *The Myth of God Incarnate* popularised the idea that the mythical genre of Incarnation language made the Church's received teaching, embodied in the Niceno-Constantinopolitan creed, incredible if not actually nonsensical. More recently, the editor of that volume, John Hick, has expressed a preference for 'metaphor' rather than 'myth' to designate the genre of Incarnation (Hick, 1993) but, as we have seen above, the reductionist consequences are unchanged and open to objection. What then are the metaphors, symbols and myths of the doctrine of the Incarnation?

The term 'incarnation' is itself a metaphor as it speaks of enfleshment. The key text, John 1.14, says that the Word 'became flesh' (*sarx egeneto*) and flesh is a central biblical metaphor for mortal humanity (cf. Matthew 16.17; 1 Corinthians 15.50). Both the Latin (*verbum caro factum est*) and the English perpetuate the biblical idiom, the image of the physical flesh as representing the whole human being. While the Incarnation is strictly speaking a metaphor, it serves as a symbol because of the weight of the tradition it carries and because it identifies Christianity as nothing else does, except the cross.

Similarly, the Pauline formula 'God was in Christ reconciling the world to himself' (2 Corinthians 5.19) is a metaphor – a spatial metaphor, one of containment or indwelling – and is perhaps to be interpreted in the light of the Pauline metaphor of the Christian's relation to Christ: 'in Christ' – a metaphor of location and incorporation.

The kenotic hymn of Philippians 2. 6–11 is a fully fledged myth because of its narrative, spatio-temporal structure. But its power to evoke and express faith is undimmed by our recognition of it as belonging to the genre of myth, for that faith is precisely a personal, existential and imaginative commitment to a person and a presence, not subscription to a formula laid down in 'literal' propositions. The truth of imagination correlates to the nature of metaphor, symbol and myth.

In the Niceno-Constantinopolitan creed we have an extremely powerful statement of the Incarnation, a piling of metaphor upon metaphor, symbol upon symbol, culminating in the myth of the Son of God descending from heaven.

> I believe ... in one Lord Jesus Christ, the only begotten Son of God, begotten of his Father before all worlds, God of God, Light of Light, very God of very God, begotten, not made, being of one substance with the Father, by whom all things were made: who for us men and for our salvation came down from heaven and was made man.

Donald MacKinnon used to quote with approval the saying of the pre-war Anglican theologian Oliver Quick that the clause 'he came down from heaven' was the litmus test of Christology, though I am sure that neither of them was unaware of the status of this image of descent from heaven as myth. Such a recognition does not rule out a doctrine of Christ's pre-existence, for that must inevitably be expressed mythically. The myth is certainly claiming much more than that Jesus of Nazareth was a human being uniquely open to God (though surely he was at least that). It speaks of the identity of Jesus with God. Now identity involves the tension of sameness and difference. The Incarnation does not mean that Jesus was God the Father walking around in human shape. There is distance from God in the image of descent and there is unity with God in the *homoousion* ('of one substance') of the Nicene Creed. There is the tension that is inescapable in the concept of identity in the finality of the eternal Son of God being made truly human.

The figurative language of the creed, based on the normative images of scripture, is not merely an expression of the Church's worship, or of the value of Jesus Christ within the faith-community. It is intended to be cognitive though not veridical. It is realist but not definitive. It denotes but does not describe. It speaks the truth but not literally. As metaphor, symbol and myth of the identity of Jesus with God, the incarnational doctrine of the creed is something which (in a realist but not literalist sense) we can and should gladly believe.

Bibliography

Abraham, W. and Holtzer, S.W., eds, 1987. *The Rationality of Religious Belief*, Oxford: Clarendon Press.

Abrams, M.H., 1953. *The Mirror and the Lamp: Romantic Theory and the Critical Tradition*, New York: Oxford University Press.

Abrams, M.H., 1971. *The Natural and the Supernatural: Tradition and Revolution in Romantic Literature*, Oxford: Oxford University Press.

Ackerman, R., 1987. *J.G. Frazer: His Life and Works*, Cambridge: Cambridge University Press.

Ackroyd, P., 1995. *Blake*, London: Sinclair-Stevenson.

Adorno, T.W., 1973. *Negative Dialectics*, London: Routledge and Kegan Paul.

Appleton, G., ed., 1985. *The Oxford Book of Prayer*, Oxford: Oxford University Press.

Aquinas, T., 1964–81. *Summa Theologiae*, Blackfriars edn, London: Eyre and Spottiswoode, and New York: McGraw-Hill.

Aristotle, 1886. *Rhetoric*, trans. J.E.C. Welldon, London: Macmillan.

Aristotle, 1987. *Poetics*, trans. R. Janko, Indianapolis and Cambridge: Hackett.

Ashworth, E.J., 1972. 'Descartes' Theory of Clear and Distinct Ideas', ed. R.J. Butler, *Cartesian Studies*, Oxford: Blackwell, pp.98–105.

Avis, P., 1986a. *Ecumenical Theology and the Elusiveness of Doctrine*, London: SPCK (*Truth Beyond Words*, Cambridge, MA: Cowley, 1985).

Avis, P., 1986b. *Foundations of Modern Historical Thought: From Machiavelli to Vico*, Beckenham: Croom Helm.

Avis, P., 1986c. *The Methods of Modern Theology*, Basingstoke: Marshall Pickering.

Avis, P., 1989. *Eros and the Sacred*, London: SPCK.

Avis, P., ed., 1993. *The Resurrection of Jesus Christ*, London: Darton, Longman and Todd.

Avis, P., 1995. *Faith in the Fires of Criticism: Christianity in Modern Thought*, London: Darton, Longman and Todd.

Avis, P., ed., 1997. *Divine Revelation*, London: Darton, Longman and Todd, and Grand Rapids: Eerdmans.

Bacon, F., 1905. *The Philosophical Works of Francis Bacon*, ed. J.M. Robertson, London: Routledge.

Barbour, I., 1974. *Myths, Models and Paradigms*, London: SCM.

Barbour, I., 1990. *Religion in an Age of Science*, London: SCM.

Barr, J., 1959. 'The Meaning of "Mythology" in Relation to the Old Testament', *Vetus Testamentum* 9: 1–10.

Barth, K., 1928. *The Word of God and the Word of Man*, London: Hodder and Stoughton.

Barth, K., 1960. *Anselm: Fides Quaerens Intellectum*, London: SCM.

Barth, K., 1972. *Protestant Theology in the Nineteenth Century*, London: SCM.

Barthes, R., 1972. *Mythologies*, London: Cape.

Bartsch, H.-W., ed., 1953. *Kerygma and Myth*, vol.1, London: SPCK.

Bartsch, H.-W., ed., 1962. *Kerygma and Myth*, vol.2, London: SPCK.

Beek, W.J.A.M., 1959. *John Keble's Literary and Religious Contribution to the Oxford Movement*, Nijmegen.

Berdyaev, N., 1948. *Freedom and the Spirit*, 4th edn, London: Bles.

Berlin, I., 1976. *Vico and Herder*, London: Hogarth Press.

Bevan, E., 1962. *Symbolism and Belief*, London: Fontana.

Bhaskar, R., 1978. *A Realist Theory of Science*, Hassocks: Harvester Press and New Jersey: Humanities Press.

Black, M., 1962. *Models and Metaphors*, Ithaca: Cornell University Press.

Blake, W., 1977. *The Complete Poems*, ed. A. Ostriker, Harmondsworth: Penguin.

Boswell, J., 1953. *Life of Johnson*, Oxford: Oxford University Press.

Brown, D. and Loades, A., eds, 1995. *The Sense of the Sacramental: Movement and Measure in Art and Music, Place and Time*, London: SPCK.

Bultmann, R., 1960. *Jesus Christ and Mythology*, London: SCM.

Burke, E., 1834. *A Philosophical Enquiry into the Origin of our Ideas of the Sublime and Beautiful with an Introductory Discourse Concerning Taste, The Works of the Right Hon. Edmund Burke*, vol.1, London: Holdsworth and Ball.

Burke, E., 1910. *Reflections on the Revolution in France*, ed. A.J. Grieve, London: Dent.

Burrell, D., 1973. *Analogy and Philosophical Language*, New Haven and London: Yale University Press.

Butler, J., 1889. *The Analogy of Religion Natural and Revealed*, London: Bohn.

Bynum, C.W., 1982. *Jesus as Mother: Studies in the Spirituality of the High Middle Ages*, Berkeley: University of California Press.

Caird, G.B., 1980. *The Language and Imagery of the Bible*, London: Duckworth.

Caird, G.B., 1994. *Theology of the New Testament*, ed. L.D. Hurst, Oxford: Clarendon Press.

Cairns, D., 1960. *A Gospel Without Myth? Bultmann's Challenge to the Preacher*, London: SCM.

Calasso, R., 1994. *The Marriage of Cadmus and Harmony*, London: Vintage.

Calvin, J., n.d. *Institutes of the Christian Religion*, trans. H. Beveridge, London: James Clarke.

Campbell, A.C., 1957. *On Selfhood and Godhood*, London: Allen and Unwin.

Cassirer, E., 1944. *An Essay on Man*, New Haven: Yale University Press.

Cassirer, E., 1946a. *Language and Myth*, New York: Dover.

Cassirer, E., 1946b. *The Myth of the State*, New Haven: Yale University Press.

Cassirer, E., 1955. *The Philosophy of Symbolic Forms*, vol.2, *Mythical Thought*, New Haven: Yale University Press.

Chesterton, G.K., 1950. *The Innocence of Father Brown*, Harmondsworth: Penguin.

Childs, B., 1962. *Myth and Reality in the Old Testament*, 2nd edn, London: SCM.

Cloud of Unknowing, The, see Wolters, 1961.

Coats, G.W., ed., 1985. *Saga, Legend, Tale, Novella, Fable: Narrative Forms in Old Testament Literature*, JSOT Supp. Series 35, Sheffield: Sheffield University Press.

Cohen, P.S., 1969. 'Theories of Myth', *Man* n.s. 4: 337–53.

Coleridge, S.T., 1884. *Table Talk*, ed. H. Morley, London: Routledge.

Coleridge, S.T., 1895. *Anima Poetae*, London: Heinemann.

Coleridge, S.T., 1960. *Shakespearean Criticism*, ed. T.M. Raysor, London: Dent, 2 vols.

Coleridge, S.T., 1965. *Biographia Literaria*, ed. G. Watson, London: Dent.

Coleridge, S.T., 1969. *Poetical Works*, ed. E.H. Coleridge, Oxford: Oxford University Press.

Coleridge, S.T., 1972. *Lay Sermons*, ed. R.J. White, *Collected Works*, vol.6, London: Routledge and Kegan Paul, and Princeton: Princeton University Press.

Coleridge, S.T., 1976. *On the Constitution of Church and State*, ed. J. Colmer, *Collected Works*, vol.10, London: Routledge and Kegan Paul, and Princeton: Princeton University Press.

Coleridge, S.T., 1990. *Notebooks*, ed. K. Coburn, *1819–1826*, vol.4, London: Routledge.

Coleridge, S.T., 1993. *Aids to Reflection*, ed. J. Beer, *Collected Works*, vol.9, London: Routledge and Kegan Paul, and Princeton: Princeton University Press.

Collier, A., 1994. *Critical Realism: An Introduction to Roy Bhaskar's Philosophy*, London: Verso.

Collingwood, R.G., 1939. *Autobiography*, Oxford: Oxford University Press.

Conquest., R., 1988. *New and Collected Poems*, London: Hutchinson.

Coulson, J., 1970. *Newman and the Common Tradition*, Oxford: Oxford University Press.

Coulson, J., 1981. *Religion and Imagination*, Oxford: Oxford University Press.

Crewdson, J., 1994. *Christian Doctrine in the Light of Michael Polanyi's Theory of Personal Knowledge*, Lewiston, Queenston and Lampeter: Edwin Mellen Press.

Crockett, W.R., 1989. *Eucharist: Symbol of Transformation*, New York: Pueblo.

Culler, J., 1981. *The Pursuit of Signs: Semiotics, Literature, Deconstruction*, London: Routledge and Kegan Paul.

Cupitt, D., 1986. *Life Lines*, London: SCM.

Davis, C., 1976. 'Religion and the Sense of the Sacred', *Proceedings of the Catholic Theological Society of America* 31: 87–105.

Davis, C., 1986. *What is Living, What is Dead in Christianity Today?*, San Francisco: Harper and Row.

Davis, C.F., 1989. *The Evidential Force of Religious Experience*, Oxford: Clarendon Press.

Descartes, R., 1968. *Discourse on Method and the Meditations*, trans. F.E. Sutcliffe, Harmondsworth: Penguin.

Dillistone, F.W., 1985. *Christianity and Symbolism*, London: SCM.

Dillistone, F.W., 1986. *The Power of Symbols*, London: SCM.

Doctrine Commission, 1938. *Doctrine in the Church of England*, London: SPCK.

Doctrine Commission, 1981. *Believing in the Church*, London: SPCK.

Doctrine Commission, 1987. *We Believe in God*, London: Church House Publishing.

Dodd, C.H., 1953. *The Interpretation of the Fourth Gospel*, Cambridge: Cambridge University Press.

Donne, J., 1950. *John Donne*, ed. J. Hayward, Harmondsworth: Penguin.

Dubrow, H., 1982. *Genre*, London: Methuen.

Duhem, P., 1954. *The Aim and Structure of Physical Theory*, 2nd edn, Princeton: Princeton University Press.

Duhem, P., 1969. *To Save the Phenomena*, Chicago: University of Chicago Press.

Duncan, H.D., 1968. *Symbols in Society*, New York: Oxford University Press.

Dundes, A., ed., 1984. *Sacred Narratives: Readings in the Theory of Myth*, Berkeley: University of California Press.

Durkheim, E., 1915. *The Elementary Forms of the Religious Life*, trans. J.W. Swain, London: George Allen and Unwin.

Eliade, M., 1964. *Myth and Reality*, London: Allen and Unwin.

Eliade, M., 1968. *Myths, Dreams and Mysteries*, London: Fontana.

Emmet, D., 1966. *The Nature of Metaphysical Thinking*, London: Macmillan.

Ernst, C., 1979. *Multiple Echo*, London: Darton, Longman and Todd.

Etchells, R., 1983. *A Model of Making*, London: Marshall, Morgan and Scott.

Farrer, A., 1948. *The Glass of Vision*, London: Dacre Press.

Fawcett, T., 1973. *Hebrew Myth and Christian Gospel*, London: SCM.

Feyerabend, P., 1975. *Against Method*, London: NLB.

Fodor, J., 1995. *Christian Hermeneutics: Paul Ricoeur and the Refiguring of Theology*, Oxford: Clarendon Press.

Fogelin, R., 1988. *Figuratively Speaking*, New Haven and London: Yale University Press.

Fowler, A., 1982. *Kinds of Literature: An Introduction to the Theory of Genres and Modes*, Oxford: Clarendon Press.

Frei, H., 1974. *The Eclipse of Biblical Narrative*, New Haven and London: Yale University Press.

Frei, H., 1975. *The Identity of Jesus Christ*, Philadelphia: Fortress Press.

Frei, H., 1993. *Theology and Narrative: Selected Essays*, ed. G. Hunsinger and W.C. Placher, New York and Oxford: Oxford University Press.

Freud, S., 1954. *The Interpretation of Dreams*, trans. and ed. J. Strachey, London: G. Allen and Unwin.

Frost, S.B., 1952. 'Eschatology and Myth', *Vetus Testamentum* 2: 70–80.

Frye, N., 1957. *The Anatomy of Criticism*, Princeton: Princeton University Press.

Frye, N., 1982. *The Great Code: The Bible as Literature*, London: Routledge and Kegan Paul.

Fukuyama, F., 1992. *The End of History and the Last Man*, Harmondsworth: Penguin and New York: Free Press.

Fukuyama, F., 1995. *Trust: The Social Virtues and the Creation of Prosperity*, London: Hamish Hamilton.

Furbank, P.N., 1970. *Reflections on the Word 'Image'*, London: Secker and Warburg.

Geertz, C., 1973. *The Interpretation of Cultures*, New York: Basic Books.

Gibson, J.C.L., 1998. *Language and Imagery in the Old Testament*, London: SPCK.

Gillingham, S., 1994. *The Poems and Psalms of the Hebrew Bible*, Oxford: Oxford University Press.

Gilson, E., 1964. *The Spirit of Thomism*, New York: Kenedy.

Goethe, J.W., 1959. *Faust: Part II*, trans. P. Wayne, Harmondsworth: Penguin.

Gombrich, E., 1969. 'The Use of Art for the Study of Symbols', in J. Hogg, ed., *Psychology and the Visual Arts: Selected Readings*, Harmondsworth: Penguin, pp.149–70.

Gombrich, E.H., 1972. *Symbolic Imagination: Studies in the Art of the Renaissance*, London: Phaidon Press.

Goulder, M., ed., 1979. *Incarnation and Myth: The Debate Continued*, London: SCM.

Gouwens, D.J., 1989. *Kierkegaard's Dialectic of the Imagination*, New York, Bern and Frankfurt am Main: Peter Lang.

Graves, R., 1960. *The Greek Myths*, Harmondsworth: Penguin, 2 vols.

Grene, M., 1966. *The Knower and the Known*, London: Faber and Faber.

Gurvich, G., 1971. *The Social Frameworks of Knowledge*, trans. M.A. and K.A. Thompson, Oxford: Blackwell.

Guyer, P., 1994. 'Locke's Philosophy of Language', in V. Chapple, ed., *The Cambridge Companion to Locke*, Cambridge: Cambridge University Press, pp.115–45.

Habermas, J., 1987. *The Philosophical Discourse of Modernity*, Cambridge: Polity Press.

Hacking, I., 1983. *Representing and Intervening*, Cambridge: Cambridge University Press.

Harries, R., 1993. *Art and the Beauty of God*, London: Mowbray.

Harris, H., 1998. *Fundamentalism and Evangelicals*, Oxford: Clarendon Press.

Harrison, C., 1992. *Beauty and Revelation in the Thought of Saint Augustine*, Oxford: Clarendon Press.

Hart, K., 1989. *The Trespass of the Sign: Deconstruction, Theology and Philosophy*, Cambridge: Cambridge University Press.

Hawkes, T., 1972. *Metaphor*, The Critical Idiom 25, London: Methuen.

Hebert, G., 1935. *Liturgy and Society*, London: Faber and Faber.

Hesse, M., 1966. *Models and Analogies in Science*, Notre Dame: Notre Dame University Press.

Hesse, M., 1988. 'The Cognitive Claims of Metaphor', *Journal of Speculative Philosophy* 2 (1): 1–16.

Hick, J., 1973. *God and the Universe of Faiths*, London: Macmillan.

Hick, J., ed., 1978. *The Myth of God Incarnate*, London: SCM.

Hick, J., 1993. *The Metaphor of God Incarnate*, London: SCM.

Hirsch, E.D., 1967. *Validity in Interpretation*, New Haven and London: Yale University Press.

Hobbes, T., 1962. *Leviathan*, ed. J. Plamenatz, London: Fontana.

Hodges, H.A., 1979. *God Beyond Knowledge*, London: Macmillan.

Hooke, S.H., ed., 1933. *Myth and Ritual*, Oxford: Oxford University Press.

Hooker, R., 1845. *Of the Laws of Ecclesiastical Polity, Works*, ed. J. Keble, Oxford: Oxford University Press, 3 vols.

Hopkins, G.M., 1994. *The Works of Gerard Manley Hopkins*, Ware: Wordsworth.

Hoskyns, E., 1947. *The Fourth Gospel*, ed. F.N. Davey, London: Faber and Faber.

Hoskyns, E., 1970. *Cambridge Sermons*, London: SPCK.

Hoskyns, E. and Davey, F.N., 1981. *Crucifixion-Resurrection*, ed. G. Wakefield, London: SPCK.

Jacobi, J., 1959. *Complex, Archetype, Symbol in the Psychology of C.G. Jung*, trans. R. Manheim, London: Routledge and Kegan Paul.

James, D.J., 1949. *The Life of Reason: Hobbes, Locke, Bolingbroke*, London: Longmans.

Jenkins, D., 1976. *The Contradiction of Christianity*, London: SCM.

Johnson, S., 1755. *Dictionary of the English Language*, London.

Jones, G., 1991. *Bultmann*, Cambridge: Polity Press.

Julian of Norwich, 1901. *Revelations of Divine Love*, London: Methuen.

Jung, C.G., 1953. *Psychology and Alchemy*, trans. R.F.C. Hull, *Collected Works*, vol.12, London: Routledge and Kegan Paul.

Jung, C.G., 1956. *Symbols of Transformation: An Analysis of the Prelude to a Case of Schizophrenia*, trans. R.F.C. Hull, *Collected Works*, vol.5, London: Routledge and Kegan Paul.

Jung, C.G., 1958. *Psychology and Religion: West and East*, trans. R.F.C. Hull, *Collected Works*, vol.11, London: Routledge and Kegan Paul.

Jung, C.G., 1973–6. *Letters*, ed. G. Adler and A. Jaffe, trans. R.F.C. Hull, London: Routledge and Princeton: Princeton University Press, 2 vols.

Jung, C.G., 1982. *Dreams*, London: Ark.

Jung, C.G., 1983a. *Selected Writings*, ed. A. Storr, London: Fontana.

Jung, C.G., 1983b. *The Psychology of the Transference*, London: Ark.

Jung, C.G., 1983c. *Memories, Dreams, Reflections*, London: Flamingo.

Jung, C.G., 1985. *Dreams*, trans. R.F.C. Hull, London: Ark.

Jung, C.G., n.d. *Aspects of the Feminine*, London: Ark.

Kasper, W., 1984. *The God of Jesus Christ*, London: SCM and New York: Crossroad.

Kaufman, W., 1968. *Nietzsche*, Princeton: Princeton University Press.

Kearney, R., 1988. *The Wake of Imagination*, London: Hutchinson.

Keats, J., 1954. *Letters*, ed. F. Page, Oxford: Oxford University Press.

Keble, J., 1877. 'Life of Sir Walter Scott', *Occasional Papers and Reviews*, Oxford: Parker.

Kelly, J.N.D., 1965. *Early Christian Doctrines*, 3rd edn, London: Black.

Kenny, A., 1975. *Wittgenstein*, Harmondsworth: Penguin.

Kerr, F., 1997. *Immortal Longings: Visions of Transcending Humanity*, London: SPCK.

Kierkegaard, S.K., 1945. *Concluding Unscientific Postscript*, Oxford: Oxford University Press.

Kierkegaard, S.K., 1946. *Philosophical Fragments*, Princeton: Princeton University Press.

Kimel, A.F., ed., 1992. *Speaking the Christian God: The Holy Trinity and the Challenge of Feminism*, Grand Rapids: Eerdmans and Leominster: Gracewing.

Kirk, G.S., 1971. *Myth: Its Meaning and Functions in Ancient and Other Cultures*, Cambridge: Cambridge University Press and Berkeley: University of California Press.

Kittay, E.F., 1987. *Metaphor: Its Cognitive Force and Linguistic Structure*, Oxford: Clarendon Press.

Knight, G.W., 1933. *The Christian Renaissance*, Toronto: Macmillan.

Knights, L.C. and Cottle, B., eds, 1960. *Metaphor and Symbol*, London: Butterworth.

Koester, C.R., 1995. *Symbolism in the Fourth Gospel*, Minneapolis: Fortress Press.

Kundera, M., 1984. *The Unbearable Lightness of Being*, London: Faber and Faber.

Langer, S., 1956. *Philosophy in a New Key*, 3rd edn, Cambridge, MA: Harvard University Press.

Leach, E., 1969. *Genesis as Myth and Other Essays*, London: Cape.

Leach, E., 1989. 'Fishing for Men on the Edge of the Wilderness', in R. Alter and F. Kermode, eds, *The Literary Guide to the Bible*, London: Fontana.

Leatherdale, W.H., 1974. *The Role of Analogy, Model and Metaphor in Science*, Amsterdam and Oxford: North Holland, and New York: Elsevier.

Lessing, G.E., 1956. *Theological Writings*, ed. H. Chadwick, London: Black.

Lévi-Strauss, C., 1968. *Structural Anthropology*, vol.1, London: Allen Lane and Penguin Press.

Lévi-Strauss, C., 1977. *Structural Anthropology*, vol.2, London: Allen Lane and Penguin Press.

Lévi-Strauss, C., 1978. *Myth and Meaning*, London: Routledge and Kegan Paul.

Lindbeck, G., 1980. *The Nature of Doctrine*, London: SPCK.

Locke, J., 1961. *An Essay Concerning Human Understanding*, London: Dent, 2 vols.

Lodge, D., 1977. *The Modes of Modern Writing*, London: Arnold.

Lyotard, J.-F., 1984. *The Post-Modern Condition: A Report on Knowledge*, Manchester: Manchester University Press and Minneapolis: Minnesota University Press.

Macaulay, T.B., 1905. 'Milton' (from *Edinburgh Review* 93 [1825]), *Lord Macaulay's Essays*, London: Longmans, Green and Co.

Macaulay, T.B., 1978. 'Mill's Essay on Government: Utilitarian Logic and Politics' (from *Edinburgh Review* 97 [1829]), ed. J. Lively and J. Rees, *Utilitarian Logic and Politics: James Mill's 'Essay on Government', Macaulay's Critique and the Ensuing Debate*, Oxford: Oxford University Press.

McConnell, F., ed., 1986. *The Bible and the Narrative Tradition*, New York and Oxford: Oxford University Press.

MacDonald, G., 1964. *Phantastes and Lilith*, Grand Rapids: Eerdmans.

McFague, S., 1982. *Metaphorical Theology: Models of God in Religious Language*, Philadelphia: Fortress Press and London: SCM.

Macquarrie, J., 1973. *Religious Language*, London: SCM Press.

Malinowski, B., 1971. *Myth in Primitive Psychology*, Westport: Negro Universities Press.

Manuel, F., 1962. *The Prophets of Paris*, Cambridge, MA.

Maurice, F.D., 1843. *Right and Wrong Methods of Supporting Protestantism*, London.

Maurice, F.D., 1904. *The Friendship of Books*, London: Macmillan.

Maurice, F.D., 1958. *The Kingdom of Christ*, ed. A. Vidler, London: SCM, 2 vols.

Meyer, B.F., 1989. *Critical Realism and the New Testament*, Princeton Theological Monograph Series 17, Allison Park: Pickwick Publications.

Milbank, J., 1997. *The Word Made Strange*, Oxford: Blackwell.

Mill, J.S., 1950. *Mill on Bentham and Coleridge*, ed. F.R. Leavis, London: Chatto and Windus.

Milton, J., 1913. *The English Poems of John Milton*, Oxford: Oxford University Press.

Mol, H., 1976. *Identity and the Sacred*, Oxford: Blackwell.

Monk, R., 1991. *Ludwig Wittgenstein: The Duty of Genius*, London: Vintage.

Moore, G.E., 1953. *Some Main Problems of Philosophy*, London: Allen and Unwin.

Morley, J., 1988. *All Desires Known*, London: Movement for the Ordination of Women/ Women in Theology.

Morris, T.V., ed., 1987. *The Concept of God*, Oxford: Oxford University Press.

Muir, E., 1984. *Collected Poems*, London: Faber and Faber.

Murdoch, I., 1970. *Bruno's Dream*, Harmondsworth: Penguin.

Murdoch, I., 1993. *Metaphysics as a Guide to Morals*, Harmondsworth: Penguin.

Murphy, F.A., 1995. *Christ the Form of Beauty*, Edinburgh: T. and T. Clark.

Murray, M., 1937. *Countries of the Mind*, 2nd series, Oxford: Oxford University Press.

Neusner, J. and Dupuis, J., eds, 1983. *The Christian Faith in the Doctrinal Documents of the Catholic Church*, London: Collins.

Newman, J.H., 1895. *Essays Critical and Historical*, London and New York, 2 vols.

Newman, J.H., 1903. *An Essay in Aid of a Grammar of Assent*, London: Longmans, Green and Co.

Newman, J.H., 1908. *The Dream of Gerontius*, London: Bagster.

Newman, J.H., 1959. *Apologia Pro Vita Sua*, London: Fontana.

Newman, J.H., 1974. *An Essay on the Development of Christian Doctrine*, ed. J.M. Cameron, Harmondsworth: Penguin.

Newton-Smith, W.H., 1981. *The Rationality of Science*, London: Routledge and Kegan Paul.

Nietzsche, F., 1873. 'On Truth and Falsity in their Ultramoral Sense', ed. O. Levy, *Complete Works*, vol.2, New York: Russell and Russell, 1964.

Nietzsche, F., 1910. *The Joyful Wisdom*, trans. T. Common, ed. O. Levy, *Complete Works*, vol.10, Edinburgh and London: Foulis.

Nietzsche, F., 1961. *Thus Spoke Zarathustra*, Harmondsworth: Penguin.

Nietzsche, F., 1968. *Twilight of the Gods and The Anti-Christ*, Harmondsworth: Penguin.

Nietzsche, F., 1982. *Daybreak*, Cambridge: Cambridge University Press.

Nietzsche, F., 1986. *Human All Too Human*, Cambridge: Cambridge University Press.

Nietzsche, F., 1993. *The Birth of Tragedy*, ed. M. Tanner, trans. S. Whiteside, Harmondsworth: Penguin.

Noll, M., 1994. *The Scandal of the Evangelical Mind*, Grand Rapids: Eerdmans and Leicester: IVP.

Ortony, A., ed., 1979. *Metaphor and Thought*, Cambridge: Cambridge University Press.

Palgrave, F., ed., 1928. *The Golden Treasury*, London: Macmillan.

Palmer, H., 1973. *Analogy*, London and Basingstoke: Macmillan.

Pannenberg, W., 1970, 1971, 1973. *Basic Questions in Theology*, London: SCM, 3 vols.

Pannenberg, W., 1985. *Anthropology in Theological Perspective*, trans. M.J. O'Connell, Philadelphia: Fortress Press and Edinburgh: T. and T. Clark.

Pannenberg, W., 1991. *Systematic Theology*, vol.1, Edinburgh: T. and T. Clark.

Pascal, B., 1966. *The Pensées*, trans. A.J. Krailsheimer, Harmondsworth: Penguin.

Pattison, G., 1991. *Art, Modernity and Faith*, London: Macmillan.

Pickstock, C., 1998. *After Writing: On the Liturgical Consummation of Philosophy*, Oxford: Blackwell.

Polanyi, M., 1958. *Personal Knowledge*, London: Routledge and Kegan Paul.

Polanyi, M., 1962. 'The Unaccountable Element in Science', *Philosophy* 38: 1ff.

Polanyi, M., 1967. *The Tacit Dimension*, London: Routledge and Kegan Paul.

Preyer, R.O., 1958. *Bentham, Coleridge and the Science of History*, Bochum-Langendreer: Heinrich Pöppinghaus.

Price, H.H., 1953. *Thinking and Experience*, London: Hutchinson.

Prickett, S., 1986. *Words and the Word: Language, Poetics and Biblical Interpretation*, Cambridge: Cambridge University Press.

Quick, O.C., 1938. *Doctrines of the Creed*, London: Nisbet.

Rahner, K., 1965–92. *Theological Investigations*, London: Darton, Longman and Todd, 23 vols.

Ramsey, I.T., 1957. *Religious Language*, London: SCM.

Richards, I.A., 1965. *The Philosophy of Rhetoric*, New York: Oxford University Press.

Ricoeur, P., 1970. *Freud and Philosophy*, New Haven and London: Yale University Press.

Ricoeur, P., 1976. *Interpretation Theory*, Fort Worth: Texas Christian University Press.

Ricoeur, P., 1978. *The Rule of Metaphor*, London: Routledge and Kegan Paul.

Ricoeur, P., 1980. *Essays on Biblical Interpretation*, ed. L.S. Mudge, Philadelphia: Fortress Press.

Ricoeur, P., 1984. *Time and Narrative*, vol.1, Chicago and London: University of Chicago Press.

Ross, J.F., 1981. *Portraying Analogy*, Cambridge: Cambridge University Press.

Rossi, P., 1968. *Francis Bacon: From Magic to Science*, London: Routledge and Kegan Paul.

Ruthven, K.K., 1976. *Myth*, The Critical Idiom 31, London: Methuen.

Sacks, S., ed., 1979. *On Metaphor*, Chicago and London: Chicago University Press.

Schaer, H., 1951. *Religion and the Cure of Souls in Jung's Psychology*, London: Routledge and Kegan Paul.

Schillebeeckx, E., 1963. *Christ the Sacrament of the Encounter with God*, London: Sheed and Ward.

Schillebeeckx, E., 1979. *Jesus: An Experiment in Christology*, London: Collins.

Schmithals, W., 1968. *An Introduction to the Theology of Rudolf Bultmann*, London: SCM.

Schouls, P.A., 1980. *The Imposition of Method: A Study of Descartes and Locke*, Oxford: Clarendon Press.

Schouls, P.A., 1989. *Descartes and the Enlightenment*, Canada: McGill-Queens University Press and Edinburgh: Edinburgh University Press.

Searle, J.R., 1979. *Expression and Meaning*, Cambridge: Cambridge University Press.

Shelley, P.B., 1888. *A Defence of Poetry*, ed. R.H. Shepherd, *Prose Works*, vol.2, London: Chatto and Windus.

Shelley, P.B., n.d. *Poems of Shelley*, ed. H. Newbolt, London and Edinburgh: Nelson.

Sherry, P., 1992. *Spirit and Beauty*, Oxford: Clarendon Press.

Shutz, A., 1967. *Collected Papers*, vol.1, *The Problem of Social Reality*, The Hague: Nijhoff.

Soskice, J.M., 1985. *Metaphor and Religious Language*, Oxford: Clarendon Press.

Sperber, D., 1975. *Rethinking Symbolism*, Cambridge: Cambridge University Press.

Stanford, W.B., 1936. *Greek Metaphor: Studies in Theory and Practice*, Oxford: Blackwell.

Steiner, G., 1975. *After Babel*, Oxford: Oxford University Press.

Steiner, G., 1989. *Real Presences*, London: Faber and Faber.

Storr, A., 1989. *Solitude*, London: Flamingo.

Strauss, D.F., 1972. *The Life of Jesus Critically Examined*, ed. and intro. P.E. Hodgson, Philadelphia: Fortress Press and London: SCM.

Sutherland, S., 1984. *God, Jesus and Belief*, Oxford: Blackwell.

Swiatecka, M.J., 1980. *The Idea of the Symbol: Some Nineteenth-Century Comparisons with Coleridge*, Cambridge: Cambridge University Press.

Swinburne, R., 1992. *Revelation*, Oxford: Clarendon Press.

Tillich, P., 1968. *Systematic Theology*, Welwyn: Nisbet, 3 vols in 1. ฿T 7S.TԿ

Thomas, D., 1985. *Under Milk Wood*, London: Dent.

Todorov, T., 1990. *Genres in Discourse*, Cambridge: Cambridge University Press.

Torrance, T.F., 1965. *Theology in Reconstruction*, London: SCM.

Torrance, T.F., 1969. *Theological Science*, Oxford: Oxford University Press.

Turner, V., 1968. 'Myth and Symbol', ed. D.L. Sills, *International Encyclopedia of Social Sciences*, London: Macmillan and Glencoe: Free Press, vol.10, pp.576–82.

Tyrrell, G., 1910. *Christianity at the Crossroads*, London: Longmans.

Ullmann, S., 1964. *Language and Style: Collected Papers*, Oxford: Blackwell.

Urban, W.M., 1939. *Language and Reality: The Philosophy of Language and the Principles of Symbolism*, London: Allen and Unwin.

Urban, W.M., 1951. *Humanity and Deity*, London: Allen and Unwin.

Van Gennep, A., 1960. *The Rites of Passage*, trans. M.B. Vizedom and G.L. Caffee, London: Routledge and Kegan Paul.

Vanhoozer, K., 1990. *Biblical Narrative in the Philosophy of Paul Ricoeur*, Cambridge: Cambridge University Press.

Vargish, T., 1970. *Newman: The Contemplation of Mind*, Oxford: Oxford University Press.

Vico, G.B., 1961. *The New Science*, trans. and ed. T.G. Bergin and M.H. Fisch, Ithaca: Cornell University Press.

Von Balthasar, H.U., 1975. *Elucidations*, trans. J. Riches, London: SPCK.

Von Balthasar, H.U., 1982–9. *The Glory of the Lord: A Theological Aesthetics*, ed. J. Fessio and J. Riches, Edinburgh: T. and T. Clark and San Francisco: Ignatius Press, 7 vols.

Von Franz, M.-L., 1980. *Projection and Re-Collection in Jungian Psychology*, La Salle: Open Court.

Von Hügel, F., 1921. *Essays and Addresses on the Philosophy of Religion*, London: Dent.

Ward, G., 1995. *Barth, Derrida and the Language of Theology*, Cambridge: Cambridge University Press.

Ward, K., 1970. *Ethics and Christianity*, London: Allen and Unwin.

Warnock, M., 1976. *Imagination*, London: Faber and Faber.

Watson, F., 1994. *Text, Church and World: Biblical Interpretation in Theological Perspective*, Edinburgh: T. and T. Clark.

Webster, J., 1985. 'Eberhard Jüngel on the Language of Faith', *Modern Theology* 1: 253–76.

Wheelwright, P., 1962. *Metaphor and Reality*, Bloomington and London: Indiana University Press.

White, H., 1973. *Metahistory: The Historical Imagination in Nineteenth-Century Europe*, Baltimore and London: Johns Hopkins University Press.

Whitehead, A.N., 1928. *Symbolism: Its Meaning and Effect*, Cambridge: Cambridge University Press.

Whitehead, A.N., 1929. *Process and Reality*, Cambridge: Cambridge University Press.

Whitehead, A.N., 1938a. *Modes of Thought*, Cambridge: Cambridge University Press.

Whitehead, A.N., 1938b. *Science and the Modern World*, Harmondsworth: Penguin.

Whitehead, A.N., 1941. *The Philosophy of A.N. Whitehead*, ed. P. Schilpp, Evanston and Chicago: Library of Living Philosophers.

Wilson, M., 1978. *The Life of William Blake*, St Albans: Paladin.

Wittgenstein, L., 1961. *Tractatus Logico-Philosophicus*, trans. D.F. Pears and B.F. McGuinness, intro. B. Russell, London: Routledge and Kegan Paul.

Wittgenstein, L., 1968. *Philosophical Investigations*, trans. G.E.M. Anscombe, Oxford: Blackwell.

Wolters, C., trans., 1961, *The Cloud of Unknowing*, Harmondsworth: Penguin.

Wordsworth, W., 1920. *The Poetical Works of William Wordsworth*, ed. T. Hutchinson, London: Oxford University Press.

Wordsworth, W., 1971. *The Prelude: A Parallel Text*, ed. J. Maxwell, Harmondsworth: Penguin.

Wren, B., 1989. *What Language Shall I Borrow?*, London: SCM.

Index of Names

Abraham, K. 120–1, 126
Abraham, W. 147
Abrams, M. H. 62, 86, 97
Ackerman, R. 127
Ackroyd, P. 3, 36, 64
Adorno, T. W. 149
Aelred of Rivaulx 84
Alston, W. P. 70
Anselm 31, 84
Aquinas, T. 61–2, 70, 72–3, 74
Aristotle 93, 94, 97, 98–9
Arnold, M. 159, 160–1, 169
Ashworth, E. J. 19
Augustine of Hippo ix, 3, 5, 30–1, 38, 61, 65, 108, 157
Avis, P. 8, 20, 23, 65, 74, 118, 119, 138, 139, 140, 141, 142, 147, 154, 173
Ayer, A. J. 16

Bacon, F. 16, 18, 19, 32, 40, 45
Barbour, I. 68, 150, 151
Barfield, D. 102
Barr, J. 169–70
Barth, K. 5, 30, 49–50, 58, 60, 62, 70, 73–4, 145–6, 164–5
Barth, M. 72
Barthes, R. 26
Bartsch, H.-W. 161, 162, 163
Beek, W. J. A. M. 86, 109
Bellah, R.150
Bentham, J. 18, 20–1, 41
Berdyaev, N. 107, 121, 150
Berlioz, H. 171
Bernard of Clairvaux 84
Bevan, E. 139
Bhaskar, R. 145, 147, 150

Black, M. 37, 94, 99–100
Blake, W. ix, 3, 5, 10, 32–3, 36, 44, 50, 61, 63, 65, 95–6, 157
Bonhoeffer, D. 134
Boswell, J. 99
Bowker, J. 150
Braithewaite, R. B. 148
Brown, D. 54
Bultmann, R. 12, 117, 123, 132, 143, 161–5, 166, 169, 172
Burke, E. 39, 40, 44, 61, 62, 63, 79
Burrell, D. 76
Butler, J. 108
Bynum, C. W. 84
Byron, G. G. 86, 96

Caird, G. B. 50, 170
Calasso, R. 126, 129–30
Calvin, J. 165
Campbell, C. A. 146, 152
Campbell, N. R. 75
Carnap, R. 16
Cassirer, E. 104, 117, 118, 131, 132, 150–1, 157
Chesterton, G. K. 54
Childs, B. 59, 60
Coats, G. W. 122, 125
Cohen, P. S. 116
Coleridge, S. T. ix, 10, 31, 34–5, 36–7, 38, 41–2, 45, 46, 61, 62–3, 64, 65, 72, 79, 80, 81, 85–8, 89, 96, 99, 106, 107, 108, 109–10
Collier, A. 145, 147
Collingwood, R. G. 123
Conquest, R. 37, 38
Coomaraswamy 116

Cottle, B. 102
Coulson, J. 31, 39, 40, 42, 63, 78, 79, 89, 159
Crewdson, J. 32, 42
Crockett, W. R. 108, 110
Crossan, J. D. 52
Culler, J. 93
Cupitt, D. 144, 146,147, 149

Dante 79, 173
Darwin, C. 131, 159
Davey, N. 54
Davidson, D. 94
Davis, C. F. 100
Davis, C. viii, 138–9
de Broglie, L. 16
Derrida, J. 24–5, 74, 105
Descartes, R. 18, 19, 32, 42, 43, 45, 99, 118
Dodd, C. H. 53, 55
Donne, J. 31, 69
Dubrow, H. 124
Duhem, P. 16–17, 146–7
Duncan, H. D. 106
Dundes, A. 125, 126, 127, 133
Dupuis, J. 71
Durkheim, E. 17

Einstein, A. 99
Elgar, E. 171
Eliade, M. 119, 131, 133
Emmet, D. 74–5
Ernst, C. 70
Etchells, R. 111

Farrer, A. 4, 5, 75
Fawcett, T. 60
Feuerbach, L. A. 7, 8, 119
Feyerabend, P. 147
Fichte, J. G. 10
Fodor, J. 57
Fogelin, R. 97, 101
Fowler, A. 124
Fraser, J. G. 28, 124–5, 127, 128, 129
Frei, H. 56–7
Freud, S. 7, 71, 99, 106, 119–20, 121, 126
Frost, S. B. 169, 170
Frye, N. 123, 124, 159, 160–1
Fukuyama, F. 29
Furbank, P. N. 97

Gibson, J. C. L. 50, 57, 58–9, 65
Gillingham, S. 51
Gilson, E. 73
Goethe, J. W. 107, 109
Gombrich, E. 36, 62
Goulder, M. 167, 168
Gouwens, D. J. 21–2, 30
Graves, R. 130
Grene, M. 32, 42
Gunton, C. 18
Gurvich, G. 106

Habermas, J. 79
Habgood, J. 54
Hacking, I. 144–5
Harries, R. 79, 80
Harris, H. A. 4
Harrison, C. 38, 61, 80
Harrison, J. 126
Hart, K. 24
Hegel, G. W. F. 79
Heidegger, M. 36
Herbert, G. 85
Herder, J. G. 38, 65
Hesse, M. 75, 99
Hick, J. 111, 153, 167–8, 173
Hilary of Poitiers 54
Hirsch, E. D. 123–4
Hobbes, T. 16, 18, 19, 40, 75, 99
Hodges, H. A. 138, 139, 142
Holtzer, S. W. 147
Homer, 97–8
Hooker, R. 41, 89, 110
Hopkins, G. M. 69, 96
Hoskyns, E. 50, 53, 54

Jacobi, J. 106
Jakobson, R.111
James, D. G. 68
James, D. J. 17, 20
Jenkins, D. 10–11
John of the Cross 84
Johnson, S. 98–9
Jones, G. 164
Julian of Norwich 83–4
Jung, C. G. 99, 106, 112, 119, 120–1, 126, 131–2, 137, 139–40, 151, 153, 154–6, 164, 165
Jüngel, E. 100

Kant, I. 10, 11, 32, 131, 148, 149, 152
Kaufman, W. 109
Kearney, R. 23–4
Keats, J. 7, 8, 11, 64, 65, 69, 79, 81, 82, 168
Keble, J. 51, 81, 86, 87, 88, 108–9
Keller, A. 154
Kelly, J. N. D. 54
Kenny, A. 15
Kerr, F. 148–9
Kierkegaard, S. 10, 29, 30, 146
Kimel, A. F. 18
Kirk, G. S. 126
Kittay, E. F. 100
Knight, G. W. 98, 111, 160
Knights, L. C. 102
Koester, C. R. 55
Kraus, K. 36
Kuhn, T. 147
Kundera, M. 119

Lakatos, I. 147
Langer, S. 97, 103, 104, 122, 132
Lash, N. 168
Laudan, L. 147
Leach, E. 57–8, 59
Leatherdale, W. H. 68, 99
Lessing, G. E. 10
Lévi-Strauss, C. 117, 121, 128–9, 132
Lindbeck, G. 167, 168
Loades, A. 54
Locke, J. 16, 18, 19–20, 40, 75, 99
Lodge, D. 111
Lonergan, B. 121–2, 155
Lowth, R. 62
Luther, M. 6, 9
Lyotard, J.-F. 28

Macaulay, T. B. 21
MacDonald, G. 119
MacKinnon, D. 174
Macquarrie, J. 143
Malinowski, B. 127–8, 129
Manuel, F. 20
Marrou, H. 61
Marx, K. viii, 7, 8
Maurice, F. D. 38–9, 42
McCabe, H. 72
McConnell, F. 57

McFague, S. 18, 52, 68
Meyer, B. F. 155
Milbank, J. 157
Mill, J. 20, 21
Mill, J. S. 20–1, 41–2
Milton, J. 41, 44, 81, 88
Mol, H. 121
Moore, G. E. 141–2, 172
Morley, J. 84
Morris, T. U. 71
Muir, E. 39
Müller, M. 127
Murdoch, I. 66, 77, 148–9
Murphy, F. A. 80
Murray, M. 18, 97, 98

Neusner, J. 71
Newman, J. H. 8, 9, 37, 42, 44–5, 46, 61, 63, 65, 66, 78, 79, 80, 109, 137, 171
Newton, J. 83
Newton-Smith, W. H. 144, 150
Nietsche, F. 7–8, 27, 99, 120, 129, 130
Noll, M. 4–5

Ortony, A. 100

Palgrave, F. 79, 169
Palmer, H. 70
Pannenberg, W. 59–60, 70, 71
Pascal, B. 44
Pattison, G. 54
Peacocke, A. 150
Phillips, D. Z. 148, 149
Pickstock, C. 25–6, 100
Plato 133, 149
Poe, E. A. 119
Polanyi, M. 31–2, 37, 42–3, 99, 121–2, 142, 149
Popper, K. 147
Preyer, R. O. 20
Price, H. H. 104
Prickett, S. 9, 62, 81

Quick, O. 5, 174

Rahner, K. 71, 110–11, 144, 153, 154, 156, 166
Ramsey, I. 66
Richards, I. A. 94, 97, 98, 99
Ricoeur, P. 51–2, 93, 98, 100, 104–5, 106

Ross, J. F. 76
Rossi, P. 19
Rousseau, J. J. 65

Sacks, S. 94
Schelling, F. W. J. 115
Schillebeeckx, E. 153–4, 155–6
Schleiermacher, F. D. E. 167, 168
Schmithals, W. 162
Schouls, P. A. 19
Scott, W. 63, 86
Searle, J. R. 93
Shakespeare, W. 88, 94–5, 160
Shelley, P. B. 33, 36, 40, 64, 69, 86, 93,
    96
Sherry, P. 80
Shutz, A. 107
Soskice, J. M. 100, 112, 147, 150
Spinoza, B. 50
Stanford, B. 93–4, 98–9
Steiner, G. 26, 38, 39, 94
Storr, A. 35
Strauss, D. F. 116–17, 153, 159
Sutherland, S. 148, 149
Swiatecka, M. J. 107, 109
Swedenborg, E. 64
Swinburne, R. 94, 146

Teilhard de Chardin, P. 54
Temple, W. 6, 54, 108
Teresa of Ávila 84
Tersteegen 71, 146
Thiselton, A. 132, 165–7
Thomas, D. 95
Tillich, P. 106, 108, 112, 197, 132, 137,

139, 150, 154, 156, 158–9, 163, 165,
    167
Todorov, T. 124
Torrance, T. F. 18
Toulmin, S. 147
Turgot, A. R. J. 20
Turner, V. 116, 133
Tyrrell, G. 46

Ullmann, S. 98
Urban, W. M. 36, 37, 68–70, 101–2, 105,
    106

Van Gennep, A. 116, 133
Vargish, T. 8
Vico, G. B. 19, 38, 43–4, 65–6, 117, 121
Voltaire 20
Von Balthasar, H. U. 3, 5, 58, 72, 79, 80,
    104, 112, 153, 154, 156, 158–9, 164–5
Von Franz, M.-L. 120, 151, 155
Von Hügel, F. 43

Ward, G. 73–4
Ward, K. 75
Watson, F. 50, 56, 57
Wellhausen, J. 159
White, H. 20
Whitehead, A. N. 9, 43
William of St Thierry 84
Wilson, M. 10
Wittgenstein, L. 14–16, 19, 39, 42, 46,
    76, 88, 127, 148
Wolters, C. 72
Wordsworth, W. 33–4, 36, 40–1, 62–3,
    64, 68–9, 80, 86, 88, 96
Wren, B. 84

Subject Index

aesthetics 6, 29, 30, 35, 57, 65, 67, 69, 76, 78, 79, 80, 81, 82, 86, 87, 89, 103, 112, 119, 120, 131–2, 154, 157, 158, 168, 170; expressivism, cognitive content of 168; vision of 157

analogy 5, 68, 70–7, 99, 109, 122, 137, 143, 144; dependence of religious language and theological discourse on 68; doctrine of 70, 137, 145; epistemological framework of 73; and metaphor 5; ontological framework of 73; role in science 99; works dialectically 71–3

anthropology viii, 116–7, 124–5, 127–8, 143

apocalyptic 169, 170

apologetics 166

art 54, 64, 65, 67, 77, 86, 104, 113, 120, 148, 149, 160

baptism 53, 65, 110

beauty 3, 6, 78–80, 104, 149, 156–7, 168, 170; of truth *see* truth, beauty of

belief, Christian vii, 3, 6, 12, 40, 56, 78–83, 101, 149; myth in 165; rationality of 139, 153; truth of 101; vital aesthetic component of 170; *see also* doctrine, faith

Believing in the Church 132, 165

Bible 44, 49–67, 68, 78, 83, 89, 95, 96, 97, 125, 130, 132, 133, 166, 172; addressed to the imagination 50; aesthetic response to biblical narrative 160; conservative evangelical view of 4, 57; containing transfigured myth 58; as definitive

revelation 58; genres of 122, 123–4; historical elements in 159, 160; images of 64, 83; as imaginative vision of God 65; interpretation of 124, 158; as intrinsically poetic 51; language of 63; legendary elements 159; literal meaning in 56, 62, 166; mythic elements in 12, 56–61, 116, 122, 126, 130, 158, 159, 162, 163, 165, 166, 169 (and God's Word 163); narrative meaning in 56; numinous eschatological symbols in 169; otherness of 49; as poetic, figurative and symbolic 61, 62, 159; revelation through viii, 3–5, 64, 65; symbolic unity of 57; uncritical, unscientific worldview of 166; *see also* scripture

Christ 9, 11, 26, 51, 53, 55, 56, 59, 64, 72, 74, 78, 79, 83, 84, 85, 88, 110, 111, 114, 117, 131, 133, 138, 139, 143, 158, 165, 170, 172–4; as artist 64, 65; embodies ideal of human life 167; as embodiment of God's revelatory and redemptive act 60; historical Jesus 154–6, 159, 161, 163; image of 155, 159; life of Jesus 160; as living parable of God 153–4; metaphors of 83, 84; as metaphor of God 65; as metaphor and symbol of God 111, 153; metaphoric identity with 111; as mother 83, 84; as myth 153; as poet and prophet 67; pre-existence of 174; resurrection of *see* resurrection; as revelation of the form of God 79; as supreme form of revelation 3; as

signum efficax of God 111; as symbol
153, 154, 155; as symbolic person 65;
symbols of 53, 55, 56, 105; as ultimate
sacrament 153
christology viii, 26, 56, 59, 64, 74, 138–9,
148, 153–6, 172; myths of 133–4, 153;
as supreme effective symbol 153;
symbolic 153–6 (and history 154–5);
symbols of 53, 55–6, 60, 134
church 5, 9, 26, 53, 59, 61, 63, 78, 85, 89,
110, 112, 132, 133, 141, 143, 166, 170;
authority of 6; literalism in 166;
mission of 160; sacramental ministry
of 112; as *signum efficax* of Christ
111; and state 45; as symbolically
insensitive 112; teaching of 140;
worship of 6, 53, 174
clarity *see* precision
Cloud of Unknowing, The 72
cognitivism, scientistic 127, 128
community 36, 37, 38, 53, 54, 68, 85, 89,
105, 115, 117, 137, 139, 141, 143, 148,
164, 167, 168, 174
context: cultural 123; literary 123; social
123
counterphenomenality 145
creed, doctrines of *see* doctrine

deconstruction 24–6
deism 9
deliteralisation 165–9
demythologisation 12, 27, 115, 117–18,
123, 132, 134, 161–5, 165–9
dialogue, ecumenical 141
doctrine viii, 3, 5–6, 9, 13, 84, 112–13,
138, 140, 168, 170; cognitive function
of 168; cultural-linguistic model of
167–8; derived from symbols of
revelatory experience 139, 143;
elusiveness of 71, 142, 170;
'expressive' view of 167, 168; human
construction of 141; imaginative
assent to 6; importance of statements
of 141; as ineradicably figurative 68;
literalism in 166; making of 68–77;
myth in 122; propositional character
of 141–2; revelation through 65;
symbolic construction of 112, 141;

symbolic provenance of 145; symbols
and *see* symbols, and doctrine
dream: beauty of 120; myth and *see*
myth, and dream; as origins of
metaphysics 120

ecclesiology 110, 143,
empiricism 16, 22, 150
Enlightenment ix, 10, 18–20, 23, 24, 27,
28, 29, 41, 63, 99
epistemology vii, 12, 26, 30–2, 42, 73,
74, 121, 148, 154, 156; analytical
tradition in 32, 40, 93, 100, 102;
biblical 58; epistemological anarchism
147; fiduciary tradition in 30–2, 40,
93, 102, 105, 137; *see also* realism
eschatology 12, 58, 59, 66, 73, 74, 125,
133, 142, 157, 160, 162, 164, 169–72;
as mythical 59, 160, 169, 170; and
myth *see* myth and; numinous
symbols 169; stated in metaphor,
symbol and myth 169; as symbolic
160, 169, 170
ethical, the 29, 30, 52, 54, 55, 76, 107,
112, 170
eucharist 65, 110, 131, 173
evocation 68, 70, 131, 144
existentialism 164

faith viii, 3, 6, 12, 40, 56, 68, 78–84, 101,
105, 122, 125, 138–9, 143, 149, 155,
163, 174; aesthetic element 78;
clarification of 163; as cognitive 78,
143; cognitive, moral and volitional
elements in 78; historical foundations
for 159, 163; imaginative-aesthetic
dimension of 6; as incarnational and
sacramental 54; language of 169
(imaginative assent to 169) (as
metaphorical, symbolic and
mythological 169); mythic elements
12, 126; mythic elements of Bible
important for 159; narrative character
of 163; operates through imagination
78; 'poetic faith' 80; revelation
through 65; statements of 148, 164;
subjectivity of 157; truth of 8, 13, 80;
'unreflective popular faith' 146
fallibility 145

feminism 84
feminist liturgy *see* liturgy and worship, feminist
figurative genres 7, 50, 166
figurative language (discourse) vii, 11, 14, 16, 17, 18, 20, 21, 27, 29, 50–1, 53, 61, 65, 68–9, 85, 112, 114, 137, 143–4, 166, 170, 174; as appropriate vehicle of divine revelation 51; Christianity embodied in 83; as cognitive 11, 144, 174; prejudice against 14, 23, 29, 114; realist but not determinative 174; revelation inextricably wedded to 65; as not veridical 174
figurative realism *see* realism, figurative
First Vatican Council (1869–70) 71
functionalism, social 127–8
fundamentalism 144, 149

genre, discernment of 122–4
God: absence of God from world 109; attributes of 70, 144; beauty of 156, 158 (embodied in Jesus Christ 158); becomes present through symbols 153; communication through imaginative mode 5, 64, 119; contact with vii; creator 9, 73, 108, 109, 165; divine action 161, 174, 165; as Father 83; glory of 79; human encounter with 12, 133, 153, 162, 164, 169, 172; humanity of 49; identity of Jesus with 174; ineffability of 70–3, 137, 139, 142; infinity and eternity of 44; as instrument of totalisation 24; interaction with world 60, 109–10, 164; knowledge/understanding of vii, 38, 72, 107, 152; love of 71–2; metaphors of 83–4; metaphysical/moral/personal nature of 56; mind of 46, 118; models of 112–13; as mother 83–4; naming of 84; non-symbolic language for 137, 138; obliqueness of invocation of 88; as personal 137; God's purpose 162, 170, 172; as poet/artist ix, 3, 5, 61, 65, 156, 157; redemptive activity of 59, 60, 73, 154, 165; relationship to 149; rule of 77; self-communication of 73, 105, 110, 153, 154; as spouse 83; symbols of

52–6, 105, 137, 152; total dependence on mercy of 171; transcendence and mystery of 51, 139, 146; triune nature of 84; as ultimate ground of all meaning 24; unique identity of 168; wisdom of 72; *see also* revelation

hermeneutics 102; fiduciary 39
Holy Spirit 9, 26, 66, 110
hymns 69, 83

idea 45–6, 107; as constitutive 46
idealism 118, 150
identity: Christian ix; community 168; formation of 105; human 11; as involving tension of sameness and difference 174; symbolic 153
illative sense 42
images 22, 23, 26, 30, 38, 40, 44, 52, 53, 61, 62, 64, 68, 75, 77, 83–4, 94, 97, 105, 107, 129–30, 132–3, 137, 142, 148, 154–5, 163–5, 168, 174; circle of 137; as cognitive 11; dichotomy of imagistic or figurative thinking/rational discourse 22, 23, 29; as irreducible 11; numinous 165; social construction of viii, 10–11; as not veridical 11; *see also* metaphor, myth, symbol
imagination vii, 3, 5, 8, 17, 20–1, 23–4, 29, 30, 33–5, 38, 40–1, 43, 50–1, 61–4, 78–82, 83, 85, 89, 93, 95–7, 99, 102–104, 107, 109, 117–20, 137, 149–50, 152, 156–7, 160, 168–9; able to transfigure impersonal universe 34; apotheosis of 30; articulation of 35–7; as creative energy 86, 109; dichotomy of logical and imaginative thinking 122; distinction of mimetic/productive/parodic 23–4; expressions of 7; as the 'holistic faculty' 79; imaginative apprehension of revelation 61; imaginative apprehension of transcendent truth 86; imaginative insight conveys truth about the world and God 152; imaginative insight expressed in metaphor, symbol and myth 152; imaginative truth 8, 21, 28, 30, 65, 83,

89, 105, 168, 174; moral 149; mythic
131; as symbolic, as best guide to
truth 157; symbol-forming power of
157; theological 149
immanentism 84
incarnation 9, 12, 54–5, 61, 77, 108,
110–11, 125, 153–4, 160, 162, 167–9,
172–4; as central paradigm of biblical
revelation 61, 160; expressed in
metaphor, symbol and myth 160; as
literal 167–8; metaphors, symbols and
myths of 173; as metaphor 111, 167–8,
173; as myth 111, 114, 167, 173;
transcendent significance of 160
incommensurability of scientific
theories, doctrine of 146, 147
instrumentalism 144, 146–50
invocation 68–70, 144

knowledge, mediated through social and
psychological structures 145

language: of faith *see* faith, language of;
fiduciary approach to 93, 102, 105;
idealist view of 105; literal 14; as
midwife at birth of belief 40; non-
symbolic 101, 137–8; philosophy of
viii, 14–19, 36–7, 39–40, 73, 75, 93,
100–1, 105, 118, 148; relation of
religious and theological to 68–70,
138, 144 (religious language as poetic
69) scientific 101; theological 149
liminality 133
literalism, misplaced 101 102, 132, 133,
142, 149, 157, 165–9, 170–4
literalistic fallacy 101
literary theory viii, 100, 125
liturgy and worship viii, 3, 6–7, 25–6, 39,
52–3, 56, 78, 83–9, 105, 117, 131, 144,
170, 174; feminist 84; imaginative
adequacy of 6–7; integrative function
of 89; liturgical experiment 89;
revelation through 65; unreflective
worship 157

materialism of Christianity 54
metanarrative 28
metaphor vii, 11, 16–22, 27–9, 43, 50–3,
65, 68, 70, 74–7, 83–5, 89, 93–102,
104–7, 111, 117–18, 143, 147, 166–9,

173; ambiguities of 76; and analogy 5;
in biblical revelation 51; as cognitive
100, 149; concealment of truth 102; as
condensed symbol 105; 'dead' 101,
167; as expression of imagination 7,
152; definitions of 93–4; distinction
of, and simile 97–8; God's revelation
conveyed in 50; heuristic power of 99;
incremental view of 93, 98–100; as
instrument of 'the truth of
imagination' 105; 'interaction' theory
of 100; logical taint of 98; a matter of
both words and thoughts 96–7;
occasion and image of 94–5;
ornamental view of 93, 98–100; as
path to truth 107; perspectival theory
of 100; as primary constituent of
language 102; as primary mental
activity 104, 118, 168; as realist 149;
role in science 99; vehicle of fresh
insight 11; as vehicle of tensive truth
98; as vehicle of truth about the world
and its transcendent ground 149, 152;
as not veridical 100
metaphysics 24, 66, 68–70, 73, 74–6, 88,
117, 122, 124, 126, 133, 138, 143, 148;
dreams as origins of *see* dreams, as
origins of metaphysics
metonymy 111
metre 86–8
mind 32, 33, 35, 42, 43, 63, 104, 151,
152; 'savage' or 'primitive' 121,
127–8; symbolic structure of 157
models 68, 76–7, 128; cognitive function
of, as primary 112; role in science 99
Modernism (Modernity) vii, ix, 10,
14–22, 28–9, 46, 83
moral, the *see* ethical, the
music 67, 69
mystery 23, 51, 71–2, 85, 139–40, 142,
149
mystical, the 15–16, 23
myth vii, 12, 17–18, 21, 23, 26–9, 37, 52–4,
56–61, 65, 68, 70, 74, 77, 83, 85, 89,
101, 104, 114–34, 137–40, 143–4, 146,
149–50, 153, 167–70, 172–4; biblical
see Bible, mythic elements; 'broken'
59, 126, 131; Christ as *see* Christ, as
myth; christological *see* christology,

myths of; cognitive and realist concept of 116–17, 126–7, 130, 149; constellate sacred symbols in narrative sequence 116, 125, 133, 158, 164, 169–70, 173; convey mystery 140; critical realist conception of 130, 149; deficient understanding of 161, 163; definition of 116, 126, 161, 169–70; denigration of 114–15, 132, 149, 166; dissolution of 131; and dream 119–22 (symbols of 119); in doctrine *see* doctrine; drive towards the universal 126, 130–1; embodying primitive and discredited worldview 161, 172; embodying sacral narrative 11; and eschatology 169; as essentially anthropomorphic 161, 172; as expression of imagination 7, 152; fallacy of myth/history antithesis 60; as false science 127; God's revelation conveyed in 50; and history 122–3, 125–6, 130–1, 133, 159–62, 170, 173; as illusion 128; and imagination *see* imagination, myth and; interprets transactions in the realm of the sacred 116; irreducible variety and complexity of 130; *kerygma* contained in 162, 172; and legends 124–6 (and saga 125); as literary genre 172; mystification of 115; narrates sacred history 131; as narrative genre 60, 158; as narrative of primeval reality 128; nature of 129–30; popular misunderstanding of 56, 166; and question of truth 131–2, 158; as primary form of revelation 158; as primitive phase of metaphysical thought 122; *raison d'être* to depict relation between God and the world, history, and community; and reconciliation of contradiction 128–9; and reality *see* reality, myth and; reconciling or integrating function of 121; reductionist view of 163; reflects human experience of the world 130; sacralises identity 105–6; as sacred and numinous 125, 133, 158; as sacred form of narrative 158; as subdivision of narrative 124; symbol

as 117–18, 158–9; as synonymous with falsehood 114, 166; tendency to dehistoricise 116; theories of 126–31 (*see also* cognitivism, scientistic; functionalism, social; structuralism); transfigured 58, 158; as unavoidable 158; unawareness of 115, 117; as unscientific 161; as vehicle of the truth of divine revelation 116–17; as vehicle of truth about the world and its transcendent ground 149, 152; as not veridical 116, 130; worldview and 161–2, 172

narrative 12, 51–3, 57, 70, 85, 115–16, 123–4, 133, 139–40, 143, 164, 170–1; biblical *see* Bible; as character of faith *see* faith, narrative character of; hostility of post-modernists to 28; non-narrativity 164; 'realistic' 57; symbolic 60, 65, 116, 166–7
narrative theology ix, 56
narrative theory ix
nature 33–4, 64, 80, 95–6, 118, 121, 128, 151
non-realism/non-cognitivism 18, 99, 147, 166
numinous, the 88, 118–19, 125, 140, 155

objectivity 16–17, 25, 42, 84, 143, 145, 157, 168, 173
ontology 12, 63, 73, 100, 107, 164
orthodoxy/orthodox faith: Christology as touchstone of 172; compatibility of mythic elements with 126
Oxford movement 39

parable ix, 51–2, 61, 65, 84, 109, 166–7; Christ as, *see* Christ, as parable
paradigm shifts 147
personalism 31–2, 84, 137, 142, 144, 152
plurality, of religions 114–15
poetry ix, 3, 5, 17, 20, 21, 33, 35–6, 39, 44, 51, 61–7, 73, 75, 80–2, 85–8, 99, 104, 117–19, 144, 150, 159–60; common source of, and religion 86–7; distinction of prose and 85–7, 118, 123; divine source of poetic inspiration 33; as evocative 68–9; as

non-cognitive 17; 'numinous' 69; as therapeutic 86
Post-Modernism (Post-Modernity) vii, ix, 11, 22–9, 83, 89
precision 42–3; limitations of 44
prophecy 35, 64, 67, 73, 138
psychology: depth 99, 140, 143, 164
purgatory 171

rationalism 21–2, 24, 40, 63, 116–17, 124, 127–8
realism 11, 32, 69, 73; critical vii, 100, 130, 137–51, 152, 154 (as socially qualified 150) (transcendent object of 152); definition of 144–5; 'depth' 145; designer 146; figurative 11, 112; metaphoric 11–12; moral 148–9; mythic 11–12, 56–7, 61, 116–17, 152–3, 158–74; naïve 144–6, 150 (as incompatible with apophatic theology 146); qualified 150–2; scientific 145, 157; 'shallow' 145; symbolic 11–12, 26, 28, 105, 108–11, 118, 149, 152–7, 166, 170 (transcendent object of 152); theological 144, 145; transcendental 150; varieties of 144–55
reality: biblical understanding of 59; construction of perception of 130; description of 84, 138; distinction of, and representation of 117–18; experience of 37, 105, 130; explanation of 143; as grounded in revelation 60; interpretation of 35; myth and 131–2; nature of viii, 15; symbolic mediation of 107; 'ultimate' 133, 146
reason 20, 41–2, 45, 78, 107, 127
reductionism 7–8, 18, 98, 111, 117, 119–20, 138, 140, 148, 153, 156, 163, 168, 173
religious experience 7, 52
repentance 66
resurrection 12, 77, 117, 125, 130, 133, 170, 172–3
revelation vii, viii, ix, 3, 18, 49–52, 54, 58, 60, 65–8, 71, 73, 105, 107, 110, 116, 124, 137, 139–40, 142–3, 146, 153–4, 156, 164, 170, 173; authority of 74; beauty of 79; given in

salvation-history 160; givenness and otherness of 73; historical forms of 163; imaginative nature of 61–4; as inextricably wedded to figurative language 65; mythic form of 60, 160; objectivity of 158; poetical character/ form of 61–4, 160; priority of vii; propositional views of 4–6, 141–2; reception of 6, 18, 141–2; sacramental nature of 61; sacred symbols of 158; unverifiability of 142
ritual 37, 116
romanticism (incl. romantic poets, movement etc.) vii, 21, 23, 29–30, 32–5, 41, 51, 62–4, 80, 86, 88, 93, 95–7, 99, 107–8, 168

sacrament 53, 54, 65, 108, 110, 133; Christ as *see* Christ as ultimate scrament; as effectual signs of grace 110; theology *see* theology, sacramental
sacred, the vii, viii, 7, 60, 68, 105, 108, 116, 141, 157; symbols of 112
salvation 66, 112, 131, 139–40, 153–4, 163; models of 113; symbols of 112
science: 15–16, 32, 42, 76, 99, 101, 104, 127–8, 132–3, 138, 144–5, 150–1, 166; critical realism in 144 (*see also* critical realism); instrumentalism in 144, 146–7, 157; language of 101; literalism in 144; myth in an age of 166; as objective and literal 17, 101; philosophy of vii, 93, 99, 157
scripture 39, 49–50, 52, 62, 65, 70, 75, 83–4; as divine-human encounter 50; imaginative complexion of 61; normative authority of 166; normative images of 174; revelation in 65, 170; *see also* Bible
secularisation 27
sexuality 84
sign 24, 26, 36, 45, 61, 73, 103, 106, 110
simile 76–7, 81, 97–9
social sciences, the 116
spirituality 84
story 84, 132, 140, 166–7
structuralism 128–9

subjectivity 16–18, 25, 42, 75, 84, 99, 150, 157, 165, 168, 173; of faith *see* faith, subjectivity of

symbol vii, 8, 10, 17, 21, 23, 25–9, 36–7, 43, 45, 53–8, 60–2, 65, 68, 70, 74, 76–7, 81, 83, 85, 89, 96, 98, 99–113, 116–17, 120–1, 123, 131–3, 144, 148, 150–8, 164, 166, 168–70, 172–3; ambiguities of 62, 106; authority of 141; as bound within the sacred universe 105; as bridge between God and world 108; capacity to consecrate 106; and Christian view of creation 108–10; and Christian view of incarnation 110–11; and Christian view of sacrament 110; as cognitive 144, 149; cognitive value of 105; connected with 'idea' 107; definition of 103–4, 106–7; distinction of, and signs 106; and doctrine 137–144; embedded in narrative 171; as enlarged metaphor 105; evil 56; as expression of imagination 7, 152; form in 103–4; imagination in 103–4; as instrument of 'the truth of imagination' 105; intuitive/aesthetic assent to 170; Johannine 52; as life blood of a living faith 105; makes revelation universally available 139; mediating transcendent reality 11, 107; metaphor and 104–6; of myth and dream *see* myth and dream, symbol of; as myth *see* myth, symbol as; normative influence of 56; numinous 116, 170; path to truth 107; philosophy of 103–4 (idealist philosophy of 118); primary material for theological reflection 106; realist view of *see* realism, symbolic; reception of 103; reference to and participation in transcendent reality 106–8; representation leading to participation in 108; reveals new truth 107; revelation conveyed in/revelatory 50, 139–40, 157; role of, in sustaining dimension of depth in human life 158; sacralises identity 105–6; as sacramental 53; sacred 141; symbolic nature of all created reality 11; truth value of 139; 'true' 104; as vehicle of tensive truth 98; as vehicle of truth about the world and its transcendent ground 149, 152

tacit dimension 122
tacit knowledge 31–2
theism: 'rational'/literal 152; 'suprarational'/symbolic 152
theodicy 164
theology vii, 24–5, 43–4, 56, 64, 73–6, 80, 83, 100, 104–5, 107–112, 116–18, 123, 132, 137–8, 140, 143, 145, 147–8, 152, 161–2, 167, 169, 172–3; affirmative 71; apophatic 71, 139, 146; creative 68–77; critical realism in 144 (*see also* realism, critical); distinction between religion and 157; feminist 113; Fundamental 157, 166; as ineradicably figurative 68, 70; instrumentalism in 147–8; interpretation of 124; as intrinsically 'problematical' 71; irreducibly metaphorical 102; liberal 49; literalism in 144, 167; as mythic 70, 167; neglected symbolism 112; objective aspects of vii; personalism and immanentism of 84; presupposes realist view of symbols 108; relativism in 144, 157; sacramental 108–12; as second order critical reflection 68; subjective aspects of vii; as symbolic 70, 137–8; of symbolic forms 157; task of 157; truth claims of 71
tradition 84–5, 141, 143; Anglican 108
transcendentalism 9
transcendent, the 106–8
Trinity, the Holy 108
truth: apprehension of in praxis 141; beauty of 78–9, 170; biblical 165; Christian claims 143; communicated in imaginative modes 64; discernment of 29; fiduciary approach to 31–2; historical 131; and knowledge 142; literal 101–2, 137, 165–9, 172–4 (*see also* literalism, misplaced); metaphorical 101–2; nature of 27, 37, 41, 65, 81;

religious 81, 149, 162; symbol and metaphor as path to 107; transcendent 140

understanding, nature of 41, 45
utilitarianism 20–1

Vatican II 115
verification principle, the 16

via affirmativa 71
via negativa 71

We Believe in God 137
women: emancipation of 84, 131; ordination of 84; *see also* feminism
words 36–40, 52, 62, 88–9, 105, 141; *see also* language
Word, the (of God), 49–50, 53–4, 74, 154, 162, 173